POLICE AND PEOPLE

A comparison of five countries

POLICE
AND
PEOPLE

A comparison of five countries

PAUL G. SHANE, Sc.D.

Associate Professor and Director,
Social Welfare/Social Work Program,
Rutgers University, Newark, New Jersey

with 42 illustrations

The C. V. Mosby Company

ST. LOUIS • TORONTO • LONDON   1980

Printed in the United States of America

The C. V. Mosby Company
11830 Westline Industrial Drive, St. Louis, Missouri 63141

Library of Congress Cataloging in Publication Data

Shane, Paul G   1935-
   Police and people.

   Bibliography: p.
   Includes index.
   1. Police—Case studies. 2. Police—United
States—Case studies. 3. Police—Israel—Case
studies. 4. Police—India—Case studies.
5. Police—England—Case studies. 6. Police—
Netherlands—Case studies. I. Title.
HV7921.S49   363.2   80-11805
ISBN 0-8016-4556-5

GW/M/M 9 8 7 6 5 4 3 2 1   02/D/220

Preface

A number of years ago while working on the Lower East Side of New York in my first experience as a social worker, I learned that a very small percentage of the population used the available social agencies. I wondered to whom the other people in this troubled community went for help. Several years later I was amazed by the idea that people would and did ask the police for help in intimate problems through the Family Crisis Intervention Unit, a police project in Upper Manhattan. I began to wonder if that was the case in other cities, and then if this was restricted to the American scene. It is well known that the United States has a complicated and often inadequate system for responding to people's distress. The result of all of my wondering was the study from which this book developed.

Americans are often accused of being ethnocentric. We seldom know of or are really interested in what goes on elsewhere, particularly in common daily activities. When looking at the everyday aspects of police work in the United States, as compared with other countries, one begins to develop a perspective that can be helpful in understanding and evaluating our own way of organizing and doing things. This book is intended to contribute to this perspective on American police work and organization. A comparative approach may also lead to a reevaluation of the relative importance of various aspects of police work. From this viewpoint, police and those in the other helping professions will begin to better understand and thereby value the contributions of our police to people in pain and trouble. A more cooperative relationship throughout the social service system would be of benefit to all.

This book is intended for several audiences: students of police work, students of the helping professions, and professionals in both fields. This is not intended as the definitive work on every component of police work in the countries studied: Britain, India, Israel, the Netherlands, and the United States. It is intended to highlight the array of tasks that police are called on to do in these countries and give the wherewithall for a reasonable comparison of police in the five countries.

For essential background a brief description of each country and its police history is provided. Most of us know little about police work, less about the development of police forces and their function in our own country, and least of all about these subjects in other countries. This leaves us poorly equipped to understand what police do and to judge how well they perform.

This book is organized in three general sections. Part One gives background information about police forces, the history of police in Britain, a discussion of police function, and the concept of social integration and its relevance to the understanding of police work. Part Two examines each of the five countries, with a background summary about each country, the history and development of its police force, and an analysis of the everyday function of the uniformed police in that country. Part Three is a two-chapter discussion of the comparisons and implications of the information provided in Part Two. Charts, graphs, and photographs illustrate and document police function in the five countries.

This book is the result of a fortuitous circumstance. In 1971-1972 I followed my interest in police work with an extended tour to find out how the police in Britain, India, Israel, and the Netherlands were organized and functioned. The focus for my examination was the service delivery systems in the United States and the congruence of police with these systems. The countries were chosen primarily because their police systems were in some way comparable to those of the United States and because their service systems were not comparable to those of the United States. It was an opportunity to actually test whether the function of police in helping people resulted from the lack of alternatives or from an inherent aspect of police work throughout other free-world countries. With naivete and then amazement I found police, both officials and rank and file, most open, helpful, and cooperative in the four countries I visited.

In the limited amount of time available it was not possible to get more than a superficial concept of any professional enterprise in a foreign country. This is particularly true of the most widely dispersed and complicated governmental service agency of all. The results of my investigation are a monument to the incredibly warm and helpful response given to my quest by people in the four countries. There was no hesitation in providing me with access to police personnel, their logs, and information systems in any of the four countries. Hospitality was more than I had any right to expect, and commonly inaccessible information was made available.

Obviously in the course of such an extended search for information the list of people who assisted is long, and I am indebted to all. Help was given in so many varied ways that it can never be completely acknowledged or credited.

The gathering of information was aided by many. Money supplied in modest amounts by the National Institute of Mental Health helped keep the body together, while the friendliness and helpfulness of the police and colleagues I met kept the morale and intellect together. Faculty and staff of the Johns Hopkins School of Hygiene and Public Health, and its departments of Mental Hygiene and Behavioral Science in particular, and Temple University, especially the Scientific and Academic Systems staff, were most helpful and supportive in the initial study. I am grateful to the many people around the world who helped expedite the collection of data and secured my personal survival requirements during the course of data collection. In particular thanks go to Sri Ashwini Kumar, Inspector General of the Punjab Police, and all the officers of that force who were so helpful and cooperative. Dr.

David Bayley of the University of Denver helped overcome a major difficulty in India and has since been an interested and helpful correspondent. Officers of the Israeli police were very helpful, and the offices of Mayors Fliman of Haifa and Kolleck of Jerusalem helped fill in necessary additional information. Particularly helpful in both countries were the people who helped translate the police logs. Officers of the police of Groningen and Nijmegen in the Netherlands and Piet van Reenen of the Study Center for Upper Police Officials were especially helpful in the Netherlands and since have contributed additional data. I would like to thank Mieke Malandra, a neighbor, who generously gave help in accurately translating Dutch material. Stanley Bailey, the Director of the Home Office Police Research Service Branch, police officials in Gloucestershire and Cheshire counties, particularly Superintendents Lodge and Williams, and the planning and social welfare departments of the respective county councils were most helpful in Britain. Dr. Franklin Ashburn, the Director of Planning and Research, and his successor, Captain Rockford, of the Baltimore City Police Department, gave invaluable help. Dr. David Camp, serving as the publisher's reviewer, provided significant assistance with detailed suggestions throughout the entire initial draft of the manuscript.

Finally I would like to express my love and gratitude to my family and friends for the understanding and support provided through some of the difficult times on the way to finishing the study and writing the book. A special thanks is extended to Robert Plummer, my beloved nephew and almost son, for helping me remember what the eternal verities are and for providing me with unstinting love.

Paul G. Shane

Contents

PART ONE

ROLE OF POLICE IN SOCIAL CONTROL AND INTEGRATION

Chapter 1

Background

And if someday you lose your way
I'll tell you what to do.
Go up to a kind policeman,
The very first one you meet,
And simply say, "I've lost my way,
And cannot find my street."
And he'll be kind and help you find
The loved ones who are looking for you.

CHILDREN'S SONG, UNITED STATES

"Chickee the cops!"

TEENAGERS' ALARM, UNITED STATES

"Stomp the pigs!"

RADICAL RALLY CRY, UNITED STATES, 1960s

Police and policework have often been received with ambivalence and ambiguity by the people. They represent alternately and simultaneously civil order, repression, and help. They are greeted variously with fear, respect, warmth, and hatred. A traditional concept of police, that of the gunslinging crime fighter and strong person, is embodied in the Western genre and games of cops and robbers, in which the strong, moral representative of the law usually vanquishes the unscrupulous terrorizer of women, children, and the helpless. But because many people behave slightly extralegally in the daily fight for existence, this same upholder of the law can be seen as a threat. Revolutionaries portray police as representatives of the "ruling class" and oppressors, even often as the enemy itself. Police often sense themselves to be embattled with and alienated from the people. They also feel themselves to be "servants" of the people. The same person who has viewed with pleasure a police officer catching the person who has just sped by will feel harassed when stopped while hurrying to make a train or appointment. Police are asked for help in myriad types of situations by the very people who at other times would rather not have police attention. It is common to hear people say, "They are never there when you want them." This ambiguity may be stronger in some countries than in others and may lean to one side or the other in different places and times, but it seems to be rather general.

2

The relationship of police to people is generally found to be quite complex and multifaceted. The function of the police is complex and multifaceted. That police function as an agency of social control is generally conceded. It is thought by some that they also function as an agency of social support. In examining the content of police work in five countries—Britain, India, Israel, the Netherlands, and the United States—many similarities are found. In all five societies police perform both social control and social support tasks. Arguments have been presented that indicate that one or the other type of task is variously more important, natural, better, or reasonable. The purpose of this book is to present facts about what police actually do in these societies. How well the tasks are peformed and the present competence of police for any particular task or function are not examined. There is, however, some examination of attempts to prepare police for various aspects of their work and of some of the results of various philosophic approaches to police function. The purpose of this book is not to argue what tasks should be included in police work but to describe the development and organization of police forces in the five countries and to examine the tasks that selected forces perform in each country. Also an attempt is made to look at social conditions that might be correlated with the incidences of some of the tasks that police do.

The development of police forces and their expansion and reorganization have often coincided with and been explained by major "law and order" crises or social unrest within the society. This is true in each of the five countries examined. The disorder in the metropolitan areas of Britain in the late eighteenth and early nineteenth centuries as a result of the urbanization and pauperization of the landless peasant and the descendant proletariate was a focal point for the development of the modern British police system.[12,p.25] Undoubtedly there were other issues that helped to crystalize and mobilize the forces working for the development of a professional police as well. These are similarly connected with major social changes, that is, the development of the middle classes and their move toward assumption of power. Similarly in India there was an increase in "dacoitism" or banditry, which accompanied the solidification of British imperial control and influence and was connected to a breakdown in traditional controls in the society. The active revolt against British control expressed in the mutiny of 1857 was the direct impetus and support for the development of the forerunners of the modern Indian police.[2,p.42] The first police to land in mandate Palestine, the predecessor of Israel, came after the anti-Jewish civil disorders of 1921. The further anti-Jewish riots of 1929 saw major reinforcements of the Palestine police force with British officers and men.[5,p.125] In the Netherlands the police developed during similar periods of social upheaval and unrest, initially with the dislocations of the fall of the republic to Napoleon in 1795 and then with the rise of the monarchy in 1813-1815 with the defeat of Napoleon. With the disorder and social unrest of the 1830s came further crystalization of police development. This was a time of changing borders and major social change in the Netherlands. Police forces came to more closely resemble modern organizations after the 1848-1850 social unrest and revolutionary movements that took place throughout Europe, including the Netherlands.[4,15] In the United States this connection also pertains. The unrest of the pauperized immigrant and native working class during the mid-nineteenth century was the direct cause of the development of the first police force in New York City. Similar social conditions were associated with the spread of police forces across the country.[6,p.15]

Ambiguity is natural under these conditions. It is therefore understandable that from the outset the police role has been ambiguous. The police was developed as a bureaucratic institution during periods of social upheaval and was seen as a force that would promote stability. It is also natural that those who were to be stabilized often looked on the stabilizing institution as representative of repression. The need for stability and the hatred of repression would understandably lead to ambiguity and ambivalance on the part of both police and the people.

The very nature of police work furthers the ambiguity and confusion. Although there is the image of gunslinger, there is also that of helper. Many investigators have observed that a large part of police work involves activities not directly related to social control. This aspect of police work has generally received little attention, although it has been noted frequently. Banton[1] discusses these tasks in his work on patrol aspects of police work in American and Scottish cities. The tasks included are (1) supportive elements, such as service calls, personal, family, and other disturbance calls, and help for physically and mentally ill and disoriented people, and (2) involvement in consensual crimes such as alcohol and drug abuse and sexual misconduct. Estimates of the proportion of police work devoted to such supportive activities and "victimless crimes" range from 50% to 90%.* Other writers have commented on the multiplicity of tasks the police perform.† I have studied police work in five countries and found this to be true in all of them. Part of this book is devoted to looking at some of the findings of this study.

TERMINOLOGY

On the following pages are defined some terms used throughout this book, including *police force, law, law enforcement, social control, social support,* and *service delivery system.*

Police force. The *police force* is an agency within the social system that is charged with particular tasks. This charge is usually given by the legislative or executive agents of the society. The charge varies from society to society but is usually a wide-ranging and relatively undefined one of enforcing the law and maintaining peace and order. Police forces are organized and paid for by the legally constituted government. They are organized with a standard bureaucratic structure. By desig-

---

*References 7, 14, 16, 19, 20.
†References 3, 6, 8-10, 17, 18.

nation the police force is part of the system of law and justice in the geopolitical area, with close ties to the judicial and correctional subsystems.

It is not possible to anticipate exactly the need for police services in any given area. Police planners have thus thought it desirable that the police have rapid and easy access to potential sites of difficulties and calls for help. Therefore they are usually placed or "stationed" in subgroups throughout the geopolitical area.

Law. The manifest task for which police forces are organized is law or norm enforcement. *Law* is the regulation of relationships between persons and groups. This often entails interdiction of behavior that is considered inimical to public safety, well-being, or morality.

Law in action involves the making of specialized (legal) decisions by various *authorized agents.* In politically organized society, human actions are regulated by those invested with the authority to make specific decisions in the name of society.[11,p.36]

In modern society law is generally codified. There is also a body of unwritten legal traditions, or the "common law." (This latter is particularly important in Britain.) Whether codified or common, the police are expected to enforce the law.

Law enforcement. *Law enforcement* is any activity designed to promote obedience and respond negatively in cases of disobedience of the law. It is activity designed to deter lawbreaking and to detect lawbreakers in appropriate situations. It is further designed to lead to the apprehension of lawbreakers and to channel apprehended suspects into the system of justice for judicial and possible corrective measures. Law enforcement is a social control function within society. It is generally considered to be the function of the police. Police are therefore generally organized as an arm of the society's legal system and assigned a social control role.

Social control. *Social control* is the attempt to "suppress or isolate disruptive behavior or to enforce proscribed behavior in the interest of the common good."[13,p.7] Quinney,[11] in discussing the establishment of order within a society, talked about the "several systems of control" that grow as a means of regulation of human conduct. "The *legal system* is the most explicit form of social control. The law consists of (1) specific rules of conduct, (2) planned use of sanctions to support the rules, and (3) designated officials [the police] to interpret and enforce the rules."[11,p.36] Quinney thus defines the police as a major part of the social control system of society.

Social support. There is evidence that police perform many tasks that are related only marginally, if at all, to social control. On examination these tasks seem to be primarily related to social support. *Social support* is the helpful response to human needs in situations of economic, emotional, environmental, or physical stress or difficulty. Social support is provided by a wide range of institutions, both formal and informal. Among the many informal, intimate supportive elements within the social system are the family and friendship networks. The formal, bureaucratic structure of society, which is primarily supportive, has a number of elements. In aggregate these elements are part of the service delivery system of the society.

Service delivery system. The supportive part of the *service delivery system* is a combination of all of the institutions within a social system that are involved in the delivery of health and welfare services to the population at large. There are other aspects to the service delivery system, for example, education. Supportive aspects include programs in health care, social service, financial assistance, family counseling, child welfare, and day care. In some societies the service delivery system is organized under government auspices. In other societies there are many independent programs, under a variety of auspices, such as public at a variety of governmental levels, private nonprofit, and profit making. In still other societies there is a mixture of organizational modes. Some societies have well-developed systems; other societies have rudimentary systems. Regardless of the type or types of organizations or degree of development that characterizes the organization of service delivery of any society, it is in fact a system. It is in fact the *support* system of the society.

Although the police role within the support system has been problematic for most observers of police work, it has been suggested that police are the basic service providers, at least in American communities.[19] It is apparent that an examination of the police role in various societies and of the range of activities with which they deal might help clarify some of the ambiguity. Such an examination is to be attempted in this book. It is hoped that it will be helpful in the further development of police work and training and the development of greater integration of police into the systems of which they seem to be a part, that is, the control and support systems.

REFERENCES

1. Banton, M.: The policeman in the community, New York, 1961, Basic Books, Inc., Publishers.
2. Bayley, D. H.: The police and political development in India, Princeton, N.J., 1969, Princeton University Press.
3. Bittner, E.: The functions of the police in modern society, Washington, D.C., 1970, National Institute of Mental Health, U.S. Government Printing Office.
4. Commissie ter Bestudering van het Politievraagstuk: Report (verslag) presented by joint request of the Ministries of Justice and Interior, October 1, 1948, The Hague, 1948, Staatsdrukkerij & Uitgeverijbedrijf.
5. Duff, D. V.: Bailing with a teaspoon, London, 1953, Long Publishers.
6. Fleming, T.: The policeman's lot, American Heritage 21(2):4, 1970.
7. Katzenbach, N. de B.: The challenge of crime in a free society, New York, 1968, Avon Books.
8. Klein, H.: The police: damned if they do—damned if they don't, New York, 1968, Crown Publishers, Inc.
9. McNamara, J. H.: Uncertainties in police work: the relevance of police recruits' backgrounds and training. In Bordua, D. J., editor: The police: six sociological essays, New York, 1967, John Wiley & Sons, Inc.
10. Niederhoffer, A.: Behind the shield: the police in urban society, New York, 1967, Doubleday & Co., Inc.
11. Quinney, R., editor: The social reality of crime, Boston, 1970, Little, Brown & Co.
12. Reith, C.: A new study of police history, London, 1956, Oliver & Boyd.
13. Sager, C. J., Brayboy, T., and Waxenberg, B.: Black ghetto families in therapy, New York, 1970, Grove Press, Inc.
14. Silver, A.: The demand for order in civil society. In Bordua, D. J., editor: The police: six sociological essays, New York, 1967, John Wiley & Sons, Inc.
15. Van Der Burg, F. H.: Preventive justice and local police, dissertation, University of Utrecht, March 22, 1961.
16. Wallach, I.: The police function in a Negro community, vol. 2, McLean, Va., 1970, Research Analysis Corp.

17. Werthman, C., and Piliavan, I.: Gang members and the police. In Bordua, D. J., editor: The police: six sociological essays, New York, 1967, John Wiley & Sons, Inc.

18. Whittemore, L. H.: Cop!, New York, 1969, Fawcett World Library.

19. Whittington, H. G.: The police: ally or enemy of the comprehensive mental health center?, Mental Health 55(1):55, 1971.

20. World Health Organization: Programme development in the mental health field, WHO Tech. Rep. Ser. 223, 1961.

Chapter 2

History of the police

Prior to a discussion of police function in the contemporary world it might be helpful to look at the development of police forces historically. The antecedents of modern police are found in all societies from the earliest times. However, it is within the last few centuries that police forces have become separate, formalized organizations in European and American societies. Police forces in the five countries discussed in this book (see illustration) have been influenced greatly by British developments. Thus the development of the British police is discussed in greatest detail. The focus is primarily on developments in England, although much of the discussion is equally valid for Scotland and Wales.

United States

ENGLAND

The functions delegated to the English police in the nineteenth century were developed over a period of more than 1500 years. Prior to the nineteenth century these functions had not been delegated to a full-time, separately organized force or bureaucratic institution. When a professional, paid police force was proposed in London and elsewhere in Britain, there was strong opposition. This opposition, primarily from the Whig or Liberal political faction, was expressed as a fear of repression and threat to democracy and freedom.[9] In London in the late eighteenth and early nineteenth centuries there had been a small experimental group of mounted patrollers, called the Bow Street Runners. Other areas of the country had been experimenting with new methods of policing at about the same time. The experimentation was tentatively moving toward the development of a paid group of men to handle policing functions. The first paid police force in Britain was the Metropolitan Police of London, formed in 1829. Following the formation of the Metropolitan Police other paid forces were formed until the country was policed entirely by paid police.

The prevailing system for the maintenance of peace, order, and law enforcement

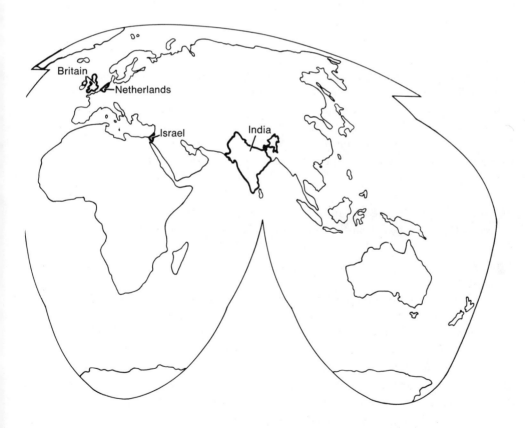

until the nineteenth century was evolved from the earliest Anglo-Saxon and Norman systems. There were three distinct developmental eras:

At first the populace, though small, was responsible for maintaining law and order. Then Justices of the Peace emerged on the scene to provide both the law and order and justice at the bar. Then, in the present era, paid "professional" police were established to maintain law and order.[7]

The early Anglo-Saxon and Norman systems of policing were based on the theory of collective responsibility. All people living in a community were held responsible for each other and by extension for the control of each other's actions. This was the "mutual pledge" system[8,p.3]; that is, all the residents of a community were "pledged" to maintain order and public peace. It was in essence a local residents' association. All adults, particularly the men, were responsible for the actions of the members of their families as well as for those of all the other members of the community or association. When a crime was committed members of the community, individually and collectively, were responsible for raising a "hue and cry" for the apprehension of the fellow group member suspected of breaking the law. If the group failed to apprehend the lawbreaker it was fined by the Crown, and all households were assessed for payment of the fine.[8,p.4] This system was later supplanted by assignment of the policing tasks within the community to specific persons.

The terminology often varied more than the practice because of the multiple cultural influences found throughout Britain. The problems of terminology tended to camouflage some simple linear developments but at the same time gave insight into the many influences that made up the British system. There was at first a mixture of the Celtic, Germanic, and Scandinavian (predominantly Danish) systems. To this, after the eleventh century, were added the Viking–Norman-French institutions. The new systems kept the original concept of collective responsibility but with a local official responsible for the organization of the system. Locally two main systems developed. In the north and west of Medieval England there were the serjeants of the peace and in the rest of the country the frankpledge or tithing system.[12] Each was based on the assumption that law enforcement and keeping of the peace were communal jobs and the responsibility of all the able-bodied men of the community. Each set one person apart to be responsible for the functioning of the system.

Gradually the tasks were assumed under general public management. Specific individuals were designated to assume responsibility for administrative functions of the government. This is illustrated by the development of the sheriff (shire [county] reeve), responsible for tax collection, law enforcement, judicial functions, and other public management tasks. The sheriff was an agent of the Crown and had jurisdiction that transcended feudal boundaries, although it cannot be denied that the sheriff also had strong ties to the feudal world of which he was a part.

This was the beginning of a national administrative system of which policing was a part.

Keeping the peace and law enforcement were not separated from other administrative functions into discrete institutional organizations anywhere, although there were many variations. With the growth of centralized political and economic authority coalescence of form and terminology developed. This was directly related to the integration of the cultural strains within the country. As the Middle Ages progressed the more clearly the systems separated into the two systems mentioned above. From one of the systems grew the constable and from the other the justice of the peace. "The English parish constable of the Middle Ages emerges as the direct lineal descendant of the ancient tythingman."[4,p.3] The serjeant of the peace is more closely related to the development of the justice of the peace. These were still not directly separate organizations, although there was the beginning of specialization of function.

In the fourteenth century a dual system separating judicial and law enforcement roles finally developed. This is seen in the partnership of the parish constable and the justice of the peace. It was to remain the essential British system for the next 500 years, lasting until the reform movement of the early nineteenth century changed the policing system entirely and introduced the modern concept of a police force. The partnership of the constable and justice of the peace brought the final melding of the previous variations into one general format for the entire country. It can be seen that this system had enormous staying power and functioned rather effectively for a long time, although later eras were to look with disdain on the system: "What the early Victorians contemptuously wrote off as the 'old police,' a working partnership of parish constable and justice, by then had endured with remarkable stability for almost 500 years.[4,p.2]

The industrial revolution at the end of the eighteenth century brought a huge growth in the urban population. This rapid development of an urban unlanded class of poor (and the simultaneous development of cheap distilled alcohol-gin[11,p.6]) put great strains on the system of constable and justice of the peace, and it was found inadequate to the task of responding to peacekeeping needs. Experimentation in new directions led to the development of modern police institutions—new institutions with roots in the old.

"Unfortunately for the facilitation of analysis, each police system did not emerge full blown at a single moment in time.[1,p.20] Features of each system developed at different rates and at different times. Some aspects appeared at a particular period of history, were submerged, and then reappeared. This natural process of maturation makes it difficult to state exactly when any given feature became institutionalized in a given system. However, it is possible to see the antecedents of current systems prior to their final emergence. The structure of the French police system is discernible in the late seventeenth century under the monarchy. This is true although the French system was institutionalized under the revolutionary governments that overthrew the monarchy. "Even its essential bureaucratic structure can be found at that time.[1,p.21] In the case of the British police there were many antecedents in the previous systems and developments. Although the development of the Metropolitan Police was revolutionary and a sharp break with existing methods, many essential concepts were taken from the system overthrown. The other factor that is important is that the provincial systems changed more slowly and with greater apparent ties to the past. The organization of the police is different from that found before. The concept of separation of judicial and administrative powers is a direct continuation. Other philosophic concepts were expressed and experimented with prior to the initiation of the new police system.

Proposals to change the British police system were discussed for a good part of the century prior to the actual reorganization. In the late eighteenth century Lord Peel and the Fieldings proposed the establishment of a paid force of men to enforce the law and keep the peace.[10,p.25] In these discussions emphasis was placed on the liberal philosophy and understanding of the nature of people. Although part of the impetus for the development of police forces was the prevalent unrest and disorder, there were other important moral, political, and philosophic considerations as well. Among these were developing political currents, represented by the Whigs, that would lead to the sharing of power by large segments of the population. Essentially, there was a movement toward a democratic form of government as we understand it today and away from the centralization of power in the hands of a small class of people. The ideas were radical in concept and in effect. They were only marginally concerned with policing and were directly concerned with political and philosophic theories about society and life in general.

The evidence that the development of police forces in Britain was concerned with broad political and philosophic issues is clear. The movement for the reform of the police was directly connected with the movement for the reform of government. Critchely states the issue succinctly:

To the concern about the breakdown of law and order . . . was now added the determination of the Whigs . . . to give [the towns] democratic forms of government; and it was this confluence of political currents—above all, the new tide of radicalism—that shaped the mold in which the first of the new provincial police forces were cast.[4,p.61]

Thus, although the arguments for the reform of police work were couched to coincide with the demand of the middle classes for protection from the violence and anger of the lower classes, it was part of the larger demand for inclusion in the governing process, which they called democracy.

Other influences shaped the future of the police. These influences also stemmed from the changes in society, that is, the development of a large middle class. There was an increasing stress on law as the basis for social interaction rather than force. During the feudal era and the era of aristocracy weapons were a standard part of the male costume, particularly when traveling. One's dignity and honor were privately protected by the weapons one wore and used. The movement away from force as a normal part of daily life is reflected in the abandonment of the weapon as an everyday accoutrement: "After ages of unquestioned presence, weapons ceased to be part of expected male attire in the nineteenth century.[2,p.19] Not only did weapons disappear from everyday life, but the expectation of their use became socially unacceptable. Duels were outlawed and, although still fought, lost acceptability as a means of supporting honor. The burgeoning participation of the middle class in governance led to leadership based on ability to advance economic and social aims rather than on ability to overcome rivals. Service and general social order were the criteria by which the middle and commercial classes assessed government.

Jeremy Bentham, who along with Patrick Colquhoun and Edwin Chadwick was one of the leading architects of the new police system in England and Wales, was a leading prophet of the withdrawal from violence as a socially acceptable means of control and interaction. He preached that punishment for criminals was to be used minimally. "Even legal punishment [is] in and of itself mischievous and defensible solely in such minimal forms and measures as we necessitate to contain those few who could not or would not see that their advantage too was on the side of cooperation rather than conflict.[2,p.21] He considered it a necessary evil until society could be transformed and perfected. The message he preached was one of a cooperative society concerned with the economic betterment and well-being of its members. This major philosophic influence on the development of police forces in Britain stressed the concept of cooperative self-interest in the abolition of violence as part of the stuff of everyday life. The ideal in modern life has become to confine violence to the sporting arena. The use of violence for the solution of daily living problems is considered archaic and naturally disruptive of the ideal life. Theoretically prisoners are no longer flogged, and deviations from the law are not met with violent punishment.

This philosphy of antiviolence has penetrated the whole concept of justice and social relations in modern society. Through the eighteenth century a major element of "the criminal process from accusation, through inquiry and trial, to punishment was considered to properly involve the systematic mortification of defendants."[2,p.18] The concept of "due process" was not accepted generally in pre-eighteenth century societies. The change is dramatically reflected in the innovations included in the Constitution of the United States. Not only is the concept of due process included, but the Fifth Amendment, prohibiting self-incrimination, is a radical innovation. Previously the concept of trial by ordeal was the norm (for example, "dunking" of suspected witches; if they drowned they were innocent, if not they were guilty and thus executed). The formation of police forces in Britain was a result of the movement away from force and violence as a way of life. It is part of what Bittner characterizes as "the rise of the sustained and thus far not abandoned aspiration of Western society to abolish violence and instill peace as a stable and permanent condition of everyday life."[2,p.17] These underlying social changes shaped and were reflected in the development of the police as an institution.

The separation of old and new as previously stated is not as sharp as one would think. Although the Victorians proudly proclaimed the new police as completely different from the old, this is not as clear as it might seem. The sharpest delineation between the two was found in London. In the provinces the "new" developed more organically from the "old." In London there was a sharp break with the past in the inception of the Metropolitan Police in 1829. This was a conscious effort to institute something new and different. There was a definite philosophy of social organization and quality of life. This was not as evident in the provinces. The same philosophy came to dominate the provincial police forces as they developed but was not clearly stated at the outset. "The direction which the reform of the police took in the provinces, although it marked a notable break with the past, nevertheless evolved more naturally out of the old system than did that of the London police."[5,p.23] The 1830s also was a very important time in the development of the police forces throughout Britain. Provisions were being made then for the establishment of regular police forces in all the counties and cities of the country. The steps were by no means uniform, nor were they consistent throughout the country. There was due hesitancy and backward glances to the past. But the end of the decade saw forces established in much of the country. As these were formed and functioned the influence of the developments associated with the Metropolitan Police became more evident.[2,p.58] It can truly be said that there is one philosophy and direction guiding the function of police forces throughout Britain.

The philosophy underlying the development of the British police system still pervades the system. It is the result of social forces current at the beginning of the nineteenth century and of the men who designed the Metropolitan Police in the 1820s. Although Sir Robert Peel guided the legislation through to enactment and gave it his name, Sir Charles Rowan is considered the dominant personality and philosopher behind it. Under the enabling legislation that resulted in the Metropolitan Police these two men were assigned the responsibility of designing the new police force. In 1829 they were appointed co-commissioners. The ideas they developed were not entirely new; ideas for the development of police forces had been under discussion for some time.

What were these ideas and how did they affect development of the new police? Basically the concept is that benevolent prevention is a more effective social control than repression. Until the inception of the new police in 1829 there had been no opportunity to apply the theory in Britain. At that point, however, some important new aspects were added to the theory. Rowan was in a unique position. He could do more than talk and write about theories of policing. His idea was that prevention was not only superior in effect but was more desirable in every way. He believed that preventive action not only surpassed repressive action but that it would surpass detection in stabilizing society and stopping crime. Prevention was previously conceived of as a tactic. Now it was raised to a philosophy and put into practice.

"Rowan gave infinitely wider scope to [the concept of benevolent prevention], visualizing prevention as being, if used practically and scientifically, superior in effectiveness not only to repression but also to detection."[10,p.135] Police were to be assigned to preventive patrol and go unarmed. Their strength was to come from a moral position, not from strength of firepower.

The theory was put into practice. From the onset the London policeman, the "bobby," went unarmed as a "friend" of the community. It was a dramatic change from the armed militia that previously did policing. The change came during a period of undisguised hostility toward the authorities on the part of the masses. The role behavior of the new police was radically different from that heretofore seen by the people. The job of the police was conceptualized as working with little power and force but cooperatively and respectfully with the population. The structure and function of the police built on this base for the next 60 years. Rowan gave a lasting imprint to the London police and through developments to the police throughout Britain. "He succeeded mightily, and as a result the implacable hostility shown the police in the eighteenth and nineteenth centuries was transformed into respect and affection."[1,p.23] The bobby, with a distinctive uniform and unique hat and wielding no gun, became a familiar person in the streets of London. This was someone to whom one could go for help and to whom one spoke, who indeed often was sought out in times of crisis. Although the bobby still usually carries no gun, there has been permission to have and use guns under certain circumstances since the mid-1970s.[13]

Several distinctive characteristics of the new police set them apart from the old. These were territorial responsibility, tight supervision, bureaucratic and semimilitary organization, and uniforms. For the first time the city was divided into beats, to which coverage was assigned in an attempt to ensure that police were spread throughout the geographic area. This also introduced a measure of accountability into police work. Not only was one assigned to a beat, he was responsible in some measure for the beat. Supervision and a modicum of training were introduced to provide greater assurance that police were doing what they were supposed to be doing and where they were supposed to be doing it. Police were given uniforms to make them distinctive and easily recognizable and visible. A hierarchical, bureaucratic system was introduced, patterned after the military (highly prestigious and successful at the time). The constable was thought of as a soldier, with sergeants, lieutenants, captains, and so forth, supervising and organizing the work.[11,p.12] The analogy, although with many faults, remains. These elements and the semimilitary organization are still notable in the British police system as well as in others throughout the world.

With fits and starts the development of a national system of policing throughout Britain, particularly in England and Wales and to a lesser degree in Scotland, proceeded. The example toward which they groped was the "new police" of the Metropolitan Police of London. This ideal combined with local tradition produced the "new police" of the provinces (and incidentally of the United States as well). In the second half of the nineteenth century the Home Secretary was successively armed with the powers to raise police standards throughout Britain. Attempts were made to reconcile supervision from the central government with management by local authorities, with the objective of setting uniform standards across the country. The results of these developments "survived with little correction until the middle of the twentieth century."[7,p.101]

The police system in Britain developed greater uniformity and slowly became more consolidated during the latter part of the nineteenth century. This was largely the result of the powers of direction assumed by the Home Secretary. The balance between national direction and local management was maintained. There was movement to merge municipal police forces into county forces. Through the pattern of financial control and standard setting the Home Office developed a major influence on the police forces throughout the country without having been given formal responsibility for the function of these forces. "By 1939 the Home Office . . . had worked itself into a position of exercising great power without formal responsibility."[4,p.219]

In 1946-1947 the independent police forces in the counties were amalgamated into larger groupings. The final amalgamation took place under the National Police Act of 1967, when each county had to establish a single force. Some independence is still accorded the police in County Boroughs, although under the direction of the county police authority. An example of the current organization of British police forces is that of Cheshire:

> The Police Act places the responsibility for providing an efficient Police service on a Police Authority drawn from elected representatives of Cheshire County Council and the County Boroughs in Cheshire. They are supplemented by Magistrates representing the Cheshire Court of Quarter Sessions and Magistrates from the constituent County Boroughs.
>
> The actual operations of the Force is the responsibility of the Chief Constable, and in that he is not subject generally to the Police Authority's direction, though he is accountable directly to them. The Home Office exercises a considerable influence, mainly on the basis of legal accountability, and partly because 50% of the cost of the police service is defrayed by Home Office.[3]

The outline of the organization of police forces outside of the London metropolitan area is police forces organized and run by the county councils under "substantial influence" of the central government through financial support and legal accountability to the Home Office (equivalent to the Ministry or Department of Interior). The Metropolitan Police of London operate directly under parliamentary authorship, through Scotland Yard (the headquarters of the Metropolitan Police) responsible to the Home Office.

The role of the police has matured but retains the essence of what Rowan and

Peel conceived 150 years ago. In 1908 a newspaper account described the police as being distinctive but

. . . related to the people whom they serve by ties of intimate personal association which are not to be found in any other country in the world. The policeman in London is not merely a guardian of the peace; he is an integral part of its social life. In many a back street and slum he not merely stands for law and order; he is the trusted handyman of our streets, the best friend of a mass of people who have no other counsellor or protector.[4,p.320]

Obviously the world of the 1980s is different from that of the 1900s, although in many aspects it is quite the same. The issues of the day are the struggle to retain personal freedom amidst the development of mass communications and restraint. The individual often is adrift in a world significantly different from that in which he or she was raised. The problems of alienation and loneliness have become endemic in modern society. Police are in the middle of the stresses and strains of modern life. They deal with the lonely and the sick, the elderly and the poor, the lost and the disoriented. They deal with those who are fighting and those who have given up. The police are at the cutting edge of the changing values and standards,

for he is much more deeply involved in society than most. At its humdrum least, he is spending his time getting to know and understand people. At its highest, . . . the police being so closely in touch with the public, and therefore so responsive to current trends and aspirations, can themselves contribute to the quality of the society of the future.[4,p.321]

Rowan and Peel would be at home with this description of the function of police in Britain.

The history of the police in India, Israel, the Netherlands, and the United States was influenced heavily by developments in Britain. These influences were either direct, as in India and Israel, or indirect, as in the Netherlands and the United States. These relationships are briefly discussed here and the histories dealt with at greater detail in the chapters in which each country is discussed fully.

INDIA

India was at least partially part of the British Empire for 250 to 300 years. Although only sections of the country were under direct British governance, the whole of India, save for a few small colonies of other European powers, was under British influence from the late seventeenth through the mid-twentieth century. It was during this period that the organization of the India Police System was developed, directly patterned after the development of the Royal Irish Constabulary. There had been indigenous forms of policing extant in the country, and in some measure these continued and were later incorporated into the developing police system.

Nearly two centuries after the British first began gaining control of the Indian subcontinent they felt forced to provide for policing functions directly under the pressure of deteriorating social control and the ineffectiveness of the native ruling classes to maintain social order and conditions fit for commercial growth. In 1792 the administration was removed from the hands of the landowners and rulers of India and vested in the governor general of India for those areas of the country under direct British control, the provinces or states of Bengal, Bombay, and Madras. This was finally given legislative approval in the late 1850s and early 1860s after the revolutionary period of the mutiny of 1857. The codes under which the policing powers of the country were regulated at the time are still the basis on which the police of India function. These forms set up a civilian constabulary with a bifurcated nature. There were an all-India officers corps and provincial constabularies. The Peelian reform of an unarmed civilian constabulary was exported to India. These constables were and continue to be stationed close to the people. They patrol their assigned areas generally on foot but sometimes on bicycles. They are found through-out the country, speaking the language of the people, from city to villlage.

The officers corps is somewhat different. It is organized on a national basis, and there is normally no mobility from provincial police force to officers corps. Officers are assigned and trained, regardless of the cultural identity with which they ma-tured. They are expected to use both the national language, Hindi, and English. Thus in many instances the officers cannot speak the language of the native popula-tion of the area in which they are stationed and serving. They often live in govern-ment housing, thus further separating them from the people of the district and emphasizing the class differences between officers and constabulary. However, it has a strengthening influence on the national identity of the police and of the nation as a whole.

Police in India are generally charged with law enforcement and maintenance of the peace. They are responsible for dealing with cognizable offenses (those dealt with in the All-India Criminal Code), noncognizable offenses (less serious crimes and misdemeanors), and complaints (non-law-enforcement tasks such as mediation of civil disagreements and various requests for service). They carry out their tasks in a country with a rudimentary and often nonexistent telephone system and with little help from motorized vehicles. Other than this, their work often resembles that of the police in Britain to an astounding degree.

ISRAEL

Israel is part of the region of Palestine that was under mandate from the League of Nations to Great Britain from 1918 to 1948. Although there were policing arrange-ments under the previous rulers, the Ottoman Empire, the British completely reorganized the police shortly after gaining control. Initially the force was made up wholly of British gendarmes on duty in the Holy Land. This first force took control in 1922. With the continuing developments and conflict between Arabs and Jews, the force was enlarged shortly thereafter and was composed of colonial and local members. In 1926 the British Police Order instituted a permanent public security force. This order remains the basic code under which policing is organized in the country, because on independence the Jewish government revested the British system as the law of the land.

The force was organized as and remains a unitary national force. Central headquarters are in Jerusalem, with districts and subdistricts throughout the country. A major shift from colonial times has been the emphasis of the police force. Prior to independence the force was responsible for maintaining law and order against a resistive local population. Since independence the force is part and parcel of a nation that considers the commonweal to be of foremost importance. The emphasis therefore is on preventive measures. This police force probably embodies Rowan's concepts of prevention most fully of any studied. Police are considered to be one of a group of cooperating social institutions; thus the service function of police is considered to be equal in importance to law enforcement, crime prevention, and peacekeeping. A special function of Israeli police relates to the precarious international situation in which the country finds itself. There are frequent acts of terrorism deriving from the unsettled situation with the neighboring countries and the Palestinian Arabs. In a sense this binds the police even closer to the population in that they must be mutually supportive in fighting terrorism.

The force is organized in a quasimilitary manner with ranks and uniforms. Originally the force was unarmed. Because of the security problem, however, arms are now an expected part of the uniform. This in a country where most civilians are expected to participate in military reserve or public watch activities, including the handling of weapons. In other aspects the philosophic and organizational influence of British concepts have married well with the Jewish ethic and national police developments.

NETHERLANDS

Although there have been many influences on the development and organization of the Dutch police, the British influence, indirectly, can be seen to be strong. The policing function of the Netherlands has developed over many centuries. There are indigenous elements that prior to organization of a police force combined executive, judicial, and law enforcement elements. These were similar in many respects to the sheriff and baliff found in the old English systems. In 1795, when Napoleon invaded and occupied the Netherlands, a police force was organized. It followed the pattern of the French police, with additional duties geared toward occupation of a foreign land and people. Prior to the French occupation there had been discussions of police forces based on the British concept of municipal police forces. The French introduced the idea of a national police force. In consideration of conditions in the Netherlands the French authorities began to develop a national police force while maintaining local autonomy. This conflict has been the constant in the development of the police since then. Since the restoration of Dutch sovereignty under the monarchy in 1813 the tension between national control and local autonomy has been almost continuous. From this tension has sprung the parallel organizations of municipal police (gemeentepolite) and national police (rijkspolitie). The country is divided into rural and urban municipalities. Those over a certain population, about 25,000, are delegated the authority to have locally controlled police forces, while the rest of the country is covered by posts and stations of the national police. The governmental responsibility and control has been reorganized several times, most recently in 1957, but still seems to be unsatisfactory, and new commissions are studying the problem and suggesting remedies. In essence the separation of police powers into the two types of forces stems from 1851.

Although there is local responsibility and authority, police operate under national regulations and subsidies. Monies for police forces come from the central government, either directly to the national police or through subsidies to the municipal police. Forces are generally uniform in strength per population. The national police force is under the supervision of the Ministry of Justice, with 6000 police serving a population of about 5 million. It is divided into over 20 districts. There are special branches for transportation sections, that is, River, Aviation, and Highway. The municipal forces are organized in 122 municipalities. These forces are in essence independent, and although there are constraints from the central government, are responsible to the local government. There are cooperative relationships between police forces, providing police coverage on a unified basis to the country. Police deal with a large number of activities, reported under the categories of public order, social concerns, criminal matters, public morality, public health, public safety, economic matters and work conditions, traffic, protection of property, and miscellaneous. The police in the Netherlands have a broader mandate than do police in other countries studied, but in actuality they do much the same work. In essence it would appear that the concept borrowed from the British of local police has become the dominant pattern of the country, while the French national police have been severely restricted in scope. The concept of civilian police operating under a philosophy similar to that of Rowan and Peel is not foreign to the function of the police in the Netherlands, although the British influence is indirect through cultural borrowing rather than direct through functional lineage.

UNITED STATES

The first police force in the United States, organized in New York City in 1845, was patterned consciously on the then new Metropolitan Police of London.[6,p.15] The second force in Boston used the same model. The organization of police forces in other cities throughout the country followed rapidly. Police organization in the counties and rural areas of the country was patterned after the county police of Britain and predates the urban police forces in some places. In the rural systems officials were called sheriffs and assistants deputy sheriffs after the old British model.

The urban forces developed a greater range of hierarchy and a more bureaucratically styled organization. With later developments the patterns for the United States began to diverge in some major respects from that of Britain. These changes were in response to cultural and social differences between the two countries. A major divergence is that in the United States the influence of central government over general policing has never been accepted.

Initially police in the United States went unarmed, as did their British colleagues; however, the police in the United States rapidly gained firepower. Revolvers were added to the uniform of the New York police in 1858, thirteen years after the inception of the force. In the 1880s the movement was generally completed with the arming of the Boston police. Since this change police in the United States are considered to be out of uniform without arms. They are even mandated in most areas today to be armed when not in uniform.[6,p.17]

There are many parallels between the American and British police. Historically the impetus for the development of the police was similar. Police in the United States were organized in response to social disruption during a period of great social change. In both countries the problems were primarily urban and coincident with urbanization and industrialization. Immigration was widespread, in Britain from the countryside and in the United States from European communities. In the early and mid-nineteenth century the cities of the United States were scenes of civil disruption and disorder. In large areas of the cities poverty was endemic and conditions of living unbearable for many of the inhabitants. At the same time the rising bourgeoisie was involved with reformist political currents driving toward increased participation in the running of society.

In keeping with the ingrained distrusts of centralized government in the United States, policing in particular was kept as a local prerogative. Those currents that were similar in both countries in moving toward the development of police forces were wedded in the United States to philosophies of local control of policing powers. The fear of autocracy was aroused by the idea of central government controlling policing. Police forces today are locally controlled and financed, with no central authority over any aspect of their function. Of course central influences over police work in the United States have developed through consultative arrangements and subsidies. One cannot say that central government runs county police forces in Britain, but there is certainly greater influence and less autonomy for local forces in Britain than there is in the United States.

Although the influences have been indirect and the result of similarity of culture and borrowings rather than imposition through colonialism, the subsequent function of police in both countries has become more similar over the years. Uniforms are similar, the distinctive hat of the bobby being a major difference, and that used only in special situations. There has been a move in Britain toward arming police in recent years, increasing the similarities. On the other hand, there are still differences. Local autonomy leads police forces in the United States to have a wide diversity in philosophic underpinnings. These range from the police in some towns in California wearing blazers rather than traditional uniforms to differentials in educational requirements, from high school diplomas to college degrees. The major difference between British police and American police is the great diversity that exists among police forces in the United States and the minor influence of central government, either national or state, on local police forces.

SUMMARY

The history and development of police forces in Britain have influenced the history and development of police forces in India, Israel, the Netherlands, and the United States. Similarities among police forces in the five countries are many. In three of the countries the functions of the police and their development are in response to a combination of local needs and traditions and the British national development of the mid-industrial revolution. In the other two, the Netherlands and the United States, the British concept of policing, along with other factors, had great influence over the development of the police. With the differences in historical development the similarities are striking and deeply rooted. In all five countries police are orgnaized in semimilitary bureaucratic organizations. A basic organization was developed when the Metropolitan Police of London was organized in 1829, and similar organizational structures are seen in all five countries. Police have territorial responsibilities, are uniformed, and are supervised. Forces in all five countries have arisen in response to major social crises within the society accompanying social change. They represent a move to a system of general law and order and social integration, away from violence. In Britain, most of India, Israel, and the Netherlands civil police are generally unarmed. In the United State and Punjab, India, civil police are generally armed, with strong controls placed on the use of the arms.

There are some major organizational differences between the various police forces in the five countries. A major difference is the level of government that has jurisdiction over policing. In Britain, where the concept of local police forces was initially enunciated, the police are organized in generally autonomous county forces with coordination, direction, and influence from the national Home Office. India has a somewhat more autonomous system of state forces, with officers in all forces part of the India Police Service. Israel has a national force with no local autonomy. The Netherlands has both a national force and rather autonomous municipal forces under government regulations. The United States has the greatest diversity of police forces and the greatest dispersion of police powers. The term *police* in the United States, however, generally refers to the autonomous local forces responsible to the local government, whether township, municipality, or county.

In general, similarities of function and general organization are greater between police forces in the five countries than the differences of sponsorship and responsibility would lead one to suspect. In all five countries the police are considered professionals. They receive special training, which is the responsibility of the sponsoring authority, although the national governments attempt to ensure some degree of minimal standards and function. They have similar missions in all five countries, peform similar tasks, and fulfill similar social functions, the more obvious being social control and the less obvious but equally important being social support. In Chapter 3 the function of the police is discussed with emphasis on Britain and the United States.

REFERENCES

1. Bayley, D. H.: The police and political development in Europe, unpublished draft, Denver, 1970, University of Denver.
2. Black, A.: The people and the police, New York, 1968, McGraw-Hill Book Co.
3. Cheshire Police Authority: The Cheshire constabulary, Wilmslow, England, 1970, Cheshire County Council.
4. Critchely, T. A.: A history of police in England and Wales: 900-1966, London, 1967, Constable & Co., Ltd.
5. Cumming, E., Cumming, I., and Edell, L.: Policeman as philosopher, guide and friend. In Quinney, R., editor: The social reality of crime, Boston, 1970, Little, Brown & Co.
6. Fleming, T.: The policeman's lot, American Heritage 21(2):4, 1970.
7. Hewitt, W. H.: British police administration, Springfield, Ill., 1965, Charles C Thomas, Publisher.
8. Katzenbach, N. de B.: The challenge of crime in a free society, New York, 1968, Avon Books.
9. Melville, W. L.: History of police in England, London, 1901, Patterson Smith.
10. Reith, C.: A new study of police history, London, 1956, Oliver & Boyd.
11. Rubenstein, J.: City police, New York, 1973, Farrar, Straus & Giroux, Inc.
12. Stewart-Brown, R.: The serjeants of the police in medieval England and Wales, Manchester, England, 1936, Manchester University Press.
13. They don't rely on just nightsticks anymore, *Philadelphia Inquirer*, December 17, 1978, p. 20A.

Chapter 3

Police function

Many writers concerned with police work have attempted to define the function of police within society and their relationship to the general population. There are often different emphases in each definition as well as questions about appropriateness of different aspects of police work. Some writers question not only the variety of tasks with which the police are involved but the priorities as well.

Since the Second World War there has been much discussion of the functions of the police and the relationship between police and public. The discussions in the United States and Britain have occasioned a plethora of books and articles.* In the Netherlands several Royal commissions have studied the organization of police forces and various routes of responsibility and authority.[12,16] In the United States and Britain there is more concern with the function of the police and the philosophy under which the police should operate. To be sure, organization and lines of authority are problematic in these two countries as well. There does not seem to be as much concern about the function of the police in India and Israel in public discussion. The issues discussed often have relevance to the issue of the relationship between police and the public.

Analysts of police work have examined all aspects of this institution. A common issue is organization: whether lines of authority should be centralized or localized. How responsible should police authorities be to the people who are policed? In the United States the issue of responsibility revolves around the institution of civilian review boards and the purposes of community relations programs. Among the most problematic areas in British and American writings are police responses to requests for aid not directly related to law enforcement.[4,37] Other issues discussed are the kinds of uniforms and weaponry police should use. Most of the discussion is concerned with how police can best achieve their goals and what these goals are. Is the focus of the police law enforcement, crime prevention, service, or a combination of the three? How can they be mixed most effectively, if they are to be mixed? The discussion takes us back to that of the early nineteenth century, prior to the development of the Metropolitan Police in London.

In this chapter various analyses of the function of police are summarized. There

---

*References 11, 15, 31, 36, 41.

is some discussion of possible explanations for the differences of opinions as well as discussion of implications of attempts to set priorities for police activities.

It is my opinion that police have several functions that are equally important and valuable to society and that these functions are not necessarily in conflict but may even be mutually supportive. These functions are support and control. To help students understand some of the related issues there is a brief examination of possible relationships between police work and mental and physical health. Since there are different opinions in these matters it is helpful for students to have them at their disposal.

As an aid to study of police tasks the sociologic concepts of function of social institutions is useful. Merton developed a useful theory of function. Although many social scientists consider Merton's concepts antiquated, I feel that there is validity and use in setting the concepts out. Merton defines "function" and the "vital or organic processes considered in the respects in which they contribute to the maintenance of the organism."[21,p.75] He suggests that there are negative and positive functions, that there are aspects of a function that are helpful to the organism and those that are deleterious. He calls the former functions and the latter dysfunctions. "Functions are the observed consequences which make for the adaptation or adjustment of a given system. Dysfunctions are those observed consequences which lessen the adaptation of a given system."[21,p.105] Merton further discusses the idea that there are both generally recognized or acknowledged and unrecognized and unacknowledged aspects of function. These are the manifest and latent aspects. "Manifest" aspects of function are those intended and recognized by the participants in the system. "Latent" aspects are neither intended nor often recognized. In brief this means that organizations and activities often do not have the effect intended. It also means that organizations and activities often are doing more than what is generally supposed. While the various concepts of the meaning of police work and effectiveness of police work are being examined it might be helpful to keep in mind the concepts of manifest and latent function and dysfunction.

In this light major questions arise in discussions of police work. Is it possible that police have more than the generally assigned social function? Are the manifest functions of police work congruent with latent functions? Are the manifest functions actually dysfunctional? Do we make a mistake when the manifest function of police is taken as the only legitimate function or even the total function? Skolnick, among others, asks a stark question: "For what social purpose do the police exist? What values do the police serve in a democratic society?"[36,p.1] In essence the question is: What is the function of police? There is no agreed on answer, nor often even an agreed on basis for discussion.

Law enforcement or social control is the generally agreed on manifest function of the police. Most laws establishing police forces and defining their tasks clearly set this forth. Police in explaining their work take this assumption for granted. Reports stress the social control aspects of police work. Regularly the newspapers examine the success or failure of police to maintain a crime-free environment. Police point with pride to decreases in the crime index and are embarrassed by increases. Another possible social function of police pointed to by various data and often mentioned in passing by commentators is social support. It is possible that police function not only as part of the social control system of society but also as part of the supportive socially integrative system. Cumming et al. noted the latent nature of this aspect of police work: "The policeman's role in an integrative system is by definition and by law explicitly concerned with control . . . and only latently with support."[15,p.147] Evidence points to the possibility that the latent support function of police may be equal in actuality to that of control. Does the latent nature of the function decrease its legitimacy? Or does it make it more difficult to do the work adequately by obscuring its nature?

The problem of what the legitimate function of police has been and is to be has been discussed by various writers from many angles. The concern with police function has involved investigators and commentators representing many disciplines, including criminology, history, law enforcement, law, mental health, political science, social science, and social welfare. It is not surprising therefore that different parts of the elephant have been described. These include views in opposition as to legitimate police function and the importance and value of the control and support functions. Quinney puts forth the general situation: "The role of the police in the community in relation to the duties of law enforcement has always been the source of a major dilemma."[33,p.113] Part of the dilemma is related to the fact that it has been very difficult to connect police work directly with the incidence of lawbreaking.

In examining definitions and expectations of police work the historical roots and continuing arguments are reviewed, particularly as they have been made in Britain and the United States. Many of the arguments offered in the late eighteenth and early nineteenth centuries in support of the establishment of the Metropolitan Police and the reform of the provincial police of England and Wales were quite direct and unambivalent. They directed themselves toward the need to protect law, order, and property rights and to suppress crime. These arguments were put forth during a period of active social unrest and disruption. It was a period during which the lower classes were beginning to question the economic prerogatives of the middle and upper classes and the sanctity of property. The middle class was beginning to assert itself against the ancient prerogatives of the aristocracy, and the class system itself was being reorganized. Concurrently there was movement toward increased involvement in the governing process by the hitherto disenfranchised coupled with a major crime wave. The earliest partisans of reforming the police were themselves ambivalent about what the task of the police would be. If, as Rowan thought, prevention was the primary job of the police, right behind it was the expectation that police could lower crime rates. He posited the proverbial carrot-and-stick approach: behind prevention is punishment. If they will not cooperate we will punish them. Unfortunately the ambivalence enters from the beginning:

The primary object of an efficient police is the prevention of crime; the next that of detection and punishment of offenders if crime is committed. To these ends all the efforts of police must be directed. The protection of life and property, the preservation of public tranquility, and the absence of crime, will alone prove whether those efforts have been successful and whether the objects for which the police were appointed have been attained.[11,p.11]

It is not clear in this approach whether the police are to effect the conditions that lead to crime or to attack crime itself or both. Included in this definition is preservation of public tranquility along with prevention and punishment. Although the definition leans toward social control, it includes elements that could definitely indicate a social support role for the police. If the resultant police were to be "friends" rather than adversaries of the people, as discussed earlier, it can be suggested that friends help rather than control. This indicates that the police were expected to act as helpers as well as lawkeepers. There are several possibilities as to why the double tack was taken. On the one hand there was strong suspicion of the antidemocratic possibilities of the police. The helping aspect might have been introduced as a means of allaying these fears. On the other hand it might result from the philosophic stand that a society cannot repress crime but can only affect the conditions under which crime thrives.

At the same time there were other major factors influencing the development of the "new" police. A historian, Critchely, analyzing the forces supporting and opposing the development of the police, sets forth some of the motivations behind the development:

Determination to suppress crime was undoubtedly one, but probably not the major or most urgent of the causes that led, first, to the reform of the borough police, and, second, to an enabling Act that permitted magistrates to reform rural police.[14,p.58]

Critchely goes on to say that the concern for law and order was a convenient cloak for the development of an institution designed to speed political change. The development of police forces was thus primarily part of the political movement designed to change the political nature of British society. He suggests that the Whigs sought the development of police as a means of moving the society toward a more democratic form. This development would loosen the reins of the "ruling" class on the sources of power and therefore its control of the population. Interestingly, opposition to the police at that time and now, particularly in the United States, rests in the belief that the police do just the opposite. It may be that the power of the police is greatly overestimated in both cases. Nevertheless a dichotomy of expectations of police work appears that seems to be unresolved and perhaps is even unresolvable.

In Britain there has been some rethinking of the role of the police, partly because of changes in society since World War II. The British police, who were unarmed except for a nightstick, have begun carrying and using guns since the latter part of the 1970s.[38] This has excited a great deal of discussion. On the one hand are some leaders of the police and segments of the population who are concerned with a growth in the use of weaponry by unlawful elements; on the other are those who are concerned about the possible repressive use of weapons and the increase in the violence quotient of British life. One newspaper caught the latter when it commented: "Policemen should manage without guns wherever possible. . . . Civil peace is a precious and envied part of British life."[38] They went on to make nefarious comparison with police in other European countries and the United States, where guns are a common part of the police uniform. From this infiltration of guns in Britain can be inferred a hardening of British law enforcement attitudes. The American paper commenting on this issue stated: "The image of the British policeman as a kindly copper helping old ladies across the road is gone."[38] Of course there has been an increase in the use of arms by the criminal element either preceding or concomitant to the development of armed police in Britain, and the average bobby still does not carry a gun. However, there is evident a strengthening of the concept that police are there primarily for social control purposes. The same kind of thinking is found in the United States.

Often in the United States the police themselves are the strongest proponents of the view of police as law enforcers. For example, when their force was threatened with a cut in manpower at the end of 1978, police under the aegis of the Fraternal Order of Police, Newark (N.J.) Lodge #12, strongly put forth the idea that with

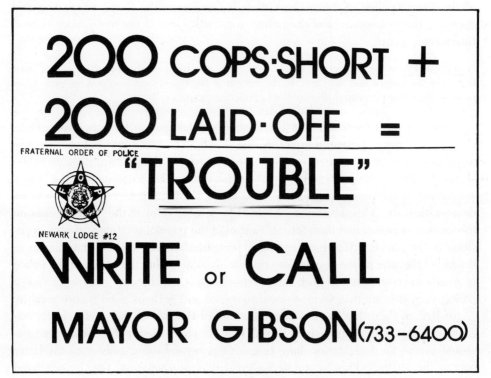

Police leaflet, Newark, N.J., 1978.

the small police force "trouble" would follow (see illustration). Leaflets warned passers-by to leave the city before dark, lock car doors while inside as well as when leaving the vehicle, and be prepared to protect themselves in case of attack, because there would be fewer police available. This was part of a "fear city campaign."[29] This might be called a hard sell and reinforces the image of the police as crime fighters. Reports of similar campaigns by other police in similar circumstances were noted in New York City during the 1960s and again in 1975.[29] The image of police as the only barrier against lawlessness has been used in other situations when police felt their strength to be threatened. This attitude increases the general conception of police as being primarily, if not solely, involved with law enforcement, and being successful at that. The manifest functional definition of police work is thereby given greater currency.

Not only police have this viewpoint. In the United States many segments of the population look on the police as protectors against lawlessness and disorder. In some communities the police are blamed for "allowing" crime to take place. A recent example of this phenomenon occurred in a section of Brooklyn, N.Y. The area of Borough Park has been populated predominantly by orthodox Jews for a number of years. The area is middle class and generally has a very low crime rate. On December 2, 1978, an elderly resident of the community was killed by several teenagers during an attempted robbery while he was on the way home from synagogue. That day, a Saturday, there was a rather emotional and at times violent demonstration at the local police station by orthodox Jewish men and boys demanding greater police protection for the community. The message was that the murder would not have occurred if the police had been doing their job in enough force.[23]

The police supported this view of the incident. A representative of the Patrolmen's Benevolent Association suggested that the recent cuts in police power because of budget problems within the city had indeed been the reason for the murder. He suggested that the police were not responsible but that the city officials were responsible. He said, "These people have a right to be angry over the lack of police protection."[26]

Let it be noted that the crime rate in that community, which had been rising for several years prior to 1978, had in 1978 decreased significantly.[26] The perception of the community that it was under attack and the experience that many of the residents may have had in communities from which they had moved may have been more a factor in the outburst of anger at the police resulting from the murder than from the reality of a worsening crime situation.

On the other hand, just a few years before large segments of the population began calling police "pigs" and condemning them for the social conditions in the country and the world. During the 1968 Democratic Party National Convention in Chicago there was a widely reported confrontation between the police and demonstrators that led to violence and further alienation of a segment of the population from the "establishment," with which they identified the police. A similar but less publicized confrontation between police and people took place in Philadelphia during 1978. In this case there was a violent resolution to a long-standing issue between the city and a houseful of members of a "radical" group that disdained civilization's comforts and ideals. The members of the group were predominantly black. When during the denouement a member of the group was killed, as was a police officer, the black leadership of the city brought charges against the police for handling the situation badly and for using violence. In addition they charged that the police often used violence on and mistreated blacks.[27] This incident, along with others, became an issue in the city elections and has resulted in strong opposition to police procedures and organization on the part of many in the city.

Yet police also present an alternate image to the community. The same campaign mentioned above in Newark included material that spoke of the service nature of police work as among the complex of services needed by urban populations. A joint front was suggested, pooling the interests of the citizen in "police, education, sanitation [and] health services" (see illustration). This leaflet may have resulted from the belief of some police that in many sectors of the community police have become controversial.

An example of the public controversy over the role police are playing in American society is the series of hearings held in Philadelphia relative to legislation intended

---

THE FRATERNAL ORDER OF POLICE SAYS:

"SAVE OUR SERVICES"

Let's Join Hands To Keep What We Pay Taxes For:

POLICE - EDUCATION - SANITATION - HEALTH SERVICE !

Join Our **RALLY** At 3:45p.m. On

DECEMBER 21st

At **PRUDENTIAL** Broad Street, Nwk.

Police leaflet, Newark, N.J. 1978.

to strengthen civilian complaint procedures for reporting police abuse. There had been numerous complaints of police abuse, particularly of minority and handicapped males, during 1977 and 1978, some connected with the incident mentioned above. There had also been several newspaper series on the negative aspects of police-people relations, one of which received a Pulitzer Prize for journalism.[17] The legislation to be discussed had been held in committee by the City Council Committee on Public Safety for "almost 2 years."[32] The demand for this legislation was supported by those in the community who were concerned with the repressive possibilities of police activity and the potential and even alleged misuse of police power. The resistance to the legislation came from those in the community who were concerned that any further controls on the police would hamper their ability to protect law and order. These hearings were indicative of the concern about abuse of police power among certain elements of the population and the support given to the police concept of themselves as the last bulwark against disorder among other elements of the population. This split has been particularly evident in Philadelphia under the mayoralty of the former chief of police but is seen in many other localities throughout the country from time to time.

The dichotomy in the view of police can be seen to be a result of the position in which the police have been placed and at times place themselves. They are seen variously as guardians of law and order or responsible for their breakdown or are identified as oppressors and symbolic of the inequities and injustices in society. The Police Foundation has been organized in the United States by the Ford Foundation to fund studies and courses to deal with some of these issues and controversies. Some of the latest thinking from this foundation is discussed later in this book, but it is enough to say here that the ferment and rethinking of police roles has been seriously attended to in the United States. Some of the changes are the result of the move toward greater participation in society of formerly disenfranchised elements, for example, women and minorities. There has been a steady increase in police women since the late 1960s and particularly during the middle and late 1970s. In 1977 police women made up 3% of urban police forces.[13] Rand Corporation studies of police work are resulting in changes in the image police have of themselves. The question has become more open: Are police really "social workers who carry guns?" as one police chief was quoted.[13]

Examination of police work based on the assumptions inherent in the manifest definition is not on the face of it unreasonable. It can lead, however, to some seemingly simple conclusions. If the job is such, the success of the job is to be measured directly from the same basis. Reiss and Bordua, in a major work published in 1969, say simply, "The legally defined end of a police department is to enforce the law. The measure of success of a police department is presumably some measure of the degree to which it has in fact enforced the law."[34,p.34] This is not simple for two reasons. One is the difficulty of measuring law enforcement. The other is the difficulty in measuring and assigning value to all the other things that police do.

An alternative analysis of police work takes an entirely different point of view. The terminology is different, as are the definitions and measurements. Whittington makes the somewhat astounding statement that the police are essentially human service workers and perhaps not either primarily or significantly controllers and law enforcers. He claims that the police are the basic service providers of the United States:

The police, in a very real sense, are the generic human service workers in the American community. For forty hours a week they share their heavy burden with a host of other medical and social agencies. The remaining 128 hours a week, when all other agencies close down, the police and emergency room of the hospital are left alone to face the multitudinous problems of the city.[41,p.55]

One may disagree with an assessment that suggests that police should do this but cannot disagree with the fact that the above is true. If it is true, are the roles of police as social controllers and service workers compatible and complementary? If this is true in the United States, does it also describe the police elsewhere? Does this aspect of police work have a legitimate function? These questions are in part the genesis of the study reported later in this book.

Others have dealt with the same issues. Saunders in writing about the distribution of police tasks suggests that there be a readjustment in emphasis. He suggests that the reality of police work is not addressed in current training and that police are not being trained to do what is a major aspect of their job. "Peacekeeping functions consume most of the officers' time . . . which is seriously neglected in training and . . . any view of the police task which undervalues the peacekeeping function [is inadequate]."[35,p.23] Black, a noted jurist, argues for a balanced conception of police work as being a composite of several activities:

If crime and law enforcement were the only responsibility of the police it would be more than a full time job. But the job goes further. A substantial part of police time and energy goes to dealing with human problems which have little to do with crime or the criminal element.[8,p.10]

Others have questioned whether police should be "stuck" with these tasks. It has been argued that police are burdened with "extraneous" non-law-enforcement activities and that they should not be expected to "waste" time on this kind of work. However, Melville, a historian of the British police, suggested at the beginning of the twentieth century that involvement in these activities is not accidental: "The object of the police is not only to enforce compliance with the definite laws of the land, but also to encourage a general recognition of the unwritten code of manners which makes for social progress and good citizenship."[24,p.xxix] It is possible to discuss forever whether and how this might be achieved. It is also reasonable to question whether any one institution in society can do this. If an institution's mandate is too broad and expectations too great, failure may well be built into the system. This does not mean that the questions raised are of no value. To question whether police are expected to have the solution to society's most pressing problems does not leave them with either complete or no responsibility. One cannot require an all-or-nothing response. The question at hand is: What are the functions of police in a democratic society? In almost all cases these functions are shared with other institutions. What is found is active disagreement as to the most appropriate and correct function for the police.

Historically police work has been composed of disparate elements in the five countries studied. From the earliest times policing has been a mixture of peace-keeping (the maintenance of a generally undisturbed and equable social condition) and law enforcement. In Britain, "as the highest maintainer of the peace, the king claimed an actual police supremacy and was not content with a mere title. . . . He had the power of enforcing the rules of the peace, of which he was the chief guardian and exponent."[24,p.1] Here the concept of peacekeeping and law enforcement are conceived of as congruent. A similar description would fit the role of the sheriffs and bailiffs within their jurisdictions. These latter had additional functions, as did their counterparts in the Netherlands, the schout and baljuw. In both cases the judicial role was added to the executive and direct policing roles. Among the range of activities these officers controlled were collection of taxes and issuing of permits.[39] In the Netherlands the issuing of permits still is performed by the police. Throughout the police have been responsible for both fighting crimes and providing various kinds of help to people. Helping aspects seem to be minimized when police were agents of unpopular governments, for example, during periods of French control in the Netherlands and British control in India and Israel.

Some analysts have seriously questioned the appropriateness of the helping or supporting activities, particularly in the United States but also in Britain and India. The helping role seems to be more completely assimilated into the concept of police function in Israel and the Netherlands and to a lesser degree in Britain. British and particularly Dutch critics of the police often seem to be less concerned with the function of police than with whether they are doing all they are supposed to do and are well organized. In order to understand the differences of opinion about police function in this particular area, the main arguments will be set out concerning the disputed police activities, the helping activities or support function.

Some writers consider non-law-enforcement activities to be an interference with the "appropriate" function of the police in social control. Bouma, an American, clearly expressed this point of view: "Not only is [the police person] the thin line between law and disorder . . . but he is saddled with a multitude of problems that are social, medical and economic rather than criminal."[9,p.25] The expression "saddled" surely gives a negative judgment to the "multitude of problems" with which police deal. In some measure one gets the impression that having to deal with these problems detracts from the police ability or availability to deal with maintaining the "thin line between law and disorder." At the least Bouma seems to infer that the police job is made more difficult than it should be because of the added problems.

Another approach is to think of non-law-enforcement work as being of utility only where it helps law enforcement activities. British critics, Martin and Wilson, are concerned with the waste of time entailed in what they call general purpose activities. They indicate that there may be times when such work is justified but that in general it has to be justified by how it affects work with crime. They even seem to be critical of the time spent in patrolling: "In the last resort all that can be said is that such use of time [for general purpose activity] has to be justified in terms either of the prevention of crime or by the availability of the constable to deal with a situation without actually having to be summoned to it."[22,p.163] This statement indicates a rather disparaging view of police involvement in these activities. Both Bouma and Martin and Wilson represent those who believe that police work outside of law enforcement and criminal activity is at best a nuisance that must be shouldered with the least disruption and at worst a positive hindrance to the real function of police, that is, social control.

On the other hand there are those who conceive of police work as only incidentally being involved with law enforcement and crime. The head of the sapper (antibomb) squad in an Israeli city suggested to me that Israelis value the helpful activities of the police much more than law enforcement activities. He said further that only the "social work" aspects of police work were of interest to most Israelis being recruited into police work. His feeling was that unless the job could be made to seem more like social work it would be increasingly difficult to keep the police ranks up to force. A similar concept has been suggested in the United States. Whittington suggests that police in the United States are really "human service workers." As was previously discussed, he calls the American urban police the frontline workers of the human service system. Other critics from the mental health and community service fields have indicated similar ideas.

Another approach to police function has been a somewhat intermediate one. The President's Task Force Report[31] takes the position that the support function is complementary to the control function but less important. It states that the support function aids the control function, although control is the primary role of police. At the very beginning the report states: "The greatly increased complexities of society and its laws today only make more important the kind of unofficial peacekeeping that Jan Jacobs has called the 'intricate, almost unconscious, network of voluntary controls and standards.' "[19,p.2] This is almost an echo of Rowan's ideas of nearly a century and a half before. The acknowledgment of the value of the various elements of their work leads to the possibility of more realistic evaluations of the police.

Narrow definitions lead to difficulties in evaluating their success and value to society. Saunders suggests that there are problems attendant to narrow definitions: "As new demands and responsibilities are [recognized] the difficulties are compounded by the general failure to understand and appreciate the complex nature of the police role and the high qualifications it requires."[34,p.34] Because of this failure police are often required to justify their function on grounds that are unrealistic and inadequately describe their functions in society. Bittner discusses the difficulties engendered by traditional analyses of proper police function also. He talks about the far-ranging results this has on the image of police and the work they do. These have had consequences beyond those affecting performance:

Because the idea that the police are basically a crime fighting agency has never been challenged in the past . . . no one has troubled to sort out the remaining priorities. Instead the police have always been forced to justify activities that did not involve law enforcement in the direct sense by either linking them constructively to law enforcement or by defining them as nuisance demands for service.[7,p.42]

This situation was found in all five countries studied. I received official reports from the Israeli police outlining the work of the police in Jerusalem and Haifa in 1970. These reports list offenses and cases investigated. There are 56 different offenses listed. The list of work done includes seven categories and numerous subcategories. The non-law-enforcement work is summarized in four or five subcategories. The law enforcement work is detailed and accounted for in several ways, for example, numbers of incidents and value and types of objects recovered. In Israel the vast majority of police work is in non-law-enforcement tasks. In Britain official reports show the same bias. The reports for 1970 of the constabulary of Cheshire do not mention non-law-enforcement work except as it relates to community relations work. Other official reports of police work in government files contain 31 categories, of which only seven relate to non-law-enforcement or patrol tasks. Here again the majority of police work activities are of a non-law-enforcement nature. In the Netherlands reports are much more reflective of the actual distribution of police work, with non-law-enforcement and patrol elements having more categories than law enforcement and crime-related categories. For the United States it is rather difficult to make any general statement except that the Federal Bureau of Investigation collects reports only on crime from local police departments and comparisons are made between cities on the crime rates. Local police departments may have more balanced report systems or systems similar to the FBI reports. In Baltimore at the time of the study the statistics kept reflected the wide variety of police tasks quite accurately.

The emphasis on law enforcement at the expense of support activities leads to further problems. One of these is that the police are made to justify their existence through an unrealistic projection of the work they do and possibly of its value to society. The report forms mentioned above for Israel and Britain are good examples of this stress. Unrealities are compounded by this approach, as Reiss points out for the United States:

The low success rate in crimes cleared by arrest creates a dilemma for the police administrators in their efforts to maintain a public image of themselves as productive in a market oriented society. It is neither sufficient nor publicly acceptable for American police to justify themselves by their roles as simply representatives of the moral or legal order. They are under considerable pressure from . . . newspapers and crime commissions and from the Federal Bureau of Investigation, who interpret the statistics in relation to their own goals.[34,p.35]

The problem is not simply one for the United States. The confusion engendered by the lack of clarity, conflicting definitions of police work, and the disregard of reality leads to a problem of self-concept among police and affects their ability to effectively function.

Reexamination and reassessment of police work and police priorities may need to be undertaken (and in some places may indeed be under way):

To view police activity solely from the standpoint of law enforcement is perhaps to miss the crux of the role of the police in the community. It may be argued that the principal function of the police is to promote peace in the community.[33,p.113]

A one-sided emphasis may be lessening the effective function of both the police and professionals in related professions. It certainly increases the difficulty of relationships as part of the social support system. It also might be increasing the difficulties of effective functioning in law enforcement. It is important to remember that there was and continues to be a general antagonism toward police in many societies, including the United States. Resistance to the institution of a police force in England was organized in terms of the repressive possibilities present in a large semimilitary organization divorced from the people. Berkley speaks of this resistance with understanding:

There was and remains much resistance to the concept of police in democratic countries. The fear always remains that they will become agents of repression and are basically anti-democratic.[6,p.9]

Such fears of necessity inhibit the relationships of the police and the people and lead to alienation of the police from the people. Evidence of the continuing strength of such feelings is the attempt to develop civilian review boards for alleged misconduct in various places in the United States (Philadelphia; New York during the 1960s). Proposals for reorganization of federal policing powers in the United States in 1978 occasioned similar fears of abuse of police power: "The centralization of law enforcement functions carries with it the possibility of further abuses, and we're always concerned about that."[30] The fear of abuse of power by police is thus not some straw man built up for the sake of argument. It is real, as real in the latter quarter of the twentieth century as it was in the beginning of the nineteenth.

To understand the responses to police work and priorities it might be helpful to understand the genesis of some of the opinions. Factors influencing opinions about what constitutes the proper focus of police work and about police can be put into three categories: internal police reactions, general societal reactions, and sociopsychological reactions.

Internal police reaction to supportive activities is ambivalent, although some of the tasks cause primarily stress. The ambivalence is caused on the one hand by perceived danger and on the other by fear of isolation from the general community. Some supportive activities have proved to be quite dangerous and difficult. (This is particularly true when the people performing these tasks are not trained to handle the passions often involved.) On the other hand police feel that their value to society is only appreciated as law enforcers. Yet there is the possibility that exclusive involvement in crime fighting and social control could lead to isolation and further alienation from general society. This conundrum is based on reality. The job of police is full of seemingly unanswerable questions and puzzles.

The danger perceived in supportive activities, particularly those involving arbitration and mediation tasks, is real. A member of the Baltimore police force described his fears and the difficulties he experiences in these types of incidents:

Most of the times you get hurt is in a family disturbance. It might be a homicide or a rape or just a lonely old lady who will fantasize a complaint just to talk to you. You don't know what you're walking into and you can't go on every call with a gun in your hand.[3]

A major part of the confusion seems to lie in the inability to take a stand prior to becoming involved in the incident. One can assume in a crime-related incident that there is a good and a bad person involved. The lines are not so clear-cut in supportive actions. That there is real danger is not be to scoffed at. Various studies have emphasized the frustration and danger involved in supportive activities in the United States. A study conducted in New York over a period of 3 years reviewed incidents that were "critical," or in which some major problem developed between police and people. The possibility exists that, with inexpert handling, police intervention can exacerbate a situation rather than resolve it. The person who conducted the study said that he:

. . . was initially struck by the extent to which the handling of relatively minor incidents such as traffic violations or disorderly disputes between husbands and wives seemed to create a more serious situation than existed prior to the police attempt to control it.[23,p.169]

The difficulty may lie somewhat in the concept that there is a need to control situations rather than to help in these situations, a carryover from the control function of police.

In some ways the ambivalence directed at supportive activities may be a result of the greater simplicity inherent in social control. Law enforcement is seen as being much more predictable than support. Support activities are related to very complex socioecological and psychological factors. Crime is seen as being much simpler. The complexity of support activities and the sense of failure and frustration that police in the United States seem to feel when confronted with this complexity is clearly stated in the President's Task Force Report of 1967: "It is when it attempts to solve problems that arise from the community's social and economic failure that policing is least effective and most frustrating."[19,p.2] I would amend the above through the caveat that similar problems are inherent in social control activities as well. As will be seen later, the same questions are raised in regard to that function. But ambivalence does not arise from a situation in which the payoff is only negative. There must be positives in the support function of police work.

The positives are derived from several sources. For many police the positive relationships within the community are what make the job worthwhile. There is also a belief that the supportive aspects of police work are the basis for whatever positive relationships the police have with the public. There are roots for this belief in the historical development of the police in Britain. The new police were designed to depend for their success by working cooperatively with the public. The repressive control aspects of police work were specifically relegated to the back room. The special role behavior of the British bobby was developed during the years following the introduction of this new type of police in 1829. In many ways the development of this new role model for police was imminently successful: "The 'Bobby' was a new kind of police officer. He was unarmed, depending for his success, indeed for his very life, upon his ability to work cooperatively with the populace. He was given little power and told to build respect. He succeeded mightily."[5,p.23] The crux of the problem of ambivalence is found here. The new police were to provide social control but also to gain respect and cooperation from the people they were controlling. The respect and cooperation were to stem from police as helpers and "friends" rather than bullies. This sets up what looks like a double bind for police.

The results of the double bind can be seen in American police going to the public when their jobs are threatened and suggesting that without them there would be lawless chaos while asking the public for help in keeping their jobs. It results in role confusion and a curious schizophrenic self-concept. There is much less of this confusion in societies in which the police role is clearer, such as the Netherlands, Israel, India, and even Britain. In the Netherlands, Israel, and Britain the helper role is emphasized, whereas in India the control role is emphasized and police are not as apt to get lost in confusion about their relations with the general public.

The second category of factors influencing conflicting opinions as to appropriate police priorities are general societal values and expectations. These often generate confusion in the minds of the police as they attempt to fulfill them, particularly as was stated for the United States. On the one hand the police are asked to perform many types of support activities; as will be seen, a majority of the requests for police are of this nature. On the other hand the police are called on to justify their existence by how well the society seems to be controlled. In all of the five countries there are similar measures for police success. The general conception of the effectiveness of the police is directly related to the crime statistics. This is most obvious in the United States but equally true in the other countries. The specificity of what is called success in the United States has been discussed by other writers. An example of the simplicity of it all is found in the following statement, not to be disputed:

There are two major ways that success gets defined for [police] departments. The first kind is a measure of aggregate success, whether of a crime rate, arrests, crimes cleared by arrests, convictions, or values of stolen property recovered. The second is the success it has in meeting public demands to solve a particular crime problem as, for example, when a crime outrages the public conscience.[34,p.34]

The police in Israel publish only the above kinds of statistics, as do the police in

Britain, the Netherlands, and India. Although the statement reflects the situation in the United States, it is generalizable to the other countries as well. And this in countries in which the police have developed rather good supportive relationships with the general public. No wonder the police of Newark, New York, and Philadelphia aim for public support by trumpeting the dangers inherent in their absence and the benefits of social tranquility that will attend increasing the forces and raising their salaries.

Success and priorities are measured as well by the rewards given for the performance of particular tasks. Rewards are in the form of public notice of a job well done (aside from salary increases) and of political recognition. Awards are given for police bravery in the line of duty, for capturing criminals, for solving heinous crimes, or for having been involved in life-threatening situations. The macho image is reinforced and broadened, as illustrated in the American film *The French Connection* and other similar police movies. The police hero is an intrepid, almost superhuman, hero on the trail of desperate and consciousless criminals. He relentlessly tracks them down against all odds, having thrilling adventures all the while and coming close to death. In the end, of course, right triumphs, and the police hero brings the criminals to justice, even in the face of a corrupt justice system. The only non-crime-oriented job for which the police get awards is bravery in saving lives. Awards are seldom given to police for rescuing marriages, making a lonely person's life less empty, helping to calm emotionally disturbed people, getting ill people to care, or helping people obtain needed care. An exception is the occasional award for helping to deliver a baby. In February 1979 forty-two officers of the Philadelphia police force were honored in a ceremony at police headquarters, all for bravery and courage. The Valor Award, the highest commendation of the police department, was given to a 5-year veteran shot while attempting to apprehend a robbery suspect. Three officers of the narcotics unit received Bravery Awards for shooting a suspect in the course of a drug-related arrest. Another officer was cited for bravery for shooting and wounding one of the robbers while stopping a robbery of a store. Thirty-four officers and two sergeants were cited for heroism in rescuing people from burning buildings. One civilian employee was cited for rescuing a fellow employee whose clothes had caught fire. The Deputy Police Commissioner told the gathered family and friends of the honorees, "Some people take vitamin C or vitamin D, but our police officers take bravery pills."[40] It is obvious that society gives acclaim to those police who are macho, intrepid, and fulfilling the manifest law enforcement functions almost entirely to the exclusion of the latent support function.

Over the past several years in the United States there has been a tendency to think in terms of soldiers when thinking of police. This is a direct result of the civil turmoil of the late 1960s and the public's revulsion to it. With the immense expenditures of money for tactical weaponry for police during that era and the continued conception that many people have of the cities as battlegrounds, there has been a shift toward greater emphasis on the control functions of police. One commentator suggested that "the impression [may be given] that the policeman is considered the soldier of the cities, doing battle on the front line."[9,p.20] The conception of the solider is not that of a supportive person (although it might be argued that soliders also have a support function). This has been accompanied by complaints of police brutality and repression, particularly from minority communities and people. The view of police as adversaries and repressors is most widespread in these communities, while the middle-class majority is led to think of police as their brutes or the forceful defenders of their rights and privileges.

Society thus reinforces the control function and not the support function of police. Incentives are given that reinforce law enforcement values, and support values are left to fend for themselves. This tends to support the negatives that police find in support activities and fails to reinforce the positive values of such work.

A third set of factors that influence the development of police priorities is sociopsychological in nature. These are the interrelationships and disjunctions between the functions of police (social control and social support) and the ambivalence and strains thus engendered. The support and control functions of police are in some ways contradictory and in other ways complementary. Preparation, both in training and psychological set, are different for both functions. For control one must learn to be strong and resolute, whereas for support one must learn to be compassionate and understanding. Yet the two functions can be seen to reinforce each other. The conflictual and complementary elements in the relationship between the two functions are difficult to reconcile. This sociopsychological conflict is a major element in the ambivalence and ambiguity found in examining police work and responses to it.

The conflictual elements between the two functions seem obvious. It is the complementary nature of the two that must be discussed. The complementary nature of the functions is bilateral although it has usually been discussed unilaterally. It is not unusual for the support function to be justified by its complementarity to control. It has been stated that the supportive elements in police work soften the blow of the control elements. Cumming et al. set the case in bold relief: "Control without potential support is tyranny and invites rebellion or despair. . , , Both elements are essential to social regulation, the one affirming the individual, the other the social order."[15,p.6] From the writings of Rowan it has been seen that this was an elemental concept behind the initial development of the British police. One can set up a number of arguments in relating the helpful function of support activities to those of control.

There has been little or no discussion of the reverse phenomenon, that is, how the control functions might complement support activities. The identification of police with authority may be the very element that leads to requests for support. As will be seen in a later discussion, many persons define mental illness and marital problems, drug and alcohol abuse, and a host of other social problems as problems of control. A spouse may call the police during a marital conflict because they are identified as control agents. The family may call for police in problems of mental illness because they are identified as control agents. The thinking is that if persons could control or wanted to control themselves the problems would be solved. How often do we ask our children and ourselves, "Why don't you just control yourself?" Obviously, there is a modicum of truth in the accusation or question. Although discussion of this issue is beyond the scope of this text, it is my firm opinion that the matter goes far beyond control and will. However, those who so define problems would be most likely to go to the civil agents of control for help in their problems.

The complementarity of control and support roles necessitates a balance that may be difficult to achieve. In Rowan's initial conception the duality and mutual complementarity was not recognized as an issue. The issue has come to the fore, primarily in the United States, in recent years. It is not even now generally acknowledged. The tension still exists between the pull to become involved in the life of the community and provide support or to withdraw from the community to enhance the impartial controller image. Quinney looks at the delicate balancing that is necessary: "Too much involvement [in the affairs of the community] might negate the possibilities of fulfilling the ideal of fair and impartial handling of cases, while too much isolation removes the police from an understanding of the needs of the community."[33,p.113] The President's Task Force also addressed a similar question. However, it looked at it from the issue of causality. The interrelationship between need for support services and the incidence of crime was suggested. The Task Force Report, without intensive discussion, posited the often declared relationship between social conditions and social disorder. It declared an interdependence between need for social service and genesis of crime. In this light it faulted proposals to remove the support function from police hands: "Proposals to relieve the police of what are essentially social services have also been lacking in the consideration of the relationship of such services to the incidence of . . . crimes."[31,p.14] From the above discussion there seems to be several complementary relationships between support and control. One is the enhancement of each function by the other. The other is the genesis of the need for each by similar social conditions.

There is in this discussion no attempt to minimize the difficulty involved in attempting to fulfill both control and support functions by the same agency and individuals. There is no doubt that role strains are engendered by the different functions and different skills needed for these functions. Cumming et al. suggest that these role strains and difficulties are at the core of the drive to specialize in one or the other: "Support and control require different skills . . . and can involve intolerable role strain. The difficulty of performing contradictory acts and adopting conflicting attitudes is one reason agents and agencies tend to become specialized in one or another aspect of the integrative process."[15,p.7] Although in basic agreement about the strains and conflicts, I would not posit the situation in such total terms. There are, as has been seen, complementary aspects to these functions and complementary skills as well.

It need not be assumed that only the police and "experts" are ambivalent about police function. The public entertains the same ambivalence. There is probably not another agency that has such intimate dealings with a large segment of the population as the police. This is particularly true in communities with the greatest social needs. This intimacy reinforces the ambivalence people feel, particularly because it takes place at times of great vulnerability: "Police deal with people when they are most threatened and most vulnerable, when they are angry and when they are fright-ened, when they are desperate, when they are drunk, when they are violent, or when they are ashamed. . . . It is inevitable that the public is of two minds about the police: most [people] both welcome official protection and resent official inter-ference."[35,p.15] Of course the very vulnerability of the public when interacting with the police gives police a somewhat skewed concept of people. When one deals pri-marily with the seamy side of people's lives, one starts to think that this is the greatest part of their lives. This gives some understanding for the ambivalence and at times disrespect that police seem to exhibit toward the public. These sociopsycho-logical factors are involved in the decision-making process through which police priorities are set.

The President's Task Force saw involvement of the police in supportive, non-punitive activities as being not only important in and of itself but also as a means of helping police and public get to know each other in less restrictive conditions. They suggested that the police be more adequately organized to perform community and human service activities so as to reduce the adversary role relationship between police and people. In addition to its other merits, the effect would be to improve police-community relations by reducing the adversary role of the police and by making them part of a broader process than merely arrest and conviction.[31,p.162] This is presumably so that the function of the police would be enhanced in all its aspects. One can see that the sociopsychological factors influencing police-people relation-ships and their respective images are complex and multifaceted.

Other factors, such as lack of alternatives, convenience, and diagnostic concepts, also are thought to influence viewpoints about the two elements of police function. Some have hypothesized that the reason police in the United States have so many supportive activities is that it is often difficult to find another agency to which people in need of help can turn. The President's Task Force of 1967 set forth this explana-tion quite straightforwardly, while at the same time mentioning the convenience of having such a ubiquitous service agency as the police:

It might be desirable for service agencies other than the police to provide . . . services. But the failure of such agencies to develop . . . suggests that the police are likely to remain, for some time, the only 24-hour-a-day, seven-day-a-week agency that is spread over an entire city in a way that makes it possible for them to respond quickly to incidents of these kinds.[31,p.14]

Other commentators also have remarked on the convenience and availability of the police for providing needed service. Kahn suggests that the police are the most available public servants and that "people, therefore, turn to them for many emergencies."[18,p.209] In Europe and Israel, and more recently in many American cities, there is added convenience in having a simple emergency number for summoning the police. This phenomenon is seen to be a growing one throughout the world. It can safely be said that generally there is a greater attempt to make the police and fire departments more easily available than any other of the well-used services within communities. This availability, it has been suggested, is a major factor in the use of police for support tasks.

Lack of easily accessible alternatives, public convenience, and the general availability of the police may not affect perceptions of police but certainly may affect usage of the police. It has been assumed in the recent development of human or social services in the United States and in other countries that services should be available and convenient. Community service centers, satellite clinics, evening hours, and other such developments can be traced to this thinking. The importance of availability is particularly noted for that part of the population who are least sophisticated and most vulnerable, the poor and uneducated.

In the foregoing, various elements affecting perceptions of police work and the priorities and responses that grow from these have been examined. The picture is that of great complexity and diverse and often conflicting currents. The results have been attempts at simplicity and a general return to manifest definitions of police work even when the actual function of the police does not correspond completely with this. It has been seen that there are two functions of police: control and support. It has also been seen that these are in some ways conflicting and contradictory but in other ways mutually supportive and complementary.

POLICE AND HEALTH SYSTEM

It may be surprising to some to think that police have a role in mental and physical health care. In the case of physical health it may be somewhat tangential, but in mental health police often have a crucial role in the general provision of care where needed. In this section the possible areas in which police might be involved in physical health care are examined, followed by a more extensive discussion of the police role in the mental health care system.

The role of police in health care in general is related to the support function of police. In a number of cities in the United States police often furnish emergency ambulance services. During the 1960s it was widely known in the black community in Chicago that certain sections of this community without private transport could get to the public hospital only by calling for a police van. One of the public housing projects, with almost 100% black population and far from the city center and the public hospital, had a police van detailed specifically for such emergencies, often maternity situations. Police are also often called when people get sick in public places or have attacks of chronic disease, for example, epilepsy or diabetes. A major function of police in many countries is to deal with the aftermath of vehicular accidents. In these situations people are often injured or in shock and need immediate care and transportation to further care facilities. The role of the police in many of the above situations is primarily to give first aid, but often they must provide resuscitation for injured or ill people. Although in these situations the police may provide care that spells the difference between life and death or between minor and major effects of a health care situation, the major societal health role still lies with health professionals.

In the case of mental health there are more intimate involvements. In support of this, mental health agencies in some areas of the United States are attempting to develop more intensive and positive relationships with the police, as suggested by the National Institute of Mental Health (NIMH). A training program for police was tested in various cities in the country to see if the police could be taught to work with "mental and social deviates" in a more helpful manner. This program was reported in *Today's Health* in 1970. It was stated that changes were being made in the way police handled such people through the efforts of this training program.[25] Implied in the above is a somewhat passive role for the police in cases of mental and social deviation. The police role is often of a more active nature. Kahn delineated this quite clearly: "Police are major case locators; they are also major channels for the members of the public concerned with reporting situations they have encountered but about which they are not sure where to turn."[2] The role of case locator is of major importance in the mental health system, particularly if it is to be active in providing service to those who need it. Often the most difficult job of mental health agencies is finding the clients who need the service most. These are generally the very persons who are least able to seek out the service on their own. This police role as part of the "intake" aspect of the mental health system is further delineated by Kahn. He sets the police role as a major referral service in which police develop evaluative abilities and become well enough acquainted with the rest of the service system that adequate direction can be given to appropriate services:

The issue is not whether police should be screening and exercising some discretion but rather how much they can and should do. . . . Brief screening and more complete evaluation and case referral are part of the same process and require the same basic qualities and attitudes. Proper referrals, whether to a guidance clinic for personality help, to a settlement [community center] for club contact, or to a court as a preliminary step toward institutionalization, also presuppose a good working knowledge of community resources and agencies, the service they offer, and their methods of operation.[2]

The President's Task Force on the Police reached a similar conclusion. They pointed to the possibility of the police support function actually becoming integrated into a broader social service system:

The possibility has been suggested that eventually the police may become part of a broader social service team which will include social workers, psychiatrists and doctors acting as an intake screening unit for all kinds of antisocial and disturbing conduct.[31]

The value of police involvement in the mental health system as well as similar support systems has been stressed by theorists and practitioners writing on police function from the viewpoint of the delivery of mental health, health, and social services. Among the most forceful writers are those who have worked with police in dealing with particular problems, such as marital conflict, minority relations, and juveniles. Others have helped develop programs for such problems in cooperation with police departments. A major effort was made in this area in New York in the late 1960s as a pilot project, and similar projects have been attempted in other police jurisdictions in the United States.

In a police precinct of New York a specially trained Family Crisis Intervention Unit was organized in 1967. The Psychological Institute of the College of the City of New York, in collaboration with the New York City Police Department, helped develop this pilot project. A volunteer group of policemen in the pilot precinct underwent 4 weeks of intensive training and then participated in weekly consultation and supervision for continuing training. The unit members, working in pairs, were available 24 hours a day, 7 days a week. They had continuing responsibility for regular police work but were available when a call for intervention in a family crisis or dispute was received in the precinct. The project lasted 2 years. A manual was developed for ongoing training of all policemen in New York in the handling of family crises such as runaway children and arguments between spouses or between parents and children.

When the rationale advanced by the Psychological Institute for the project is examined, some interesting lapses appear. Bard suggested the project to the police as a means to reduce assaults on policemen and to decrease the incidence of family crisis calls.[4] Publications for professionals in the mental health field suggested that police could be used as front-line troops in the struggle for a mentally healthy society. The intervention of police in family crises, which were described as crucial periods of intervention with important impact on the total life of the family, was to be a step in providing mental health services to the family. The somewhat opportunistic split in the sales pitch indicates that Bard did not consider the police to be concerned about the mental health of the public, although this was a major benefit of the program proposed. Apparently the police were not trusted to respond to human service needs at all. It appears that only some concern with police self-interest could induce them to try the program.

More recently some of the New York police force have become involved in another major social health problem. There has been a large increase in the number of young teenagers running away from home to the large cities of the United States. New York is a major magnet for such young people. In April 1978 there was a report in *The New York Times* of a special project developed by the Port Authority Police. In 1976 this department began a Youth Service Unit under federal subsidy as an experiment. The unit is composed of two-person teams, a plainclothes officer and a social worker. The aim of the unit is to intercept some of the young people entering New York before they reach the streets and probable trouble and serious exploitation. It is estimated that in 1978 approximately 20,000 runaways were in New York on any given day. The work of the unit is described as "preventive" by the director of the squad. It is an attempt to prevent the common transformation from runaway to prostitute or drug addict.[10] There is obviously another aspect to the work of the unit. It not only prevents crime but also gives disturbed youngsters another chance to make some positive growth in their lives and families a chance to deal with painful issues. It is in actuality a source of support for the people with whom it comes in contact.

The role of the police in mental health is not limited to the United States. The World Health Organization (WHO) suggested that police have a role to play in the maintenance of mental health service systems. In 1961 WHO published a report on the development of mental health service systems. In this report there was mention of the function of police in such a system, albeit briefly. The concern of this section of the report was with training of police to deal with problems related to mental health. In the following excerpt several of the possibilities are outlined:

It is essential the police officer be taught how to deal with the mentally ill. It is particularly important that they be given adequate instruction in the management of suicidal persons. Since in many cases the police officer is one of the first contacts of potentially delinquent children, he should receive instruction, as explicit and complete as possible, in dealing with them as their delinquent behavior develops.[42,p.34]

This broader involvement of police has been cultivated in a number of instances. Most of them have been part of the evolution of police work in the United States over the past several years and were in some measure responses to the ferment and questioning of society's values and function that took place during the 1960s and early 1970s. A previously mentioned article in *Today's Health* describes programs being developed around the United States under grants from the NIMH.[28] The programs are concerned with drug and alcohol abuse, homosexuality (three areas that have traditionally been extensively dealt with by the police in the United States), and development of liaison with community mental health facilities. It supports the impression that there has been some support for the formation of constructive relationships between police and mental health professionals.

An article written in 1969 reports a study of police activity in mental health service throughout the United States.[16] It reports that police do indeed carry a heavy load of service to people with mental health problems. It cited a study carried out in Baltimore that found that police were the first to be contacted in 50% of the emergency admissions to mental hospitals. The study was oriented to examining why some people take their behavioral and psychological problems to the police and others turn to apparently more appropriate medical and psychiatric facilities. There are major differences between those going directly to emergency rooms of hospitals and other medical resources and those going to the police for such aid. The differences have to do solely with views of mental illness and of the police. No demographic or other social differences are found between the two groups. The police are seen as the easiest and most convenient resource by all but one of the families that used the police as the referral agents. The group using police to aid in receiving treatment deny that it is illness with which they are dealing. They state that they call the police because they think that the patient is not in control of himself and if only he could be controlled everything would be all right. This suggests a somewhat unsophisticated approach to mental illness on the part of those calling the police for help as opposed to those who obtain emergency treatment for acute episodes of mental illness.[20] It can be concluded that many people who need help in a variety of situations, which they themselves define as problems of control rather than need for treatment, turn to the police as a convenient and available resource.

SUMMARY

In this chapter an overview of police work and responses to police work by the public and various professionals is provided. Some of the interfaces between the police and the service delivery system, particularly in regard to mental health services, are discussed. Also briefly mentioned are possible reasons for requests for police provision of supportive service. Attitudes, both pro and con, toward supportive police activities are included. Possibilities of more planful interaction between the police and other service deliverers are introduced. The police are seen to provide services that often act as entrance to the supportive service system. Some of the societal forces of which the police support function may be a result, as well as the consequences of this function, should also be examined. A social process that appears to be closely related to the supportive function of the police is social integration.

REFERENCES

1. Articles on disturbances and murder in Borough Park, *New York Times*, December 2-6, 1978, p. 1.
2. Balch, R.: The police personality: fact or fiction? J. Criminal Law Criminol. Police Sci. 63:1, 1972.
3. *Baltimore Sun*, January 16, 1973, p. A20.
4. Bard, M.: Training police as specialists in family crisis intervention, United States Department of Justice, Washington, D.C., 1970, U.S. Government Printing Office.
5. Bayley, D. H.: The police and political development in Europe, unpublished draft, Denver, 1970, University of Denver.
6. Berkley, G. E.: The democratic policeman, Boston, 1969, Beacon Press.
7. Bittner, E.: The functions of the police in a modern society, Washington, D.C., 1970, National Institute of Mental Health, U.S. Government Printing Office.
8. Black, A.: The people and the police, New York, 1968, McGraw-Hill Book Co.
9. Bouma, D.: Kids and cops, Grand Rapids, Mich., 1969, Wm. B. Eerdmans Publishing Co.
10. Catching runaways before the street gets them, *New York Times*, April 13, 1978, p. B1.
11. Church Assembly Board for Social Responsibility: Police: a social study, Oxford, England, 1967, Church Army Press.
12. Commissie ter Bestudering van het Politievraagstuk: Report (verslag) presented by joint request of the Ministries of Justice and Interior, October 1, 1948, The Hague, 1948, Staatsdrukkerij & Uitgeverijbedrijf.
13. Cop on the beat: a dying breed? *Philadelphia Inquirer*, December 17, 1978, p. 1H.
14. Critchely, T. A.: A history of police in England and Wales: 900-1966, London, 1967, Constable & Co., Ltd.
15. Cumming, E., Cumming, I., and Edell, L.: Policeman as philosopher, guide and friend. In Quinney, R.: The social reality of crime, Boston, 1970, Little, Brown & Co.

16. Fijnaut, C.: The rebuilding of the Dutch police, Neth. J. Criminol. **18,** June and October, 1976.

17. The homicide files, *Philadelphia Inquirer,* April 24-27, 1978.

18. Kahn, A.: Planning community services for children in trouble, New York, 1963, Columbia University Press.

19. Katzenbach, N. de B.: The challenge of crime in a free society, New York, 1968, Avon Books.

20. Lieberman, R.: Police as a community mental health resource, Comm. Mental Health J. **5:**111-120, 1969.

21. Linton, R.: Culture and mental disorders, Springfield, Ill., 1959, Charles C Thomas, Publisher.

22. Martin, J. P., and Wilson, G.: The police: a study in manpower, London, 1969, William Heinemann, Ltd.

23. McNamara, J. H.: Uncertainties in police work: the relevance of police recruits' backgrounds and training. In Bordua, D. H., editor: The police: six sociological essays, New York, 1967, John Wiley & Sons, Inc.

24. Melville, W. L.: History of the police in England, London, 1901, Patterson Smith.

25. Mental health training program prompts police, Today's Health **48:**84, 1970.

26. More policemen in Borough Park—temporarily, *New York Times,* December 6, 1978, pp. 1, B3.

27. Move shootout articles, *Philadelphia Inquirer,* August 1978.

28. National Institute of Mental Health: First United States mental health mission to the Soviet Union, Washington, D.C., 1965, U.S. Government Printing Office.

29. Newark police officers appeal to fear, *New York Times,* November 22, 1978, p. A1.

30. Plan to reorganize U.S. law enforcement is studied, *New York Times,* May 24, 1978, p. A20.

31. President's Commission on Law Enforcement and the Administration of Justice, Task Force on the Police: Task Force report: the police, Washington, D.C., 1967, U.S. Government Printing Office.

32. A public hearing on police "crisis," *Philadelphia Inquirer,* December 12, 1978, p. 1.

33. Quinney, R.: The social reality of crime, Boston, 1970, Little, Brown & Co.

34. Reiss, A. J., Jr., and Bordua, D. J.: Environment and organization: a perspective on the police. In Bordua, D. J., editor: The police: six sociological essays, New York, 1969, John Wiley & Sons, Inc.

35. Saunders, C. B., Jr.: Upgrading the American police, Washington, D.C., 1970, The Brookings Institute.

36. Skolnick, J. H.: Justice without trial: law enforcement in democratic society, New York, 1967, John Wiley & Sons, Inc.

37. Stewart-Brown, R.: The serjeants of the police in Medieval England and Wales, Manchester, England, 1936, Manchester University Press.

38. They don't rely on just nightsticks anymore, *Philadelphia Inquirer,* December 17, 1978, p. 20A.

39. Van Der Burg, F. H.: Preventive justice and local police, dissertation at the University of Utrecht, March 22, 1961.

40. Well done: police department pays tribute to its own, *Philadelphia Inquirer,* February 28, 1979, p. 3B.

41. Whittington, H. G.: The police: ally or enemy of the comprehensive mental health center? Mental Health **55:**55, 1971.

42. World Health Organization: Programme development in the mental health field, WHO Tech. Rep. Ser. 223, 1961.

Chapter 4

Social integration

Various writers have said that social integration is one of the functions of police. Cummings et al. described the control function of police as being part of an integrative system within society.[8,p.147]

There is further evidence that the police are involved in the social integration process in modern society. In Japan it has been observed that "so many of the people the police see regularly, and to whom only they attend, are defeated, bedraggled, and helpless. Some have been abused by their own vices, some by circumstances they could not control. All are pitiful and lost, the hope gone out of their lives."[3,p.31] The police observed in Japan spend much of their time dealing with these, the flotsam and jetsam of a society that has become modern and urban in the very recent past, with those whose moorings have been broken by the social changes of their society.

John Clark has also described police work in terms of social integration. He talks about police work affecting the position of society on an isolation to integration scale. In this he suggests that police work "contributed to the overall unity and welfare of a society."[6,p.126]

The concept that police are important in the integration of the entire society, in its welfare, so to speak, is explored briefly here. First, however, it is necessary to discuss what is meant by social integration. The term itself comes from more generalized concepts. The adjective *social* is derived from the Latin, *socialis*, which in turn is derived from *socius*, meaning companion, ally, associate. It entered the language in the mid-1500s, according to the Oxford Dictionary, and has had a variety of uses in the intervening period. Webster's dictionary defines social as "of or having to do with human beings living together as a group. . . ." Integration is a noun derived from the Latin *integrationem*, meaning renewal or restoring to wholeness, from *integer*, meaning untouched, entire, or whole. It entered the language in the early 1500s, according to the Oxford Dictionary. It is currently defined by Oxford as "the making up of a whole by adding together or combining the separate parts of elements." Social integration therefore could be said to be the condition or process of adding or bringing human subgroups and individuals together into a whole society.

The context of the need for and value of social integration as a concept needs to be examined in understanding social function. I will posit further a concept of "social need" related to social integration that is measurable within social areas and which can be quantified. It can then be correlated with police work within an area to see if there is any observable connection between the two.

The history of human social development has been one of constant change in terms of social organization and processes. Historically there have been some periods of rapid social change and relatively quick growth, although usually these factors have moved rather slowly. The past few hundred years, the modern era, however, has been a period of extremely rapid, one might say unprecedented, change and growth. Many of the changes are related to industrialization, the concomitant exponential increases in population, and the concentration of the population in urban centers. These changes have been occurring worldwide, although in some areas (Western Europe and North America) they have taken place over a period of 200 to 300 years and in other areas (Asia and Africa) they have taken place primarily in the past 25 to 50 years.

It took most of human history for the world's population to reach 1 billion in about 1840. It has taken a little more than a century for this to increase to 4 billion. It is expected to again double around the end of the twentieth century. For example, the population of India was around 125 million in the 1820s. In 1928 it had reached over 300 million. Fifty years later the population had again doubled to over 600 million. It is expected to again double in about 25 years. The United States population was 76 million in 1900 and reached 215 million by 1979.

Along with population increases, societies all over the world have become increasingly urbanized and industrialized. The changes from rural to urban have been startling in North America and Europe. In the 1850s the vast majority of the population, over 90%, was rural and farming. In the mid-1900s the vast majority, almost the same proportion, was urban and suburban, depending on nonagricultural work for sustenance.

The demographic changes alone are cataclysmic. Add to this the changes in technology over the past 150 years, which have reached some societies only within the past 25 to 50 years, and it can be seen that rapid is a pale description of the rate and nature of social changes in the recent past. It can be expected that the effects of these changes on the nature of society and social institutions have been great. These effects have been examined by many scientists and philosophers. One notable effect has been the growth of new and complex institutions responding to the weakening in importance of the primary support system (that of kinship and intimate community). Contemporary society is seen as one in which a somewhat fluid, impersonal, and broad organization of social groups has increasingly replaced, or at the least complemented, relatively stable, personal, and highly segmented social organization.

Modes of social control, social integration, and socialization must of necessity change with overall changes in society, especially those so sweeping as have been briefly outlined. Since Nietsche it has been maintained that the development of "modern" or "mass" society has been largely accompanied by alienation and disorganization. The term *mass society,* in fact, is often used perjoratively to describe the alienated and alienating organization of human life in the urban, industrial world.[15]

Against mass society is posited an idyllic, integrated past. The German terms *gemeinschaft* and *gesellschaft* have been adopted to describe the alternative conditions. It has become popular to state that from a gemeinschaft, an idyllic, warm, integrated, supportive condition, society has developed into a gesellschaft, an alienated, mechanized, cold condition unresponsive to human needs. The peasant society and feudalism have been thought of as examples of gemeinschaft. Mass, urban, industrial society has been used to characterize gesellschaft. This mass society is a territorially extensive society with a large population. It is highly urbanized and industrialized. It has been suggested that in this society power must be concentrated in the hands of an "elite," which manipulates an alienated, exploited mass prone to respond to demagoguery and with few ties to anything other than survival.

There is an alternative stand to the negative view of modern society. Shils is an opponent of the position that modern society has "become" alienated and unresponsive. He claims that this position is primarily a product of the reaction to the French Revolution and the egalitarian philosophies with which it is associated. He suggests that "modern" society is actually a consensual society and that the previous societies of feudalism and early capitalism were exploitative and alienating. He says that the consensual society is *historically* a new concept of governance and that it is developing throughout the world, albeit at different rates. Shils sees the growth of modern society as having occurred through the integration rather than isolation of aggregates of humans living in geopolitical areas into social systems in which the parts are interdependent. This modern society has arisen through the death of the isolated, self-contained, and self-supporting community.[15] He further states that the mass society is the first society in which the majority of the population is more than a primarily ecological part of the system, somewhat like cattle.[15] Specific to the mass society in Shils' view is the establishment of consensually legitimate institutions, within which much of the conflict of the society takes place and which imposes limits on this conflict:

Hence, despite all internal conflicts, bridging and confining them, there are, within the "mass" society, more of a sense of attachment to the society as a whole, more sense of affinity with one's fellows, more openness to understanding among men, than in any earlier societies of our planet's history.[15]

The conflict between the gesellschaft view of modern society and Shils' "consensual" view of modern society might be amenable to resolution. This is particularly possible when society is thought of as an organism constantly developing and adjusting to the changing demands of the environment of which it is an integral part.

Development of "modern" society has been accompanied by changes in the means of sustenance and the ability to provide for large numbers of people on a rather continuous basis. It has allowed for changes in the means utilized to promote social integration and the welfare of the people. In the localized society of the village and small community, integration was promoted through personal, intimate, and "informal" mechanisms and institutions, such as family and neighbors. The ecological system could not support anything more. As the ecological system and therefore the scope of society has broadened, the function of the process of social integration has been increasingly delegated to more "formal" institutions, public and semipublic organizations. In the process feelings of alienation and anomie or normlessness have been widespread. But the participation of larger and larger aggregates of people in the larger business of life has also taken place. In examining police history the parallels are clearly seen.

There were local personal mechanisms for policing and the containment of conflict in the premodern world. With the development of larger and larger social aggregates in the past century and a half there has developed the institution of police forces, dedicated to impartial service, containment of social conflict, and generalized response to human need.

There have been a number of attempts to operationalize the concept of social integration. They have all run into great difficulties. There has been confusion as to whether social integration is a condition of society, remaining fixed over time,[1,p.168;2] or a process within society, dynamic and changing. It has been suggested that it is an expression of the mechanisms that groups develop for coping with stress[7] or expressed by the mutual assistance patterns of society.[11]

Social integration has both universal and relative aspects. Durkheim set forth the universalist conception of social integration.[9,10] Others have suggested that the variables involved are specific to each culture, developing as a particular adaptation to particular sets of societal circumstances.[11] Coping mechanisms vary as environmental stresses vary.[7] The particular integrative adaptations developed within black American subculture have received attention recently.[4,12]

Some scientists suggest that elements of the process in one culture or social area are "better" than those of another.[13,14] Alternatively it is suggested that the social integration process operates in all functioning groups and societies with differing specific elements. This position suggests that only the dying group, for example, the Ik of East Africa, is not socially integrated.[5]

A more precise terminology in the study of social integration might be developed through the empirical analysis of the integration process. I believe that the process of social integration operates through a number of channels, both informal, voluntary ones and formal, socially (public) organized ones. One difference between societies and social subgroups is the degree to which voluntary and public channels are used in the integrative process. Most modern, large, industrial societies find informal, intimate social bonds inadequate to satisfy survival and comfort needs. These societies therefore have relied to a growing degree on formal structure and agencies of society to provide support. For the purposes of this discussion a composite of indicators of need for formal public input into the support system of the society at a cross-sectional period is called "social need."

To define social need in this manner does not posit a judgment on the state of social integration within the social area. There is no implication that the need for greater or lesser use of informal and formal channels at a particular time makes one society or subgroup "better," "worse," or more viable than another society. This approach to analysis of social integration thereby reduces cultural bias.

Social integration is defined as that social process concerned with the support and nurturance that humans need to survive. Human society is the response to the need of humans for each other for survival. It is the assumption of this text that all societies are socially integrated. A difference between groups is in the amount of interdependence needed for survival as well as the balance between informal, voluntary supports and formal, public supports. Indications of need for formal, public supports is called the "social need" of the area for the purposes of this text.

Social integration can be understood on several levels, individual (psychological), small group (social psychological), and societal (sociologic). The emphasis here is on the sociologic or societal aspects. This is the conceptualization of the process whereby the interdependence within a population welds that population into a functioning group. The process can be examined in terms of "social need." Social need has a relationship to physical and mental health. It is suggested that the supportive activities of the police are an important formal response to social needs and therefore are socially integrative and important to community health.

REFERENCES

1. Abu-Lughod, J. L.: Testing the theory of social area analysis: the ecology of Cairo, Egypt, Am. Sociolog. Rev. 34:168, 1969.
2. Aiken, M., and Alford, R.: Community structure and innovation: the case of urban renewal, Am. Sociolog. Rev. 35:650, 1970.
3. Bayley, D. H.: Forces of order: police behavior in Japan and the United States, Berkeley, Calif., 1978, University of California Press.
4. Billingsley, A.: Black families in white America, Englewood Cliffs, N.J., 1968, Prentice-Hall, Inc.
5. Calhoun, J. B.: Plight of the Ik and Kaiadilb, Smithsonian 3:8, November 1972.
6. Church Assembly Board for Social Responsibility: Police, a social study, Oxford, England, 1967, Church Army Press.
7. Coleman, J. S.: Resources for social change, New York, 1971, Interscience, John Wiley & Sons, Inc.
8. Cumming, E., Cumming, I., and Edell, L.: Policeman as philosopher, guide and friend. In Quinney, R.: The social reality of crime, Boston, 1970, Little, Brown & Co.
9. Durkheim, E.: Suicide, Glencoe, Ill., 1951, The Free Press.
10. Durkheim, E.: The division of labor in society, Glencoe, Ill., 1947, The Free Press.
11. Granovetter, M. S.: Alienation reconsidered: the strength of weak ties, unpublished draft, Cambridge, Mass., 1969, Harvard University, Department of Social Relations.
12. Hill, R. B.: The strength of black families, New York, 1972, Emerson Hall Publishers, Inc.
13. Leighton, A.: The character of danger, New York, 1963, Basis Books, Inc.
14. Leighton, A., et al.: My name is legion, New York, 1959, Basic Books, Inc.
15. Shils, E.: The theory of mass society, Diogenes 39:45-53, Fall 1962.

PART TWO

DEVELOPMENT AND FUNCTION OF POLICE IN FIVE COUNTRIES

Chapter 5

Britain

The United Kingdom of Great Britain and Northern Ireland is situated in the British Isles off the Northwest coast of Europe, with the North Atlantic on the North and West. Separating the British Isles from the mainland are the North Sea on the East, the Strait of Dover on the Southeast, and the English Channel on the South. England shares the island of Great Britain with Wales and Scotland and is the largest in size and population of the components of the United Kingdom. The population of England is about 46 million (1972), and the remainder of the population of the United Kingdom is about 10 million. The government is a constitutional monarchy with a hereditary monarch (currently Queen Elizabeth II). The monarchs are descendants of William the Conqueror, the Norman prince who defeated the Anglo-Saxon royal house in 1066. The English people are descendants of the original Celts and Picts who were conquered by the Romans in the early centuries of the Christian era, invading settlers from Scandinavia and northern Germany, French and Norman settlers during the Middle Ages, and various immigrant groups from Europe and the areas of the world that were part of the English empire until after World War II. The language is basically Germanic with strong Latinate elements introduced by the Norman invaders and settlers. Celtic peoples have remained in Ireland, Scotland, and Wales, although they are also predominantly English speaking.

The United Kingdom under English domination was among the most successful European colonial powers from the seventeenth century until the second half of the twentieth century. Often the names England and Britain are used interchangeably, but this is not correct. The earliest development of the Industrial revolution with its concomitant urbanization took place in Britain. That it is an island country was instrumental in the development of shipping and naval power. For a long time the United Kingdom was the wealthiest country in Europe, until World War II put a severe drain on the economy and the loss of the Empire after the war brought other economic losses. Currently the country has severe economic problems with major devaluations of currency and inflation. The country is governed by elected officials and a parliament under the Queen. Control of the Parliament and therefore the government has alternated between the Labour Party, which is mildly socialistic, and the Conservative Party, which is mildly for free enterprise. A third party, which until the 1920s was a major force in the political life of the country but

now holds a balance of power, is the Liberal Party, somewhat between the two major parties. Only members of the House of Commons are elected by popular franchise, and the prime minister and cabinet are always members of that body. The major religious organization is the Church of England, which is Anglican or Protestant Episcopal, whose clergy are paid by the government and to which the monarch must belong. The population is overwhelmingly Protestant Christian in affiliation, although there is freedom of religious practice and substantial Roman Catholic, Jewish, Muslin, Hindu, and other communities. The population is relatively homogeneous, with strong regional variations, both in dialect and culture. Since World War II there has been an influx of immigrants from Europe as a result of persecutions and economic difficulties in Eastern and Southern Europe during the twentieth century and from various parts of the farflung empire, primarily from South Asia, Africa, and the West Indies. These latter immigrants, many of whom are not Christian and most of whom are generally dark-skinned (listed in official documents as "nonwhite Commonwealth origin") have introduced an element of heterogeneity into the population, particularly in the industrial urban areas, which has been accompanied by aspects of racism.

Police work was studied in the counties of Gloucestershire and Cheshire. Both are in the western part of England, adjacent to heavily urbanized and industrialized areas. They are not heavily industrialized and contain rural and urban sections. Both counties contain port cities. Gloucestershire is situated on the southeastern border of Wales, and Cheshire on the northeastern border of Wales. Cheshire contains ancient Roman ruins, and Chester is one of the oldest cities in England. The population of both areas is mainly English and Anglicized Welsh. In addition there are immigrants or descendants of immigrants from other parts of the empire. In no area of the two counties does this latter population make up more than 5% of the population. There are also residents who have come from other counties. In each county there is one major city, Gloucester in Gloucestershire, and Chester in Chesire, and a number of other urbanized areas. Cheshire has a total population of 1,335,000 (1971), of which 207,600 live in areas classified as rural and 1,128,500 live in areas classified as urban. Gloucestershire has a population of 644,251 (1971), of which 375,921 live in rural areas and 268,330 live in urban areas.

The counties were designated as study sites by the director of the Home Office Police Research Bureau. The Bureau had conducted a pilot study of the distribution of police work load in these two counties in 1970 (Figs. 1 and 2). The director of the Bureau held that it would be too cumbersome to request such data in other jurisdictions or to redo such a study. The police data for Britain, then, are those collected in the Home Office study of police work load in 1970. Data were divided into three subsections for each county: rural, urban foot, and urban car beats. Within the two counties data were available for 65 local authorities, divided into urban and rural. Local authorities in Britain are political entities and also serve as agencies for collection of all sorts of demographic and socioecological data (similar to cen-

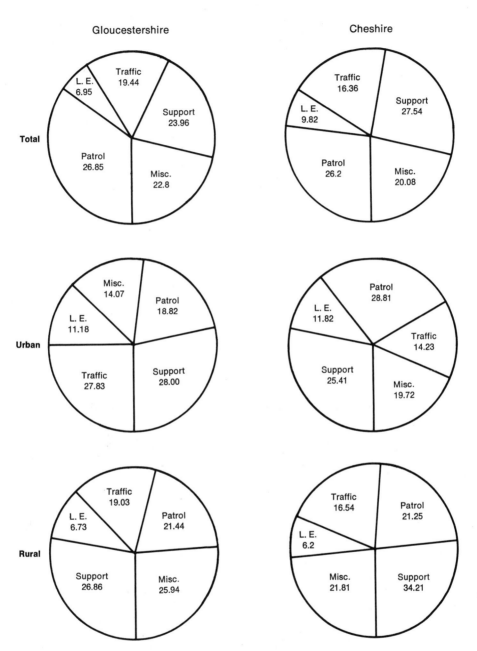

Fig. 1. Police work in Britain: percent distribution.

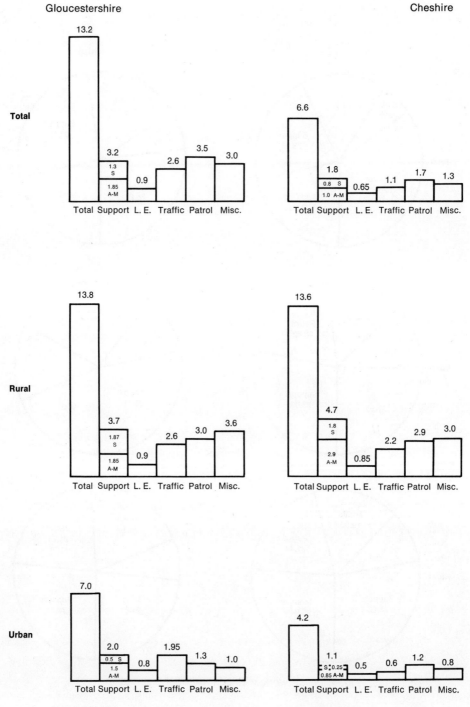

Fig. 2. Police work in Britain: incidence per 1000 population per month.

sus tracts in the United States). Local authorities are classified either as rural or urban. The definition of urban is connected with density of population and development. Although urban and rural authorities are not necessarily contiguous, data have
been collated by these classifications, primarily because that is the way the police
data were prepared by the Home Office. The data are examined primarily for the
counties as a whole, but some of the differences between urban and rural districts
are noted. (NOTE: There is some minor discrepancy between the sum of the rural
and urban beat figures and the countywide figures; this must result from some additional cases handled on a nonbeat basis.)

POLICE
History

Inasmuch as explication of the developmental history of police in England and
Wales is contained in Chapter 2, the following is a brief resume of the history of
the modern police in England. The system was compounded of indigenous patterns of law enforcement and those that were brought by succeeding waves of immigrants or invaders, including Celtic, Roman, Norse, Anglo-Saxon, and Norman
French. All of these contributed in their time to the development of policing arrangements in England. During the eighteenth century, under the pressures of
rapid urbanization, industrialization, and agricultural developments, the traditional
system, in effect for hundreds of years, was found to be grossly inadequate, particularly in London.

At the beginning of the nineteenth century, Parliament moved towards re-
structuring the police system of London. Under the tutelage of the Fieldings, Lord
Peel, and others, a new system, the Metropolitan Police of London, was designed
and put into effect in 1829 with headquarters at Scotland Yard. Sir Robert Peel
and Sir Charles Rowan were the first co-commissioners. They believed that social
control was more effective with benevolent prevention rather than repression. They
further believed and proved that patrolling and development of relationships between the police and the people were the means by which prevention could be
effected. The police were to be a professional, politically independent, hierarchical,
disciplined force. They were to be uniformed but without weapons other than a
wooden nightstick. Further distinctive characteristics of the organization of the new
police were strict supervision and territorial responsibility, the assigned beat concept, and through this accountability.

Developments outside London moved less decisively. In the provinces it took
some time for the traditional police to evolve into forces similar to that of London.
Throughout there has been a conscious effort to balance local autonomy with supervision from central government and thus create uniformity throughout the country.
The process of consolidation of independent borough and municipal forces took
many years. The Home Office was given power to influence and coordinate but
were not responsibile for local policing. In 1946-1947 independent police forces in

the counties were amalgamated into larger forces, and in 1967 the National Police Act set up county forces amalgamating all smaller forces under the direction of county police authorities. Each force is headed by a chief constable. In essence, although legally independent and responsible to local authorities, all county police forces are similarly organized throughout England and Wales and, with slight variations, in Scotland and Northern Ireland. The largest force in the country is the Metropolitan Police of London, with over 20,000 men and women, covering an area of 784 square miles and a population of over 8 million. There are similar forces throughout the country, many covering larger geographic areas, but none with the numbers of personnel or population.

Organization

The organization of county police authorities throughout Britain is similar. The Cheshire Police Authority is an example:

Senior county command: Chief Constable,
                            Deputy Chief Constable
                            Assistant Chief Constables
Administrative officers
Line officers: Chief Superintendent
                            Superintendent 1
                            Superintendent 2
                            Chief Inspector
                            Inspector
                            Sergeant
                            Constables

There are also a number of "civilians" working in the stations. There are seven operational divisions, each with one to three subdivisions. There are also three centralized sections: Administration, Criminal Investigations, and Traffic. The officers in the Criminal Investigations section have the same rank as officers in other sections, but with the added title of detective, for example, detective chief superintendent. Within each operational division there are also administration, criminal investigation, and Traffic sections, with similar sections in the subdivisions.[1,p.4]

The Police Act gives the responsibility for the running of an effective police force to the Police Authority. The membership of the Authority is taken from elected representatives of the county councils and the county boroughs. These members are supplemented by magistrates representing the County Court of Quarter Sessions and from the county boroughs. The chief constable is responsible for the actual operation of the force. Although accountable directly to the Authority, the chief constable is not directly subject to their direction. The Home Office of the national government has a great deal of influence, largely because there is legal accountability but also because half the cost of the police service is subsidized by the Home Office.[1,p.4]

The force resulted from the merger of a number of independent and fragmented forces that had developed since the early and mid-nineteenth century. In 1946-1947 the number of forces was reduced to four. This was followed in 1967 under the Police Act by amalgamation into a unitary force for the entire country.

Operation

The main operation of the uniformed police is patrolling. Prior to 1966 most uniform patrolling was organized by beats and was on foot. In 1966 motorized patrolling (called "Panda" or unit beat patrolling) was introduced along with radio direction and reporting. It is designed for more efficient use of available personnel. Further aims stated by the Authority are:

1. To cultivate a closer and better relationship with the public and encourage a greater involvement with everyone
2. To provide a quicker response to calls for assistance
3. To improve the flow of information to and from the public as an aid to detection
4. To create confidence, interest, and challenge within the police service[1,p.8]

Each constable has a radio and transmitter. There is also a collator at headquarters, recording and analyzing information received from beat patrollers, criminal investigations, and the public and then feeding it to the patrol officers. (See Table 5-1.)

The *Traffic Department* operates as a separate section within the divisional or-

Table 5-1. English police data categories and variables included in each category

Category	Activity	Category	Activity
Support		**Norm enforcement—cont'd**	
Arbitration-mediation	Civil and domestic disputes Complaints and nuisances	Traffic	Process, ss 2, 3, and 77 RTA Process, other traffic
Services	Sudden deaths Accidents, nontraffic Missing persons Diseased animals Stray animals		Accidents, fatal Accidents, injury Accidents, damage only Breathalyser tests
		Preventive patrol	Process, nontraffic Warrants and summonses Burglar alarms Stop and search
Norm enforcement			
Primary law enforcement	Breaking, locked premises Breaking, other premises Theft from vehicle Other thefts Theft of vehicle All assaults Willful damage All other crimes Arrests, criminal Arrests, other	Miscellaneous	Fires Property, lost and found Applications for and inquiries about licenses Inquiries for other stations

ganization. About 10% of the force is detailed to this department, with the objectives of keeping the roads safe and helping keep passage free and quick.

Policewomen are organized in a separate section but are dispersed throughout the force. This section was instituted in 1946, although women were working in a limited capacity prior to that in some forces. The Sex Discrimination Act of 1975 mandated full integration of women into police forces, among other institutions. According to the Public Information Officer of the Gloucestershire Constabulary, such integration has taken place throughout the country. Women have the same conditions of service and are given the same training as men. They have a special role, however, "in relation to women and children whether offenders or complainants and are most suited for the 'welfare' type of problem which confronts the Police."[1,p.16] Generally policewomen have the same duties as men and work as detectives, traffic patrol officers, prosecuting officers, and in general patrol work. However, there are some operational limitations on the full participation of policewomen in the police system. They are often shielded from participation in public disorder situations that can be foreseen, such as political demonstrations. The lack of upward mobility is explained by the fact that many women have short careers with the police service. "In addition Chief Officers may consider the percentage of female officers in any force should be limited. There are no strict rules governing this at present."[4] Further, in examining police annual reports it can be seen that women generally are assigned to traffic, youth, and sometimes vice work. In 1979 in Gloucestershire the traffic division was staffed with 36 traffic wardens, of whom 27 were women.[2] This contrasts with a total of 79 new members of the force in the same year, of whom 19 were women.[2] Women make up about 6% of the total strength of the force in Cheshire. Women are thus becoming more accepted in police work throughout the country, under law, although their role is still somewhat restricted by remaining biases.

Dogs are used in selected patrol beats and in special investigative work. There is also a communications center centered around the Information Room. These facilities are designed to enhance the function of the unit beat patrol officer.

Analysis of tasks

Police work data are given for Gloucestershire and Cheshire (Table 5-2) and for the rural and urban authorities in the two counties (Table 5-3). All categories but traffic are shown with subcategories. It is readily apparent that the incidence of police work per population is substantially higher in the rural districts than in the urban districts, in both counties and in general. A second readily apparent fact is that law enforcement is the smallest major category of police work, both in percentage of total work and in incidence per population. Preventive patrol and support tasks are about even in the overall county figures (which include all police work) but the support activities are the major category in rural and urban beat figures. In overall police work the tasks are distributed about 25% each for patrol and support, 20% for traffic and miscellaneous, and under 10% for law enforcement. By beats the distribution is slightly different. Here the work is distributed about 25% for support, about 20% each for patrol, miscellaneous, and traffic, and again about 10% for law enforcement. Within the pooled districts, rural and urban, incidence of support activities is from three to five times that of law enforcement. Although incidence of law enforcement tasks is slightly higher in rural than in urban districts, incidence of support activities is much higher in rural than in urban districts. More than 50% of patrol activities were for stop and search in all districts except Cheshire urban, where they were 45%.

A more detailed examination of the information shows a wide range of police activities in all categories of work. There are some major differences in police activities in Britain not found elsewhere. One apparent difference is the involvement of police in incidents dealing with animals. The British are known for their concern for animals, which might be a factor in the involvement. Another factor is the rural nature of parts of the counties. Of interest, the major issue in animal incidents in the rural areas was diseases of animals, while in the urban areas the calls deal with stray animals primarily. It is not known whether these are complaints or requests for help. Other support activities appear similar to those in the other countries studied. There are the many calls for intervention in civil and domestic disputes, highest in the large urban Cheshire authorities. There is the much higher incidence of nuisance complaints, being four to six times higher than incidence of disputes. The other activities in which British police are involved in support activities are accidents, including nontraffic (or injured people), and sudden deaths and missing

Table 5-2. Police work in Britain, 1 month, 1970

	Gloucestershire (pop. 644,300)			Cheshire (pop. 1,335,000)		
	Num-ber	Per-cent	Incidence per 1000	Num-ber	Per-cent	Incidence per 1000
Support						
Arbitration-mediation						
23 Civil and domestic disputes	162	1.91	0.251	341	3.35	0.221
28 Complaints and nuisances	1027	12.08	1.594	1327	13.02	0.860
SUBTOTAL	1189	13.99	1.845	1668	16.37	1.081
Services						
17 Sudden deaths	38	0.45	0.059	84	0.82	0.054
19 Accidents, nontraffic	68	0.80	0.106	69	0.68	0.045
22 Missing persons	104	1.22	0.161	165	1.62	0.107
24 Diseased animals	357	4.20	0.554	566	5.55	0.367
25 Stray animals	281	3.31	0.436	254	2.49	0.165
SUBTOTAL	848	9.97	1.316	1138	11.17	0.738
TOTAL	2037	23.96	3.162	2806	27.54	1.819
Law enforcement						
Criminal matters						
1 Breaking, locked premises	48	0.56	0.075	110	1.08	0.074
2 Breaking, other premises	34	0.40	0.053	127	1.25	0.082
3 Theft from vehicle	40	0.47	0.062	55	0.54	0.036
4 Other thefts	175	2.06	0.272	203	1.99	0.132
5 Theft of vehicle	45	0.53	0.070	86	0.84	0.056
6 Violence/assaults	57	0.67	0.088	58	0.57	0.038
SUBTOTAL	399	4.69	0.62	639	6.3	0.479
7 Willful damage	85	1.00	0.132	141	1.38	0.091
8 All other crimes	34	0.40	0.053	68	0.67	0.044
9 Arrests, criminal	29	0.34	0.045	90	0.88	0.058
10 Arrests, other	44	0.52	0.068	63	0.62	0.041
SUBTOTAL	192	2.26	0.30	362	3.55	0.271
TOTAL	591	6.95	0.917	1001	9.82	0.649
Traffic	1652	19.44	2.564	1667	16.36	1.081
Patrol (preventive)						
13 Process, nontraffic	111	1.31	0.172	51	0.50	0.033
21 Warrants and summonses	355	4.18	0.551	858	8.42	0.556
29 Burglar alarms	231	2.72	0.359	351	3.44	0.228
30 Stop and search	1585	18.65	2.460	1410	13.84	0.014
TOTAL	2282	26.85	3.542	2670	26.20	1.731
Administrative						
Applications and licenses	496	5.84	0.770	508	4.99	0.329
Miscellaneous						
18 Fires	74	0.87	0.115	122	1.20	0.079
20 Property, lost and found	394	4.64	6.120	364	3.57	0.236
27 Enquiries	974	11.46	1.512	1052	10.32	0.682
TOTAL	1442	16.96	2.238	1538	15.09	1.009
TOTAL WITHOUT TRAFFIC	6848	81.56	10.629	8523	83.64	5.525
TOTAL WITH TRAFFIC	8500	100.00	13.194	10190	100.00	6.606

Table 5-3. Police work in Britain: rural and urban

	Rural Gloucestershire (pop. 376,000)			Urban Gloucestershire (pop. 268,300)			Rural Cheshire (pop. 207,600)			Urban Cheshire (pop. 1,335,000)		
	Number	Per cent	Incidence per 1000	Number	Per cent	Incidence per 1000	Number	Per cent	Incidence per 1000	Number	Per cent	Incidence per 1000
Support												
Arbitration-mediation												
23 Civil and domestic disputes	108	2.08	0.287	47	2.51	0.175	50	1.77	0.241	249	4.45	0.187
28 Complaints and nuisances	586	11.27	1.559	353	18.82	1.316	319	11.30	1.537	846	15.13	0.634
SUBTOTAL	694	13.35	1.846	400	21.33	1.491	369	13.07	1.778	1095	19.58	0.821
Services												
17 Sudden deaths	29	0.56	0.077	8	0.43	0.030	20	0.71	0.096	58	1.04	0.043
19 Accidents, nontraffic	50	0.96	0.133	15	0.80	0.056	16	0.57	0.077	48	0.86	0.036
22 Missing persons	48	0.92	0.128	45	2.40	0.168	25	0.89	0.120	113	2.02	0.410
24 Diseased animals	346	6.65	0.920	11	0.59	0.041	433	15.33	2.087	4	0.07	0.003
25 Stray animals	230	4.42	0.612	48	2.56	0.179	103	3.65	0.496	103	1.84	0.077
SUBTOTAL	703	13.51	1.869	127	6.77	0.473	597	21.14	2.877	326	5.83	0.244
TOTAL	1397	26.86	3.715	527	28.09	1.964	966	34.27	4.655	1421	25.41	1.064
Law enforcement												
Criminal matters												
1 Breaking, locked premises	25	0.48	0.066	21	1.12	0.078	19	0.67	0.092	83	1.48	0.062
2 Breaking, other premises	27	0.52	0.072	6	0.32	0.022	28	0.99	0.135	87	1.56	0.065
3 Theft from vehicle	30	0.58	0.080	9	0.46	0.036	16	0.57	0.077	33	0.59	0.025
4 Other thefts	121	2.33	0.322	50	2.67	0.186	31	1.10	0.149	125	2.24	0.094
5 Theft of vehicle	27	0.52	0.072	17	0.91	0.063	15	0.53	0.072	62	1.11	0.046
6 Assaults	27	0.52	0.072	23	1.23	0.086	6	0.21	0.027	36	0.64	0.027
7 Willful damage	44	0.85	0.117	40	2.13	0.149	25	0.89	0.120	103	1.84	0.077
8 All other crimes	24	0.46	0.064	6	0.32	0.022	14	0.50	0.067	44	0.79	0.033
9 Arrests, criminal	13	0.25	0.035	12	0.64	0.045	13	0.46	0.062	40	0.72	0.030
10 Arrests, other	12	0.23	0.032	26	1.39	0.097	8	0.28	0.039	48	0.86	0.036
TOTAL	350	6.73	0.931	210	11.19	0.783	175	6.20	0.843	661	11.82	0.495

Continued.

Table 5-3. Police work in Britain: rural and urban—cont'd

	Rural Gloucestershire (pop. 376,000)			Urban Gloucestershire (pop. 268,300)			Rural Cheshire (pop. 207,600)			Urban Cheshire (pop. 1,335,000)		
	Number	Per-cent	Incidence per 1000	Number	Per-cent	Incidence per 1000	Number	Per-cent	Incidence per 1000	Number	Per-cent	Incidence per 1000
Traffic	990	19.03	2.633	522	27.83	1.946	467	16.54	2.251	796	14.23	0.596
Patrol, preventive												
13 Process, nontraffic	73	1.46	0.202	29	0.155	0.108	18	0.64	0.087	29	0.52	0.022
21 Warrants and summonses	219	4.21	0.582	84	4.48	0.313	185	6.55	0.892	624	11.16	0.467
29 Burglar alarms	126	2.42	0.335	51	2.72	0.190	58	3.01	0.279	238	4.26	0.178
30 Stop and search	694	13.34	1.846	189	10.07	0.704	339	12.00	0.634	720	12.86	0.539
TOTAL	1115	21.44	2.965	353	18.82	1.316	600	21.25	2.892	1611	28.81	1.207
Miscellaneous												
18 Fire	50	0.96	0.133	7	0.37	0.026	25	0.89	0.120	85	1.52	0.064
20 Property, lost and found	250	4.81	0.665	53	2.83	0.198	96	3.40	0.463	228	4.08	0.176
26 Applications and licenses	394	7.58	1.048	16	0.85	0.060	228	8.07	1.099	166	2.97	0.124
27 Enquiries	655	12.59	1.742	188	10.02	0.701	267	9.45	1.287	624	11.16	0.467
TOTAL	1349	25.94	3.588	264	14.07	0.984	616	21.81	2.969	1103	19.72	0.826
TOTAL WITHOUT TRAFFIC	4211	80.97	11.199	1354	72.17	5.047	2357	83.46	11.359	4796	85.77	3.593
TOTAL WITH TRAFFIC	5201	100.00	13.832	1876	100.00	6.992	2824	100.00	13.609	5592	100.00	4.189

persons. Of interest, there is a higher incidence of accidents and deaths in rural districts and of missing persons in urban districts, particularly in Cheshire. To compute, using only support activities as a basis, arbitration and mediation work constitutes 85% of all support activities excluding those dealing with animals. This is true in both urban and rural authorities. Thus the major difference between urban and rural authorities in support activities is the heavy involvement of police in incidents dealing with diseased and stray animals in rural districts and a much lighter involvement in such activities in urban districts. Again in urban districts the incidence of missing persons is greater than that of both deaths and accidents, whereas in rural districts the three are somewhat similar in magnitude. The percentage of support activities and law enforcement activities within the categories is shown in Tables 5-4 and 5-5. It can be seen that in Britain the vast majority of support activities dealing with human beings is in the arbitration and mediation of various types of disputes and complaints.

Table 5-4. Support and law enforcement activities as percent of total incidents

	Gloucestershire		Cheshire	
	Number	Percent	Number	Percent
Support				
Arbitration-mediation				
Disputes	162	7.95	341	12.15
Nuisance complaints	1027	50.42	1327	47.29
SUBTOTAL	1189	58.37	1668	59.44
Service				
Sudden deaths	38	1.87	84	2.99
Accidents, nontraffic	68	3.34	69	2.46
Missing persons	104	5.11	165	5.88
Diseased animals	357	17.53	566	20.17
Stray animals	281	13.79	254	9.05
SUBTOTAL	848	41.63	1138	40.56
TOTAL	2037	100.00	2806	100.00
Law enforcement				
Breaking, locked premises	48	8.12	110	10.99
Breaking, other premises	34	5.75	127	12.69
Theft from vehicles	40	6.77	55	5.49
Other thefts	175	29.61	203	20.28
Thefts of vehicles	45	7.61	86	8.59
SUBTOTAL	342	57.87	581	58.04
Assaults	57	9.64	58	5.79
Willful damage	85	14.38	141	14.09
All other crimes	34	5.75	68	6.79
Arrests, criminal	29	4.91	90	8.99
Arrests, other	44	7.45	63	6.29
SUBTOTAL	249	42.13	420	41.96
TOTAL	591	100.00	1001	100.00

Table 5-5. Support and law enforcement activities as percent of total incidents: rural and urban

	Gloucestershire				Cheshire			
	Rural		Urban		Rural		Urban	
	Num-ber	Per-cent	Num-ber	Per-cent	Num-ber	Per-cent	Num-ber	Per-cent
Support								
Arbitration-mediation								
Disputes	108	7.73	47	8.92	50	5.18	249	17.52
Nuisance complaints	586	41.95	353	66.98	319	33.02	846	59.54
SUBTOTAL	694	49.68	400	75.90	369	38.20	1095	77.06
Service								
Sudden deaths	29	2.08	8	1.52	20	2.07	58	4.08
Accidents, nontraffic	50	3.58	15	2.85	16	1.66	48	3.38
Missing persons	48	3.44	45	8.54	25	2.59	113	7.95
Diseased animals	346	24.77	11	2.09	433	44.82	4	0.28
Stray animals	230	16.46	48	9.11	103	10.66	103	7.25
SUBTOTAL	703	50.32	127	24.10	597	61.80	326	22.94
TOTAL	1397	100.00	527	100.00	966	100.00	1421	100.00
Law enforcement								
Breaking, locked premises	25	7.14	21	10.00	19	10.86	83	12.56
Breaking, other premises	27	7.71	6	2.86	28	16.00	87	13.16
Theft from vehicles	30	8.59	9	4.28	16	9.14	33	4.99
Other thefts	121	34.57	50	23.81	31	17.71	125	18.91
Thefts of vehicles	27	7.71	17	8.10	15	8.57	62	9.38
SUBTOTAL	230	65.72	103	49.05	109	62.29	390	59.00
Assaults	27	7.71	23	10.95	6	3.43	36	5.45
Willful damage	44	12.57	40	19.05	25	14.28	103	15.58
All other crimes	24	6.86	6	2.86	14	8.00	44	6.66
Arrests, criminal	13	3.71	12	5.71	13	7.43	40	6.05
Arrests, other	12	3.43	26	12.38	8	4.57	48	7.26
SUBTOTAL	120	34.28	107	50.95	66	37.71	271	41.00
TOTAL	350	100.00	210	100.00	175	100.00	661	100.00

In law enforcement activities the rural districts have a higher incidence than the urban districts, although the rates vary from approximately 0.5 to 0.9 per thousand population. The lowest incidence for law enforcement activities, indeed for all police work, was in Cheshire urban. However, in percentages of police work the urban districts had slightly more than 11% of the activities of the police involving law enforcement, whereas the rural districts had over 6% of police activities involving law enforcement. This may have something to do with the high rate of involvement in incidents dealing with animals in rural areas. Of interest, the category of willful damage was the largest in all nontheft criminal incidents. Actually, in all but Cheshire rural it was the second largest law enforcement activity with which police had to deal, and for the county as a whole it was the second largest category. In general, law enforcement tasks constitute a small percentage of police work in these two counties, less than 10%, with the majority involving thefts of all kinds.

An interesting aspect of police work in these two counties in Britain is the high involvement with what are administrative and preventive patrol activities. Stop and search constitutes one of the largest single types of police activity, even more of the total forces than that of the beat police. Another major task is inquiries for other police stations. One wonders what these might be, but they represent over 10% of police tasks in all areas. Other major types of police work found in these categories are burglar alarms, about 3% of police work overall; warrants and summonses, between 4% and 11%; lost and found property, about 4%; and applications and licenses, about 8% in rural authorities and 1% to 3% in urban authorities. Thus it can be seen that the British police have a large number of semi-law-enforcement and administrative activities. These activities are interstitial between social control and integration.

An examination of the specific details of police work shows some interesting data. The incidence of police work is two to three times greater per population in the rural areas than in the urban areas, varying between 13.6 and 13.8 per thousand in the rural sectors and 4.2 and 7.0 per thousand in the urban sectors. This is true with variations in all categories of police work. The proportions of police work in different categories is not as consistent in the urban rural distribution. It is my contention that comparisons are most reliable when incidence is examined rather than percentage. The following paragraphs deal more specifically with the types of activities police undertake in law enforcement and support tasks.

Law enforcement varies from slightly more than 6% of the total in the rural sections of the counties to over 11% in the urban sections. However, the incidence is still higher in the rural sections than in the urban sections, being 0.84 to 0.93 per thousand in the rural sections and 0.5 to 0.78 per thousand in the urban sections. The types of criminal activities found in police work during the month studied were breaking into locked premises, other breakins, various thefts (of vehicles, from vehicles, and others), assaults, damage to property, a collection of other crimes (in no case more than 0.75% of the total or slightly more than 5% of all law enforcement activities), and various criminal and other arrests. Tables 5-6 and 5-7 give the specific breakdown of all data, both for rural and urban sections of the counties and for the relationship between the various subcategories within law enforcement.

Support activities constitute from 25% to over 34% of police work in the various sections of the counties. Some of the specifics are discussed in the more general discussion. In this section are presented some of the incidence figures and how they vary between urban and rural sections. In Gloucestershire the incidence for arbitration-mediation and services was approximately the same in rural sections, 1.85 per thousand population and 1.87 per thousand respectively. As noted previously, heavy involvement with animal-related incidents accounts for much of the service

Table 5-6. Summary distribution of law enforcement and support activities in Gloucestershire and Cheshire Counties, 1970 (1 month)

County	Police activity	Number	Percent of total incidents	Incidence per 1000 population per month
Gloucestershire (pop. 644,300)	Primary law enforcement	591	6.95	0.917
	Total support	2037	23.9	3.162
	Arbitration-mediation	1189	13.99	1.845
	Service	848	9.97	1.316
Cheshire (pop. 1,335,000)	Primary law enforcement	1001	9.82	0.649
	Total support	2806	27.54	1.819
	Arbitration-mediation	1668	16.37	1.081
	Service	1138	11.17	0.738

Table 5-7. Summary distribution of law enforcement and support activities in Gloucestershire and Cheshire Counties, rural and urban districts, 1970 (1 month)

Districts	Police activity	Number	Percent of total incidents	Incidence per 1000 population per month
Gloucestershire rural (pop. 376,000)	Primary law enforcement	350	6.73	9.31
	Total support	1397	26.86	3.715
	Arbitration-mediation	694	13.35	1.846
	Service	703	13.51	1.869
Cheshire rural (pop. 207,600)	Primary law enforcement	175	6.20	0.635
	Total support	966	34.21	4.653
	Arbitration-mediation	369	13.07	1.777
	Service	597	21.14	2.876
Gloucestershire urban (pop. 268,300)	Primary law enforcement	210	11.19	0.783
	Total support	527	28.09	1.964
	Arbitration-mediation	400	21.33	1.491
	Service	127	6.77	0.473
Cheshire urban (pop. 1,335,000)	Primary law enforcement	661	11.82	0.495
	Total support	1421	25.41	1.004
	Arbitration-mediation	1095	19.58	0.821
	Service	326	5.83	0.224

activities in rural sections. There is also a rather heavy involvement in incidents related to missing persons and nonvehicular accidents, presumably injured persons. The incidence of missing persons is highest in the urban sections, particularly in Cheshire, where it is two to three times that of other sections, both rural and urban. A rather limited range of service activities is reflected in the police data for these two counties, although what is present is an important part of police work. This may be a product of the reporting process. It may also be a product of the socialized medical system and the well-organized welfare system, both of which are closely allied with the police in providing service to the population.

The relationship of various types of police work to socioecological factors does not show the same pattern as found elsewhere, although there are similarities. When the data for the two counties are compared, the incidence of law enforcement incidents and support incidents vary directly with each other. This is true within the counties between rural and urban districts as well. However, the support functions of the police show a greater difference than the law enforcement activities between districts and counties. There is also evidence of a direct relationship between social need and the incidence of support police activities.[5] Although the support activities of the police are rather restricted, there still appears to be a direct relationship between the social need and level of social integration and the demands made on the police for, and thereby their performance of, social support activities fulfilling a socially integrative function. Police in Britain provide both a measure of social control and social integration within society. Much of this is done though the intermediary administrative activities with which they deal and which make up a larger percentage of their total work load.

There appears to be a higher social need in the rural areas of these two counties than in the urban areas, as indicated by higher rates of renters, unemployed, and widowed or divorced men and by more crowded living conditions. There seems to be about the same percentage of transiency within the rural and urban areas, and they are equally diverse in population. The difference might not be enough to explain the greater magnitude of police work in the rural areas but might be partially indicative of the differences between the rural and urban areas. The distribution of police work indicates that police maintain both control and support functions in these areas. There is indication that the social need is higher in Gloucestershire than in Cheshire, as seen in the greater incidence of both support and law enforcement activities.

Activities of uniformed police are divided among five major classifications in the two counties examined. Patrol and support tasks account for over 50% of total activities of the police in both counties. In one there are slightly more patrol tasks; in the other there are slightly more support tasks. In both counties the least amount of work of the uniformed police is devoted to law enforcement in connection with lawbreaking. The activities with which police deal range from violent crimes and assaults (a small percentage, 6% to 10% of total law enforcement) to thefts, traffic-related incidents, helping people in need, helping settle disputes of various kinds, dealing with lost and found property, answering defective burglar alarms, serving warrants and summonses, applications for licenses, general inquiries, and stop-and-search activities. Police in Britain still deal with most of these problems on a beat basis, either foot or automobile, and with no weapon other than a nightstick. The incidence of police work seems to be related to the social conditions of the area, in particular the integrative symptom of social need.

Police in Britain are involved in major social problems that are almost always the result of the crossover between control and integration; for example, child abuse. In order to better understand the phenomenon of child abuse, the Juvenile Liaison Department made a study of the nature of the families of half of the reported child abusers in Gloucestershire over a period of 4 years, 1973 to 1976. Of these cases only 13% had been referred initially by the police. Only 30% were investigated by the police. However, the police department felt that it had a stake in all of the instances of child abuse for a variety of reasons not clearly stated. It is thus clear that police in Britain have institutionally accepted a role that is both normative and integrative in nature.[5]

Problems

British police authorities have addressed many of the major problems of policing in the reorganizations of the forces since World War II. The concepts of Rowan and Peel have stood the British police in good stead. Whether they will be equal to the social changes of the years to come is not clear. A problem faced by many forces throughout the country is that of recruitment. Many forces are understaffed, although not to a degree that renders them ineffective. Both the forces of Cheshire and Gloucestershire report that they are not up to approved strength. To deal with this problem forces have begun to introduce mechanical supports to police and replaced police with civilians in certain positions. These developments may not be serious and in fact may be positive factors in the future development of police in Britain.

A problem looming on the horizon, and already arrived in some areas, is related to changes within the society, both in population and in economic conditions. The influx of immigrants from the Commonwealth has introduced a measure of heterogeneity unknown for many generations. The nativist response to the immigrants has often been violent and antiestablishment in nature. There has also been a general deterioration of economic conditions within the country related to inflation, the loss of the colonial markets, and other social and economic factors too complex to analyze here. This deterioration has reintroduced a measure of class warfare that had been dormant during the past generation. It has also led to a decrease in respect for authority and an increase in violence. The fact that police have been given a limited use of guns as a result of increased incidence of use of guns by criminal elements indicates a major change in society. How the police will deal with these changes is the challenge and problem of the future.

SUMMARY

Although there is a long history of policing functions in British society, modern police forces date from 1829, when the Metropolitan Police of London was founded. Police forces in other areas of the country were fashioned from older forms and new ideas during the ensuing years. Aside from the Metropolitan Police, founded under legislation of Parliament, other forces were local and autonomous. There was a great deal of resistance to government control for fear of tyranny. In the twentieth century there have been a series of consolidations under the impetus of national legislation overseen by the Home Office. In 1946-1947 independent police forces in the counties were amalgamated into larger forces, and in 1967 county police authorities were set up under national legislation, forming county police forces. The county forces are organized in divisions and subdivisions with several shared administrative and special service sections. There are several special functions within the county force, but the central function to which most personnel are devoted is patrolling. In the mid-1960s motorized patrolling with radio backup was introduced to substitute for foot patrol. There has been a move to balance motorized patrols and foot patrols since then. Women, organized in separate sections, function throughout the force, with duties similar to those of men but with special recognition in work with women and children.

Over 50% of police work is devoted to patrol and support activities. Under 10% of police work is devoted to law enforcement during a typical period. The remainder is devoted to traffic and administrative activities. There is evidence that police work is directly related to the social need of the community. Police in Britain fulfill both a social control and social integration function, with much of their work interstitial to both functions.

The major problems of police forces at this time are understaffing and recruitment. To accommodate for this they have turned to technology. This may not be an adequate substitute for people in much of police work. The problem of understaffing does not appear to be too severe, however. Another problem developing in larger metropolitan areas is the introduction of violence and intergroup tension in the society. Police have, after 150 years without guns, been given guns in limited situations. The foremost challenge of the coming years for police forces may be the use of guns and dealing with an increasingly hostile and heterogeneous society.

REFERENCES

1. Cheshire Police Authority: The Cheshire Constabulary, Cheshire County Council, Wilmslow, England, 1970, Richmond Press Ltd.
2. Gloucestershire Constabulary: Chief Constable's report on the police establishment with criminal and other statistics for the year ended 31 December 1978, County Police Headquarters, Cheltenham, England, February 1979.
3. Gloucestershire Constabulary: Child abuse, Gloucestershire, England, 1977, Juvenile Liaison Department, Northside Division.
4. Public Information Officer, Gloucestershire Constabulary, personal communication (letter), March 8, 1979.
5. Shane, P. G.: The social functions of a civil agency, unpublished thesis, Baltimore, 1975, The Johns Hopkins University.

Chapter 6

India

India (Bharat in Hindi) occupies the larger part of the Indian subcontinent, which it shares with Bhutan, Nepal, Sikkim, Pakistan, and Bangladesh in southern Asia. The country is the third largest in area in Asia (3,205,000 sq km [1,260,000 sq mi]) and one of the largest in the world (about one third the size of the United States). It has the second largest population in the world, with probably the highest population density of the large nations of the world. The climate is tropical and subtropical, the Tropic of Cancer passing through the center of the country. The subcontinent is almost completely surrounded by immense mountain chains and water, the southern part being in effect a large peninsula. The northern crescent of the country is the southern slopes of the Himalaya mountains, an almost impassible barrier to the northern part of Asia and arctic weather. To the southeast is the Bay of Bengal. The southern point extends into the Indian Ocean. To the southwest is the Arabian Sea. To the northwest is Pakistan. To the north is Afganistan, China, and Tibet. To the northeast is Nepal, Sikkim, Bhutan, and China. To the east is Burma, with Bangladesh extending into the northern part of India. In the northwest is a semidesert opening between mountains and sea to western Asia through Pakistan. To the east there are passes through the mountains to southeast Asia through Bangladesh and Burma. A spine of mountains runs through the country north to south. Much of the area of the subcontinent is semidesert or desert. About 22.5% is forest or jungle.

HISTORY

The Indian subcontinent, the birthplace of two of the world's great religions, Hinduism and Buddhism, has an ancient cultural and historic tradition. Civilization on the subcontinent is one of the oldest in the world, going back at least 5000 years. Although well protected geographically, the wealth of India has inspired numerous invasions, almost all through the northwest opening into Western Asia, with consequent cultural changes. The last invaders prior to the British were the Moguls, Moslems from the Iranian plains, descendants of Mongol invaders of western Asia. Several of the Mogul emperors were great builders and left magnificent palaces, mosques, and forts as their legacy to India. They also left the debilitating Moslem-Hindu cultural conflict. In the late fifteenth century European nations began building commercial empires in Asia and other parts of the world, and India's riches

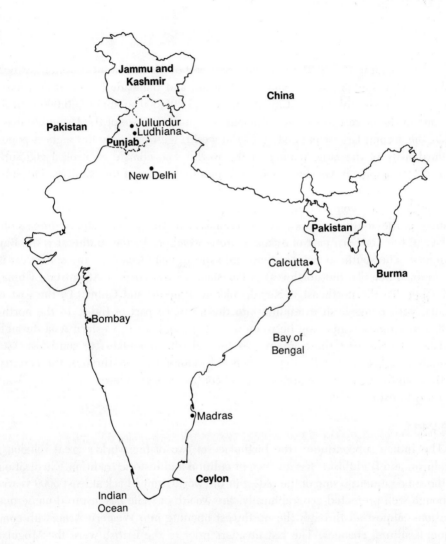

Jammu and
Kashmir

China

Pakistan

•Jullundur
•Ludhiana
Punjab

•New Delhi

Pakistan

Calcutta•

Burma

•Bombay

Bay of
Bengal

•Madras

Ceylon

Indian
Ocean

became a prime subject of exploitation and colonialism. This invasion came from the sea.

The Portuguese were the first to establish trading posts in India at the end of the fifteenth century. They were followed quickly by the British, Dutch and French. The British first arrived in any force in 1609 and quickly gained colonial dominance. They founded Madras and Calcutta and gained control of Bombay. In the seventeenth and eighteenth centuries the British trading companies, most notably the East India Trading Company, were the most successful in gaining spheres of influence and control in the subcontinent, and until the twentieth century the dominant colonial force in India was British. By 1774 the British government had taken direct control over the affairs of the subcontinent, Lord Hastings was appointed first Governor-General, and a civil administration was set up. Although about three fifths of the subcontinent were still under the rule of the local aristocracy, Britain provided the direction.

The British encountered many instances of resistance to colonialism. One of the most violent episodes occurred in 1857 and was directly responsible for the form that the Indian police system still has. Resistance to British power became particularly strong after World War I under the leadership of Mohandas "Mahatma" Gandhi and the philosophy of nonviolent resistance (stayagraha). In 1935 Britain promulgated a constitution for India as a result of a massive campaign of "civil disobedience" organized by Gandhi and the Indian Congress Party. The Moslems, under the leadership of Mohammed Ali Jinnah and the Moslem League, took the position that separate Moslem and Hindu states needed to be created. They claimed fear of Hindu domination and suppression of Moslems in an independent India.

Britain announced in 1947 that the subcontinent was to be given independence. Although August 15, 1947, was designated Indian Independence Day, the British did not withdraw until June 1948. India at independence became a member of the British Commonwealth. The subcontinent was divided into two dominions—Pakistan, in two sections separated by 1600 km (1000 mi) in the east and northwest for the Moslems, and India, which was to be secular. Several sections of the country were divided as well. These were Punjab in the northwest and Bengal in the east. Some areas were left in dispute.

In the process of partition there was much bloodshed and hardship on all sides. A legacy of distrust and several consequent wars have been the results. The last war between India and Pakistan was in December 1971 and lasted 2 weeks. It resulted in the division of Pakistan into two Moslem countries, Bangladesh in the east and Pakistan in the west. Since 1971 relationships between the three countries have stabilized but are not particularly cordial. All three have inherited problems of development, poverty, and overpopulation. All three are primarily rural, village-oriented societies. India declared itself a republic, but maintained membership in the commonwealth, under a new constitution promulgated in 1950.

CULTURE

The vast majority of the population of India is of Indo-European origin with admixtures of Mongoloid strains in the north and east. There are numerous pockets of aboriginal peoples in the mountainous central areas and the jungles of the northeast. Most of the religious groups of the world are represented in India. There are over 500 million persons of Hindu background, about 80 million Moslems (the largest Moslem population in any country), 15 million Christians of various denominations, 11 million Sikhs, 4 million Buddhists, and 3 million Jains, Zoroastrians, Animists, and Jews. There are 14 main languages, 12 of which derive from Sanskrit, with hundreds of dialects. The southern languages are of Dravidian origin, representing the languages of pre-Indo-European populations. About 50% of the population speak Hindi, a Sanskrit-based language and the official language of the country. English is still used for much of the government work and instruction in higher education, although only a small proportion of the population speaks English.

The culture of the country is based in the villages, where about 80% of the population is estimated to live. The caste system is particularly strong in the villages, although it remains a fact of life throughout the culture. This is a hereditary class system, generally endogamous and with traditional social roles and work. Most of the poorest elements in the population are members of the lowest, nonscheduled castes, called by Gandhi, Harijans, or children of god. Traditionally, contact between Harijans and members of scheduled castes is limited and highly regulated. Harijans have traditionally performed work considered contaminating by other castes, and social intercourse and contact are restricted and practically prohibited. Non-Hindus form separate caste groups. It is government policy to break down the restrictions of caste, but they are still very strong. The population of India is quite diverse in language, caste, and religion, although there are overriding cultural strains that bind it together.

POLITICS

India is a republican, federal union of 21 states and nine union territories. The states are based on dominant language or ethnic group. The government is parliamentary, with two houses (Council of States and House of the People). There is also a president, elected for 5 years. The prime minister, representing the majority party of the parliament, is the political power in the government. The federating states have similar parliamentary systems headed by governors appointed by the president. Although India is a multiparty democracy, until 1976 politics were dominated by the Congress Party, the party of Gandhi and Jawaharlal Nehru and his daughter Indira Gandhi. At that time, for a number of reasons, a coalition of parties representing a wide range of political ideals was given the popular mandate to govern. This election was seen as a reaffirmation of the power of the democratic ideal in Indian life, because it was in part a reaction against a movement to centralize power in the hands of the prime minister and various abuses of this power in terms of limitations on freedom of speech and assembly. The guiding philosophy of Indian government since independence has been a social-democratic concept of the role of government. In the world community India has been a member and leader of the nonaligned states. Its size and the stature of the prime minister in world affairs have given India an important position in world politics and developments. The difficulties of developing an overpopulated, poverty-stricken country has taken much of the energy of the present government.

ECONOMY

India is a nation of villages and villagers, with 80% living in rural communities. Although about 70% of the population is engaged in agriculture, many live at bare subsistence levels. The goal of India is self-sufficiency in food production. There are periodic problems with drought, but the agricultural development of the country has proceeded with the "green revolution," the use of irrigation and fertilizers. The process was most successful earliest in the Punjab and other areas in the north-west. There has also been development of industry, and India is an important supplier of various manufactured goods to countries in Africa and Asia. Textiles has long been important; one center of the modern clothing industry, particularly knitgoods, has been the Punjab. Major steel mills have been put into operation, some of them the largest and most modern in Asia. The first nuclear power plant was built in the late 1960s–early 1970s near Bombay. Since then other such plants have been in-augurated. India is also a major source of raw materials, including coal, manganese, and bauxite, among others. Though there are still major problems of poverty in both city and village, there has also been the growth of a modern technologic society since independence. These two sit side by side in many areas of the country.

POLICE

The information about content of police work was gathered in Jullundar and Ludhiana, two of the largest and most industrialized cities of the Punjab. Punjab is a state in the northwestern part of India. It is the remains of an older and much larger Punjab, partially through division west to Pakistan and east to India. The east was further divided between speakers of Punjabi and Hindi. Punjabi, closely related to Hindi, is the language of the state. Punjab is the only state in which Sikhs are a majority (it is their home area), although there is a large Hindu minority. The Sikhs are followers of a religion formed almost 500 years ago in this border area. It is a martial religion that some claim was founded to provide military protection for the rest of India. Others claim that it was started in an attempt to reconcile Islam and Hinduism. Punjab is relatively affluent, being the center of the most successful agricultural section of India as well as the most highly industrial. Thus immigrants have been attracted from other parts of India. The caste system is not as deeply ingrained in Sikhism, and Punjabis generally have relegated caste among themselves to a minor role. However, the non-Punjabi immigrants have in essence taken the role of the nonscheduled castes elsewhere, inasmuch as almost all were of that social strata prior to migrating. These immigrants perform the unskilled, manual labor in both agricultural and nonagricultural work. It is said that there are no poor Punjabis but that there are many poor people in the Punjab.

Although still primarily agriculture and village oriented, in many ways the Punjab is not representative of the rest of India, even having a slightly deviant police structure. There is no bifurcation of police function and organization. The armed police fulfill all police functions. Police carry weapons as well as the lathi. They often live in cantonments but also live in the community if they wish. They man the police stations and posts and provide defensive power when it is deemed necessary. They also investigate crimes, hunt for lost children, interpose in village quarrels, and patrol the streets and alleys. The combination of the two forces into one in the Punjab is, naturally, related to historic factors. In part it may be a result of martial traditions of the Sikhs and the hostile border.

History

The Indian police forces have been influenced substantially by the British police system. Much of India was under British rule until 1947, and the rest was under strong British colonial influence. The development of the Indian Colonial Police system was a British colonial activity. The early development therefore reflected much of the ferment and philosophic deliberations of the early British system, particularly that of the Metropolitan Police of London. There were major differences, however, arising from the cultural setting and the colonial nature of the institution. Native Indian antecedents influenced the development of the colonial police forces as well.

The constant throughout India's history has been the village and the caste system. This social organization has endured many conquerors and changes in power, variety of language, and cultural modifications. The adaptations have had the effect of giving Indian institutions and culture a bimodal quality based on the rural village-oriented system and the system the dominant power at any one moment organizes. Police history has the same bimodal quality. There has been the policing function of the village and local social system and that of the imperial power. "Police history can be seen . . . as the expansion and contraction of an imperial power always set upon an impermeable stratum of village institutions."[2,p.39] These factors have had important effects on the perception the people have of the police. The connection with the imperial power has earned the police a connection with repression and oppression. Fairness and justice usually are not associated with foreign conquerors and imperial powers. The connection goes back into history and continues until this day. The central government was and often still is seen as removed and oppressive. Police share this stigma. "Police in all periods of Indian history have been represented as oppressive and unfair."[2,p.40] This has left a serious problem of community relations with which the post-independence police have had to deal.

The organization and function of the modern Indian Police Services is directly descended from the British organized and run Indian Colonial Police. Although based on a bimodal cultural system, it was a product of the British imperial control of India. The police legacy to the independent country is composed of three major elements. The first is the structure of the system. The police system today is organized in almost the same way as it was organized after reforms in 1861. The second is the concept of the role of police within the society. "'Proper' police duties today are very much what were considered 'proper' police duties under the British."[2,p.50] The third is the attitude of the public and government officials and policymakers toward the police. These three elements underlie most of police work in India today.

The British did not form a colonial police service when they began to take power in India, and it was some time before there was admission that they were anything other than traders. The British were first among several European colonial nations with interests in India and had special rights in areas of India as early as 1609. Slowly they assumed the dominant colonial position in the subcontinental area. By the latter half of the eighteenth century the British had three "presidency" provinces in which they assumed direct governmental control: Bengal in the northeast, Bombay on the west coast, and Madras in the southeast. For some time they tried to rule using the native government system.

The government system of India was based primarily on the village government of elders, the panchayat, and the various feudal landholders, maharajahs, princes, and so on. The village system assumed all responsibilities dealing with daily life. The princely system was essentially superimposed on the village system for the benefit of the princes. Of course, some princes were concerned about their subjects and ruled benevolently. Much of the ruling was done through the panchayat. Both systems had policing powers, the princes through assumption, the panchayat through social necessity. Coincidental to the increase in British influence throughout the subcontinent was the decreasing ability of the prince and panchayat systems to maintain peace.

During the middle and latter parts of the eighteenth century there was large-scale growth of dacoitism and other signs of social unrest and disruption. The dacoits were armed bandits, generally working in groups that attacked villages and travellers. Often they assumed a pose similar to that of Robin Hood but generally were quite disruptive and destructive and not too successful in protecting the poor. The villages became poorer and poorer, trade was disrupted, and there was a general deterioration of social conditions throughout the subcontinent. The village panchayats became less able to maintain order and the society of the people, let alone that of the traders and their interests. The landowners and princes also lost control in many areas. The British, through the East India Company, stepped into the breach. The Company was later supplanted by the British government. Some time elapsed before order was put on a sustained, legislative basis. The development of some policing system answerable to British needs was inevitable.

The British had experience in developing colonial police forces. They had organized the Royal Irish Constabulary long before they reorganized the police system of London. It was in the three presidency provinces—Calcutta (Bengal), Madras, and Bombay—that the first colonial forces were developed. The Governor General of India, Lord Cornwallis, used the Royal Irish Constabulary as a model for the organization of similar forces in India.[2,p.43] In 1792 he gave the East India Company the power to police, having taken "police administration out of the hands of the large landowners and established in their place a police force responsible to the agents of the Company."[2,p.41]

The resultant police forces were not yet a system. The organization of the police system for British-governed India took place in small increments. As in England, the system was organized under the stresses of social disorder and revolutionary activity on the subcontinent. A major act of rebellion, the Mutiny of 1857, shocked the British into giving final legislative basis to the colonial police. It gave the impetus for the enactment of a series of laws and a set of standards under which the policing of Indian colonies would thenceforth take place:

Reforms that had been maturing for many years with pragmatic, bureaucratic thoroughness were suddenly enshrined in law. The Government of India Act of 1858, the great Indian Legal Code, the Code of Civil Procedure–1859, the Indian Penal Code–1869, the Code of Criminal Procedure, and the Police Act of 1861.[2,p.41]

These enactments still exert important influence on modern India. The Police Act of 1861 put policing under provincial control and established four principles of police organization that are still operative in the Indian police system:

1. Military police were to be eliminated, and policing was to be entrusted to a civil constabulary.
2. Civil police were to have their own separate administrative establishment headed by an inspector general in every province.
3. The inspector general was responsible to the provincial government, as the superintendent was to the civilian collector.
4. The superintendent was to supervise village police.[2,p.47]

These principles were the basis for civilian police forces, organized by province. The superintendent under the inspector general, headed police districts within the province. At a later time a quasimilitary police force, the "armed" police, was developed in the provinces to respond to civil disorder. The civilian police force became known as the "unarmed" police. Specific differences between armed and unarmed police are discussed later. The general village and town constabulary continued to be the unarmed police. The exception to this is found in the Punjab, where only one police force assumes both functions.

From the establishment of the principles of 1861 further developments throughout India continued. There remains a basically provincial organization of police forces. There is no national police force, although the officer corps is national. In each state there is a police force directly responsible to the state government. The inspector general of the police in each province is responsible to the provincial government and the superintendent to the district government. The only national element within the police are the commissioned officers.

This element adds complications to an already complicated system. Because the officers corps of the colonial police was the province of the British, it was organized on a national basis. At its inception all the officers were British. They were assigned to the provincial forces, which were composed of both Britons and Indians. Obviously in a colonial system the lower the rank the more certain it was to be filled by an Indian, or vice versa. Training and recruitment for the officers corps was separate from that for the provincial corps. This situation still exists. Ranking officers in provincial police systems belong to the national Indian Police Service (IPS). This is an entirely separate system from the provincial forces, although the commissioned officers of the provincial forces are members of the IPS. Assignments are made to provincial forces by the IPS, as are reassignments. In essence the function of the IPS is to unite the state forces into a national system. The function of the provincial or state police is to ensure local responsibility and self-government.

Tension between nation and state is a constant in India. India's states are in some ways analogous to countries in a united Europe, often based on lingual and cultural differences. Thus an attempt to build a nation must take into account a culturally diverse and lingually diverse population, often separated regionally. Regional feelings are strong and conflict with national feelings, which are also strong.

One byproduct of the national officers service and the state police forces is that officers often are assigned on a cross-cultural basis. Thus many officers are not native to the area they serve. This means that the regional language may be foreign to them. The two languages of national usage are Hindi, the legal national language, and English, the language of the colonists. Hindi is strongly resisted in the south and is spoken and understood mainly in the northern two-thirds of the country. However, because the officers are from the educated classes, they generally speak English.

The interplay between regional and state power and responsibilities and influences is central to the police forces. The IPS leads to national influence and some indirect control of the state forces by the central government. There are, of course, other national influences on the state police, generally financial and legal. The state governments receive partial subsidies for the operation of the state forces. The forces also were formed and operate under national law and standards. There are differences other than language between forces, but these are less important than the similarities across the country.

Three structural characteristics distinguish the Indian police: "control by state government, horizontal stratification, functional separation between armed and unarmed police."[2,p.52] All of these were characteristics of the colonial police forces. The first two are common to the organization of Indian government in other spheres as well. In all spheres the division of power between the states and the central government is changeable. There are controls that the central government exerts on the states, and there are ways the state governments can avoid the dictates of the central government. Parallel to the IPS is the all-India Civil Service. This service contains the top civil servants of the nation, as the all-India Police Service contains the top ranking police officials of the nation. Once assigned, they are responsible to the state government. Thus in the country the national hierarchical system (somewhat similar to the caste system) and the local cultural system are in a sort of balance.

Like the colonial system, the present national system has high standards. There are several well-organized, high-caliber training schools throughout the nation for IPS recruits and continuing education for those in service. "India was one of the first nations to provide systematic training of a high quality for officers and aspirants to high rank."[2,p.48] During most of the colonial period Indians were not permitted into the IPS or its training facilities. Since independence the corps has for all intents and purposes been completely Indianized. The standards have been maintained.

During the colonial period the training facilities were very good. Fingerprinting, one of the major advances in police work throughout the world, was developed by Sir Edward Henry, an inspector general of police in Bengal.[2,p.48]

Training for police officials today tries to maintain the standards of the colonials while responding to the needs of an independent nation. Regional training colleges serve students from several states. One of the emphases of the colleges today is the responsibility of the police service to build the nation and help the people develop standards and well being. There is an attempt to teach the police officers to look on themselves as interdependent with the general population. An excerpt from a police community relations manual illustrates this: "In socialistic pattern of society, the police and the public are to a great degree dependent upon each other."[4] Materials used in one training college are not necessarily replicated in other colleges, but national standards indicate that there is similar material at all colleges. Included are materials relating to law enforcement, community relations, and all other aspects of police work.

Training for police in the state forces is the responsibility of each state. This training varies from state to state, and each state has training facilities for its police force. There are further hierarchial differences within the state forces similar to those between the IPS and the state forces. The constabulary is composed of many people with minimal education. This reflects the average educational level of the general population. Thus training programs and materials must be tailored to that level. On the other hand, noncommissioned officers generally are university educated, so for them there is a separate network of state police training facilities. In essence the system is three tiered. The Indian Police Service, run by the national government, selects, sets conditions of service for, trains, and assigns commissioned officers. The state governments select, set conditions of service for, and train noncommissioned officers and the constabulary.[2,p.52]

Organization

The bifurcation of police into armed and unarmed (civil) branches is a special characteristic of the Indian police system. This is not unique to India, but does not exist in the other countries discussed in this book. It is another example of the influence the colonial period had on the development of the Indian police system. The cantonments in which armed police and the army live were built and developed by the British for the colonial government. As was previously stated, the armed police were developed after the major development of police forces in the subcontinent, as a direct response to the resistance of the population to the colonial system.

There are similarities between the two types of state police forces. For example, both have officers assigned by the national IPS. Both have two tiers of state police personnel: noncommissioned officers and constabulary. The armed police are organized more closely after military style than are the unarmed police. Their areas of concern are security and defense. The armed constabulary more closely resemble the troops in the army than the constabulary of the civil police. The personnel of the armed police live in the cantonments, often with the army. They carry weapons and have vehicles similar to those of the army. The people have little contact with the armed police except in cases of civil disorder. The armed police supervise and if it is thought necessary respond to public demonstrations, intercaste strife, and other types of mass disruptions. To many Indians there may be little discernible difference between the armed police and the army.

The unarmed civil police are uniformed and generally without firepower. They may, and often do, carry a baton or lathi (a bamboo staff). They are assigned to police posts or stations, spread throughout the police district to enhance their ability to respond to problems as they arise. The constabulary generally patrol their areas on foot or on bicycles. It is not unusual for constables to hitch rides to get to their posts. They generally live within the community rather than in cantonments. In normal circumstances these are the police with whom the population has contact. Most of the work of the civil police is preventive patrol. Bayley describes their function as follows:

They hunt for lost children, investigate crimes, patrol streets, regulate traffic, interpose in village quarrels and generally respond to the articulate needs of the mass of the people for police assistance. They are to be found distributed across the face of India, in metropolis, city, town and remote village.[2,p.59]

There is a great similarity between the unarmed police and the civilian police of Britain, and as shall be seen, similarities with the police in the other countries is also strong.

Ranking

Command organization in India is bilevel in that there is one command level in the state forces and another, higher level in the IPS. The rank order in the Indian police force is given in the following list.

Indian Police Service: Inspector General
Deputy Inspector General
Superintendent
Assistant Superintendent
State force: Deputy Superintendent (equivalent to Assistant Superintent, IPS)
Inspector
Subinspector
Assistant Subinspector
Head Constable
Constable

The three inspector ranks in the state forces are known as nongazetted officers (non-commissioned officers).[2,p.76]

There are four entrance levels to the Indian police. The lowest ranking levels are constable and head constable. Rarely does one move from head constable to inspector status. Entrance to the state forces can also occur at the assistant sub-inspector or subinspector level or at the level of deputy superintendent. Although it is possible to move from deputy superintendent into the IPS, this is not common. It is estimated that about one fourth of the openings for the IPS each year are reserved for deputy superintendents in the state forces. However, there may be a few dozen openings in any year but many hundreds of deputy superintendents waiting for these jobs. There is also direct entrance into the IPS at the assistant superintendent level after tests qualifying the candidate. All IPS officers have university degrees, as do deputy superintendents in the state forces.[2,p.81]

Strength

India had 761,600 police, both armed and civil, at the end of 1976. Approximately three fourths of these, or 582,700, were civil police. With a population of about 600 million at the time, there was approximately one police person per 1000 population. Of these no more than a few thousand are IPS officers. It can be readily seen that the vast majority of police serve in the provincial forces.

Equipment

In general the Indian police have little equipment. There are only a few motor vehicles per district, and most police patrol on foot or on bicycles or find other transportation. Most stations have wireless sets. Also rifles, muskets, and revolvers are available for the armed police. The basic weapon of the civil police is the lathi or nightstick. There is a gradual development of scientific aids to criminal investigations. The Indian police therefore rely more than most Western police on their own powers of persuasion and authority to achieve their aims.

Women

Women are part of both the IPS and the state forces, but not in large numbers. In the IPS, notwithstanding the resistance of the men, women hold command positions. The highest position held by a woman in the IPS in 1978 was that of superintendent, in charge of the Parliament Street station in New Delhi. This is a very important police station, covering the major government buildings in the city. It is in an area where demonstrations are not uncommon. This policewoman therefore assumes command of armed police when necessary as well as the everyday command of uniformed, unarmed police. The common assignment for women in the IPS, however, is to research units rather than to command posts. The women in the IPS are struggling to assume command positions. In the state forces the policewomen are generally in the lower ranks and almost exclusively assigned to reception work. They are not even used as juvenile workers in the few forces in which such units exist. They are generally at the constable level.[1]

Relationship with community

Historically in India the police have been mistrusted and alienated from the general population. The colonial element, British and pre-British, is a major factor in this situation. The police forces were used by the British in the struggle against the movement for independence. This only served to intensify popular distrust of the police and the identification with oppression and repression:

The independence struggle pitted police against national movement. The Indian policeman against Indian freedom fighter. Because the police bore the brunt of repressive actions, memories were planted in the minds of the people that even today fundamentally affect relations between the two.[2,p.49]

In general people think of the police as being brutal and venal. I was often warned by Indian friends and acquaintances about the dire consequences of having anything to do with the police. It was a matter of great public discussion in the villages when police constables were seen visiting me. This made me a suspect in the village and in fact precipitated a minor international incident. Because the people believe that bodily injury is a consequence of normal visits to police stations, anyone who is not injured is considered an agent of the police and somewhat sinister. These feelings of distrust are quite deep and pervasive. On the other hand, police are often asked to provide assistance in times of personal trouble.

The police authorities are concerned about this fear and negative feelings, and there have been some attempts to develop police-community relations activities. The whole has been placed within the avowedly somewhat socialistic philosophy of the central government. A major emphasis of the training material is to help police see themselves as partners of the people. This is rather difficult in a system that has traditionally been representative of the rulers. The approach now is that police need to develop a cooperative relationship with the public. All of this is done within the framework that law enforcement is the police job. In training, recruits are taught that if they help the public the public will help them fight crime. The aim for the relationship between police and the people is that it be mutually helpful. Some remains of paternalistic thinking can be found, however, as in the introduction to the training materials in police-community relations of the training college of the IPS in the Punjab:

The police cannot discharge their duties to maintain law and order without the backing, goodwill and cooperation of the public. The ideal to be aimed at is that every police officer of whatever rank should be regarded by every law abiding person as a wise and impartial friend and protector against injury to his person and property. This confidence begets police the necessary cooperation for successfully combating crime. The police are in a position to perform many nonregulatory functions during the course of their duties and small courtesies and services rendered to individual citizens would go a long way in building up goodwill for the police and an appreciation of their difficulties. They must always willingly offer their services for various causes, i.e., natural calamities, floods and fires, etc.[4]

The emphasis on helping the general public in various ways can be seen, but it is geared to the benefit that police will gain from this help in better relations with the public.

According to Bayley, however, the police in reality do helpful things regularly. Bayley makes the point that the more helpful the police are the more the public asks for help. He also points out that "police are continuously called upon to perform a host of services for members of the public that have nothing at all to do with maintaining law and order and preventing crime."[2,p.186] Bayley surveyed face-to-face contacts between police and private citizens. One point studied was the differential between police-public contacts in different settings. He found four times as much contact in urban areas than in rural areas. He also found that people who had had good experiences with the police were more likely to approach police for help. Bayley thus proposes that a measurement of success in the development of positive relationships between police and the public is the amount of help the public asks the police for. "It is one of the peculiarities of police work that the more cordial their relations are with the public the greater becomes the number of extraneous demands made upon them by private citizens. One might indeed propose that a useful test of the rapport between police and public would be the volume of non-enforcement requests made of the police."[2,p.186] It seems that the farther from traditional society a community is, the greater the demands made on the police for help. In all, the differential in urban-rural contacts, the repeat requests when there had been positive responses, point to a natural demand in less traditional society for police help. It might point to a special position for the police in Indian society.

The ongoing task of the central society in India has been to build a nation with a unitary identity. There are few governmental institutions, as yet, that are viable for the vast majority of the Indian people. The police are among these few. They are vitually everywhere, in villages and in the cities. They are at the front lines of the formation of a nation. One might postulate that the degree to which they permeate the society and respond to the needs of the people has a bearing on the future of the nation. Will the nation finally meld the traditionally separate sources of power, the village and the imperial power? Bayley says:

Police are one of the most pervasive governmental agencies in the country. In the mid '50's police stations were third only to primary schools and post offices in their proximity to all villages. The police are there all the time, for and as the government, day in and day out.[2,p.179]

The police in India therefore represent a link to a unified nation and society as well as being representatives of law and order. They have also represented conflict with central authority historically. A dilemma of the police, as well as that of the central government, is the resolution of the conflict between the ruler and the village society. The role police play will be of great importance in how the people view the nation. They have a task that is greater than getting cooperation in enforcing law. They have a task that may help build a cooperative and successful society.

Function

Information about police work was gathered through interviews with police officials and translated transcriptions of all incidents in the daily log sheets for 1 week for each city. The daily logs are maintained in each police station and post. They are kept on a 24-hour basis by the police clerk (munshee) with the help of an assistant. There is a clerk or assistant on duty at all times in all police stations and posts. In the Punjab records are kept in Punjabi, the native language of the state, although there may be inserts in Hindi, English, or Urdu because many reports are written by officials of the police.

Police in India fulfill several functions within society. The two major functions are social integration and social control. They also perform a number of the interstitial tasks, between control and integration or support, found elsewhere. In the following discussion the content and relative involvement of the Punjabi police in each type of activity are examined separately after a general discussion.

Analysis of tasks

Total incidents with which the police were involved during the week studied were 142 in Jullundur, or 2.2 per 1000 population per month, and 193 in Ludhiana, or 2.1 per 1,000 per month (Tables 6-1 and 6-2). Slightly less than one half in Jullundur and three fifths in Ludhiana were law enforcement or social control incidents. Of these almost one half in Jullundur and two thirds in Ludhiana involved moral issues such as alcohol and drug abuse and gambling. Only one third in Jullundur and one sixth in Ludhiana were what would be considered criminal, and these were thefts. Social integration activities composed one third of the total in Jullundur and one fourth in Ludhiana. Of these the large majority involved arbitration-mediation. The remainder of the incidents were scattered among traffic, patrol, and miscellaneous activities. It would appear that there is a relatively low crime rate in these two cities and that the primary offense is theft. A major involvement of the police in both cities is with sale and use of drugs and alcohol. A second important characteristic of the police work studied is the high involvement in ar-

Table 6-1. Police tasks in India (November 6-13, 1971)

	Jullundur			Ludhiana		
	Number	**Percent**	**Monthly incidence**	**Number**	**Percent**	**Monthly incidence**
Social control						
Law enforcement						
Theft, motor vehicle	3	2.1		4		
Theft, nonvehicle	15	10.6		14	7.3	
Thief	2			4		
SUBTOTAL	20	14.2	0.31	22	11.4	0.24
Arrest	3			3		
Antisocial elements				1		
Vagabond arrest	1			2		
Army deserter	1					
Public nuisance						
Firearms without license				1		
Impersonation of official				1		
Habeas corpus				1		
Embezzlement				2		
Escaped convict				1		
Security				1		
SUBTOTAL	5	4.3	0.08	13	6.3	0.14
Morals						
Rape	1					
Alcohol abuse	22	15.6		19	9.8	
Drug abuse	1			33	17.1	
Gambling	5	3.5		25	13.0	
TOTAL	29	20.4	0.45	77	39.9	0.85
Support						
Arbitration-mediation						
Landlord-tenant	7	5.0		4	2.1	
Land disputes	9	5.0				
Family	6	4.2		1		
Neighbors	7	5.0	0.11	15	7.8	
Business	7	5.0		6	3.1	
Employer-employee	1					
Street	2			6	3.1	
Mentally ill person	1					
With injury (Jullundur included with others)	7	5.0	0.11	4	2.1	0.04
SUBTOTAL	40	28.2	0.62	36	18.7	0.40
Arrest for breach of peace	10	7.1	0.15	7	3.6	0.14
Services: individuals in need						
Drunks	3			3		
Quarrels with drunks				3		
Mentally deficient person, lost	1					
Injured person	2			3		
Identification of wandering person	1			6		
Death				3		
SUBTOTAL	7	4.3	0.11	12	3.1	0.13
TOTAL	47	33.1	0.73	48	24.9	0.53

Table 6-1. Police tasks in India (November 6-13, 1971)—cont'd

	Jullundur			Ludhiana		
	Number	Percent	Monthly incidence	Number	Percent	Monthly incidence
Lost and found	11	7.8		12	6.2	
Traffic						
Complaints				5		
Accidents	7			2		
SUBTOTAL	7	5.0	0.11	7	3.6	0.08
Hospital						
Statement of legal act				3		
Miscellaneous				4		
TOTAL	142	100.0	2.19	193	100.0	2.12

Table 6-2. Police tasks in India

	Jullunder (pop. 285,000)				Ludhiana (pop. 401,000)			
	Num-ber	Per-cent	Incidents per 1000 population Week	Month	Num-ber	Per-cent	Incidents per 1000 population Week	Month
Social control								
Primary law enforcement								
Theft	20	14.1	0.07	0.31	22	11.4	0.06	0.24
Miscellaneous	5	3.5	0.02	0.08				
Arrests, breach of peace	10	7.0	0.04	0.15	13	6.7	0.03	0.14
Morals	29	20.4	0.10	0.45	77	39.9	0.19	0.85
SUBTOTAL	64	45.1	0.22	0.99	119	61.7	0.30	1.31
Support								
Arbitration-mediation (no arrests)	40	28.2	0.14	0.62	36	18.7	0.09	0.40
Services: individuals in need	7	4.9	0.02	0.11	12	6.2	0.03	0.13
SUBTOTAL	47	33.1	0.17	0.73	48	24.9	0.12	0.53
Traffic	7	4.9	0.02	0.11	7	3.6	0.02	0.08
Patrol	13	9.2	0.05	0.20				
Miscellaneous								
Lost and found	11	7.7	0.04	0.17	12	6.2	0.03	0.13
General		27.8			4	2.1	0.01	0.04
Legal statement in hospital					3	1.6	0.01	0.03
SUBTOTAL	11	35.5	0.04	0.17	19	9.9	0.05	0.20
TOTAL	142	100.00	0.50	2.19	193	100.00	0.48	2.12

bitration-mediation activities and the low involvement in other service-related activities. Specifics relating to each category of police work follow.

Law enforcement (Social control). During the period under study the police in Jullundur and Ludhiana were involved in a number of law enforcement activities categorized in four subcategories. The one that might be called primary law enforcement includes thefts and apprehension of thieves. In Jullundur there were three thefts of motor vehicles and 15 other thefts, and two thieves were apprehended. This is a total of 20 cases, or 14.1% of incidents, for a rate of 0.07 per thousand population for the week and 0.31 prorated for the month. There were five miscellaneous law enforcement incidents, including three arrests, one vagabond arrest, and one army deserter, or 3.5% of total, for a rate of 0.04 per week and 0.15 per month. There were 10 arrests for breach of peace, 7% of total. Thus all law enforcement other than morals included 36 incidents, 25.4% of total, for a monthly rate of 0.56 per thousand population. In Ludhiana there were 42 incidents of primary and secondary law enforcement, or 21.8% of total, a rate of 0.46 per thousand population

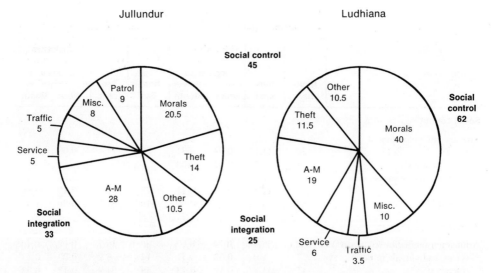

Fig. 3. Police work in India: percent distribution, November 1971.

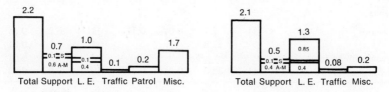

Fig. 4. Police work in India: incidence per 1000 population per month.

per month. These included 22 thefts, four of motor vehicles, and 14 other, and arrest of four thieves. There were 13 miscellaneous law enforcement incidents, 6.7% of total, comprising nine kinds of incidents, including three arrests, two vagabond arrests, two embezzlements, and one case each of antisocial elements, unlicensed firearms, impersonation of an official, habeas corpus, escaped convict, and security. In addition there were seven arrests for breach of peace.

The other major category of law enforcement incidents were in the area of morals. These incidents were concerned with alcohol, drugs, gambling, and one rape. In Jullundur 22 of the 29 incidents were related to illegal possession of or sale of alcohol. In Ludhiana there had been a major drug bust just before and during the period under examination (I was shown a room full of raw opium and other drugs in the central station). The figures for morals offenses reflect this, with 27 incidents, 35.9% of total, of which 19 were related to alcohol, 33 to drugs, and 25 to gambling. These combined for an incidence of 0.85 per thousand population per month.

Law enforcement incidents made up a relatively high percentage of total incidents for the period. In Jullundur 45.1% of all incidents were related to law enforcement or social control. In Ludhiana 61.7% of all incidents were related to law enforcement. The rate per month 1 per thousand in Jullundur and 1.3 per thousand in Ludhiana (Figs. 3 and 4).

Support (social integration). The major aspect of socially integrative incidents in which police in Jullundur and Ludhiana were involved were arbitration-mediation activities in which no arrests were made. These incidents covered a wide range of relationships and problems. A further discussion of the role of the police in this area follows in a general discussion of police work. In Jullundur 18.2% of 40 incidents were arbitration-mediation activities, an incidence of 0.62 per thousand population per month. These included seven landlord-tenant conflicts, nine land disputes, six family crises, seven disputes with neighbors, seven business disagreements, two conflicts in the street, one employer-employee conflict, and one incident involving a mentally ill person. Of these disputes at least seven led to actual violence and resulted in some injury. In Ludhiana 36 incidents, or 18.7%, were concerned with arbitration-mediation, a rate of 0.4 per thousand per month. These included similar types of disputes with a slightly different distribution: four landlord-tenant, one family, 15 between neighbors, six each business and in the street, and four leading to injury.

Involvement in other support activities is much lower, both in number and in kind, than found in some other places. In Jullundur there were seven incidents, 4.9% of total, a rate of 0.11 per thousand per month. These included three drunks, one lost mentally deficient person, one injured person, one wandering person, and one injured person in the hospital. In Ludhiana this type of activity was marginally greater. There were 12 service-related incidents, 6.2% of total, 0.31 per thousand per month. Of these, six involved drunks and six were hospital related, three dealing with injured people and three with death.

The types of incidents related to social integration and support behavior represent a significant part of police work in the two cities. In Jullundur they represent 33.1% of all police work, 47 incidents per week, a rate of 0.73 per thousand per month. In Ludhiana they represent 24.9% of all police work, 48 incidents per week, a rate of 0.53 per thousand per month. The major difference between the two cities is the lower incidence of arbitration-mediation incidents in Ludhiana. In both cities, however, arbitration-mediation made up the great majority of support activities.

Interstitial activities make up the smallest part of the police job in both cities. Traffic-related incidents are minor aspects of the activities of Indian police. This is related to the low number of motor vehicles in the country, although these are often lethally used. Much of the traffic in India outside of Delhi and similar cities is non-motorized, with either human or animal power propelling it. Of the motor vehicles many are 2-cylinder scooters and small cycles. In Jullundur there were seven accidents, or 5% total incidents, for a rate of 0.11 per thousand population per month. In Ludhiana there were also seven incidents, five of which were traffic complaints, or 3.6% of total for a rate of 0.08 per thousand per month. Miscellaneous activities, lost and found making up the majority, were 8% and 10% in both cities. Logged patrol incidents were very few although patrol is a major aspect of police work in India. The Indian police regularly check on what they call "bad characters and strangers." They also spend a good deal of time on the beat.

I had an experience in Agra that indicates the knowledge Indian police have of their beats. My pocket was picked in a crowded area. The loss was discovered several miles away in a different section of the city, near a tourist attraction (the Taj Mahal). The constable on duty there was informed of the matter and the victim was directed to the police station. While waiting for transportation I observed the constable approach a middle-aged man, inform him of knowledge of the deed and strongly suggest that the material be returned to the train station within two hours. Of course, the man vociferously insisted upon his innocence of the deed and any knowledge of it. Within three hours the material was found at the train station and forwarded to the owner through police and consular intermediaries with almost all belongings, including most of the money, intact. This is not to suggest that one should not be careful while visiting India and allow one's pocket to be picked. This does suggest that the constable in this case certainly knew his business.

In both cities the incidence and proportion of police work related to social integration is higher than that for social control if morals-related activities are not counted. The incidence of both law enforcement activities (excluding morals) and integrative activities is higher in Jullundur. The incidence of moral incidents in Ludhiana is not necessarily a reliable indication of normal affairs, because of the special drug situation in process during the time of the study.

Other aspects of police work in India must be examined. There are several elements that enter into the interaction of police and people in this society that are absent in other more European societies. These are the powerful social force of the caste system, an ingrown feudalism translated in modern times into a semblance of the class system. Although the government is committed to the eradication of the caste system and the disabilities that flow from it, there are still powerful social and cultural currents supported by caste. The bipartite nature of the Indian police is partially a product of this system and in turn is supported by it. The constables of the state police are generally without high standing in the community. They might be considered on the level of the lower middle class in European society. Officers on the other hand are middle to upper middle class. It thus follows that people of higher social standing would be reluctant to deal with constables on a voluntary basis and for many problems would rather deal with an officer, a person of higher social standing, perceived as more powerful. This supposition is supported in discussions with police officials.

Three major categories of police work are recognized in India: (1) cognizable offenses, from the all-India Penal Code (IPC), including the major crimes such as murder and robbery, dealt with uniformly throughout India; (2) noncognizable offenses, such as forgery and adultery, for which a magistrate or judicial order is needed before police can proceed; and (3) complaints, which include problems in which no offense has in reality been committed. Police officials indicate that this last category has shown proportionately the greatest increase in the 1960s and 1970s.[3] Complaints are actions instigated by an applicant, usually with an accusation of assault, although "95% prove to be neither cognizable nor noncognizable in nature."[3] Complaints are usually dealt with by officers rather than constables when the nature of the issue is clear. They often are issues resulting from unrest and require mediation of social contracts between parties of previously unequal social levels.

The changing social relationships resulting from the movement toward democratization of the society and the breakdown of previously unbreachable social barriers have increased social tensions. These social tensions are found throughout the country and in every police district and subdistrict. The police are called on to deal with many of the expressions of the social tension. In a country that is predominantly rural one would expect that many of the social changes regarding the relationships between social classes and men and women would be expressed through issues regarding working of the land. This seems to be true.

In the past the landowners set the daily wages and the workers and tenants worked at that level. There are now many incidents where the semiskilled and unskilled low-caste workers refuse to accept the landlords' decisions. This leads to major social clashes, and all available weapons are used. These include social boycotts instituted by workers against landlords and various measures utilized by the higher caste and class landlords. In these cases the local police official is called on to act as arbitrator. It is not a legally delegated function of the police. It is, however, related to the maintenance of public peace and order. Police officials in these cases arbitrate the dispute and develop a written contract stating the terms agreed on. The contract is signed by the parties to the dispute, as well as by the police official, and then kept at police headquarters. Although the use of such contracts helps

stabilize potentially volatile situations, there are no legal grounds for these trans-
actions. The police are involved to lend the prestige, power, and sanction of the
government to the contract and to increase the probability that the provisions agreed
on will be adhered to by all parties.

Another major problem with which the police are involved is the changing relationships between men and women. It is estimated that half of the mediation problems with which police deal are related to family matters, usually women rebelling
against the situation in which they are put. Marriages are generally arranged, often
without the involvement of either partner to any great extent in the decision. It
has become more common in the past few years for women to rebel against the ar-
rangement either before or after marriage. Informants state that women running
away often do so with or to a paramour. The family often seeks the help of the police
in returning the woman. The police cannot force the woman to return, but often
some sort of compromise can be worked out.

Another area in which police provide mediation between conflicting or potentially conflicting parties is in the relationships between castes and communal groups.
Religion and communal affiliation are not private affairs in India. Often tensions develop over celebration of holidays and holy days. As in other countries the holiday
of one group may be celebration of victory over one of the others. Police officials
are often the arbitrators between the various religious communities. Some issues
with which they deal are arrangements to ensure peaceful public celebration of
holidays and broadcasting of religious services over loudspeakers from temples.
There have also been public communal demonstrations relating to political issues,
language recognition, and other such issues. Police officials also often act as me-
diators when there are issues of land use and ownership. In a primarily rural and
agricultural society, the importance of this issue and the emotion with which it can
be approached are understandable.

It is estimated by police officials that 30% to 40% of their work is related to these
mediation-arbitration issues. This is a generally unpublicized aspect of police work
and is not entered in the daily logs, for what reason I cannot say. Most situations
are handled at local headquarters and by the police officers of the IPS. The arbitration agreements, duly signed and notarized, are held in the police files. Any party
to the agreement can come to the station, complain of breaches of the agreement,
and request police support for adherence to it. Because the police are vested with
a great deal of power in the popular mind, this is further incentive to adherence to
these signed and notarized agreements. This aspect of police work apparently dates
from preindependence, as does much of the rest of police function and organization.

It is clear from the information received that police in India perform tasks similar
to those of the other police studied. It is also clear that the support aspects of police
work are not as well integrated into the work of the constabulary in Punjab as they
are in other countries studied. It is evident that support work is perceived by some
police officials to be an important, although often undocumented, part of police
activity. According to the perceptions of the major informant, there is a connection

between the changes that Indian, and specifically Punjabi, society is undergoing and between developments in police work.

Socioecological relationships

Some of the differences between police activities and incidence rates in the two cities might be explained through socioecological data. Jullundur has a more homogeneous population and is less industrialized than Ludhiana. Ludhiana had a much higher rate of population growth over the 10 years prior to the study, with a density per square kilometer almost twice that of Jullundur. The two cities had been the same size for many years, but between 1961 and 1971 Ludhiana increased its population so much that it was almost 60% larger than Jullundur. This might explain the higher incidence of law enforcement activities in Ludhiana, particularly those involving morals.

Problems

Police in India have several problems, two of which are unique to the Indian situation and one that is similar to problems experienced by police in other countries, particularly the United States. The latter is primarily a public relations problem. The police have a rather poor public image and are not particularly well liked by the general population. This problem, stemming in part from the colonial experience, interferes with the integrative function of the police. It also interferes with the positive preventive activities of the police. In the development of a national consciousness and indentification with the central government and state governments, a positive relationship between the police and the people would be an asset.

The other problems with which police are faced are primarily technologic and caused primarily by the poverty of the country. India has a very poor communications network, with few telephones, rarely interurban service, and most villages with no phone connection at all. There are also very few motor vehicles outside of the urban centers. Most people, including the police, walk from place to place. These technical matters prevent any rapid response by police to situations either of a social control or social integration nature. As the country develops there will undoubtedly be an increase in the modern technology available to the police.

SUMMARY

The modern police forces of India are direct descendants of the Indian Colonial Police. This force was initially modeled after the Royal Irish Constabulary. It was begun in 1792 during a period of social unrest and disorder and was reconstituted in the late 1850s and early 1860s, another period of social disorder and unrest. The reorganization that took place at that time essentially established the format of the modern Indian police. These reforms established a civil police force with separate administration responsible to provincial civilian government, organized by districts. Perpendicular to the provincial police system a subcontinent-wide officers corps was organized, the ancestor of the Indian Police Service. The provincial or state forces ensure local responsibility and authority. The national officers corps ensures national standards and identification. In most states there is differentiation between armed and unarmed police. The former, dealing with problems of security and local defense, is organized in a more directly military fashion. The latter, although uniformed, are generally unarmed except for a nightstick (lathi). The unarmed or civil police correspond to similar police forces elsewhere. There are few women in the police forces of India at this time.

The police of India are charged with the maintenance of law and order and keeping the peace. Although police in India do many helpful, supportive things, the majority of their work is devoted to patrol and dealing with law enforcement. Law enforcement activities make up 50% or more of recorded activities. Many of the support activities are devoted to arbitration-mediation tasks related to conflicts stimulated by changing social relationships and status, for example, disputes between landlord and tenant farmer, worker and employer, and men and women. A rather high percentage of these conflicts, between 10% and 15%, lead to violence and injury. In all, the incidence of activities, whether law enforcement or support, is rather low, being slightly more than 2 per thousand population per month.

In Punjab the police data show that performance of support activities is a smaller part of police tasks than that of primary law enforcement. The greatest single activity in which police are involved is patrol. The largest amount of support activities are involved with arbitration-mediation. Police in Punjab operate under conditions not common in the other countries studied. There is a rather rudimentary telephone system, and most people do not have access to telephones. Police are generally without motorized transport to accomplish their tasks and cover their rounds. Information from police officials emphasized the involvement of these officials in support activities and suggested a relationship between the support tasks and the changing nature of society in India, particularly the changing relationships between traditionally subordinate and superordinate elements in society.

There are a few main problems in police functions in India. Two of these, inadequate communications links and transport, are probably common throughout the underdeveloped or developing world. Another problem not unique to India is the negative view of the public toward police and police work. There has been an attempt in the training process to help police deal with this problem.

In general the police of India are rather professional and have a high standard of training and function, although they suffer from the poverty of a poor nation. They do uphold the democratic ideals of that nation but have some colonial habits and legacies that will probably be shed over the coming years.

REFERENCES

1. Bayley, D. H., personal correspondence, April and May 1979.
2. Bayley, D. H.: The police and political development in India, Princeton, N.J., 1969, Princeton University Press.
3. Kumar, A., Inspector General, Pubjab Police, private conversation, 1971.
4. Relations between police and public, training materials, Police Training College, Northern Zone, Phillauer, Punjab, India, 1967.

Chapter 7

Israel

The State of Israel is on the southeastern shore of the Mediterranean Sea in the Middle East. It is bounded by Lebanon on the north, Syria, Jordan, and the Gulf of Eilat (Aqaba) of the Red Sea on the east, and Egypt and the Mediterranean on the west. It has a population of about 3.5 million and an additional 1.25 million in territory occupied during the 1967 war. The languages of the country are Hebrew and Arabic, although many people speak at least one other language, indicative of the heterogeneous origins of much of the population. In the occupied territories the population is predominantly Moslem Arab, with Christian and Druze minorities. The rest of the country is predominantly Jewish, with Moslem, Christian, and Druze minorities. The Jewish population has increased from 650,000 in 1948 to more than 3 million in 1978, largely through immigration from more than 70 countries in Europe, Asia, Africa, and the Americas. This heterogeneous population is generally divided into two major cultural groups, the Ashkenazim from Europe and the Americas and the Sephardim from southern Europe, Asia, and Africa. In addition there is a growing native-born population, the Sabras. The Arab population is primarily rural, whereas the Jewish population is heavily urbanized, albeit with significant rural and agricultural elements.

HISTORY

The State of Israel was legally constituted on May 14, 1948, when its independence was declared in Tel Aviv. Prior to that the United Nations had voted to divide Palestine, an area under League of Nations mandate to Britain, into Jewish and Arab states. The declaration of independence was accompanied by invasion from neighboring Arab countries and the flight of approximately two thirds of the resident Arab population of about 1 million. This produced a problem of refugees that has not been resolved to this date (1979). At the same time about 650,000 Jews left the Arab countries, many of them settling in the new state, which then comprised 12,800 sq km (8000 sq mi).

The history of the country is much older than this, having been recorded for over 5000 years. Much of the Bible relates to events that occurred in this area. It was first settled by tribes who are counted as the ancestors of the modern Jews and Arabs at about the time that it entered into recorded history. For much of its history

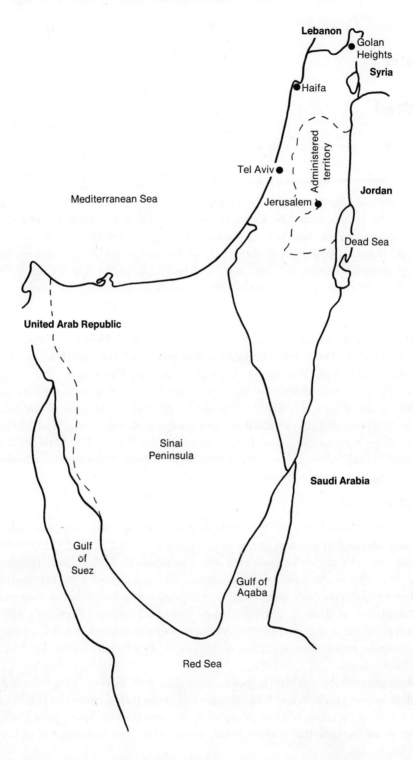

Lebanon

Golan
Heights

Syria

Haifa

Administered
territory

Tel Aviv

Jordan

Jerusalem

Mediterranean Sea

Dead Sea

United Arab Republic

Sinai
Peninsula

Saudi Arabia

Gulf
of
Suez

Gulf of
Aqaba

Red Sea

it was the crossroads of the Middle East, being on the main trade routes between Egypt, Babylonia, Anatolia, Arabia, and Greece. In approximately the thirteenth to twelfth centuries before the Christian era (BCE) Hebrew tribes developed a concept of nationhood and a country in the area. Until the second century Christian era (CE) this group was dominant in the region, although often under political domination by larger, more powerful neighboring empires. After a series of revolts against Roman rule in the first and second centuries a large part of the Jewish population was deported to join fellow Jews already living in other parts of the world. A residual population of Jews remained within the land, along with Canaanites and Philistines. After the Roman conquest the land remained as part of the Roman and then the Byzantine empire but was conquered by the armies of Mohammed from Arabia in the sixth century, when the population became arabized and predominantly Moslem. In a series of crusades in the twelfth and thirteenth centuries Christian armies from Europe attempted to free Palestine from the Moslems. These were successful for a time, but eventually the area returned to Moslem control. In 1516 it was conquered by the Moslem Ottoman or Turkish Empire and remained part of that entity until the end of the First World War. At the end of the nineteenth century a movement was begun among Jews of Europe to reestablish a Jewish commonwealth in the ancestral homeland. This movement brought increasing Jewish immigration into the area as it was redeveloped agriculturally and economically. Concomitant with Jewish immigration there was immigration of Arabs from surrounding areas. The population at the end of the nineteenth century was made up of approximately 30,000 Jews and 250,000 Arabs. In 1917 the British government issued the Balfour Declaration, promising to open the land to Jewish settlement and to develop a Jewish homeland, and about 13 years later issued the Passfield White Paper, giving the land to the Arabs. The Jewish population continuously increased from the 1920s to the 1940s as a result of legal and illegal immigration, primarily from Europe. Because the League of Nations had awarded Britain a mandate over the area at the end of World War I, the British controlled the area until the declaration of independence in 1948, by which time there was a Jewish population of 650,000 with a complex of organizations that were in essence an underground government (the Yishuv).

After 1948 there was a period of major Jewish immigration into the country, building the Jewish population from 650,000 to 2,500,000 within 20 years. At the same time there was a major effort at developing the economy of the country to provide for this population increase. Between independence and 1979 there have been four wars and constant hostility between Israel and its Arab neighbors. The Arabs have claimed that the Jewish state is not legitimate and that the area should be Arab. In June 1967, during the Six-Day War, Israel gained control of all the land west of the Jordan River, the Golan Heights to the northeast of the Sea of Galilee, and the Gaza Strip and the Sinai Peninsula. Only the Gaza Strip and West Bank area had significant populations, some of them in refugee camps, many from the flight of Arabs from Jewish-controlled areas in 1948. These areas are still under Israeli control except for parts of the Sinai that have been returned to Egypt. The eventual sovereignty of the occupied areas is a major source of argument between Israel and its Arab neighbors. Israel is primarily concerned about security in light of the historic active hostility and attacks made by Arabs against it and the communities that preceded the establishment of the country. The neighbors are concerned about the rights of the Arab population of the area, the return of land that they consider theirs, and the establishment of an "alien" presence in their midst. Much of the warfare has consisted of guerilla attacks on Israel, Israelis, and Israeli institutions by representatives of the Palestine Liberation Movement. At present the conflict seems to be almost unresolvable. It has led both sides to increasing concerns about security and defense. It has also contributed to the continued isolation of Jews and Arabs from each other within Israel itself and the unresolved position of Arabs within the country, although they are guaranteed full civil rights by law.

Economically the country has made great strides since 1948. It is a major supplier of agricultural products to Europe. It has also become a center for light industries dependent on technology and a trained work supply. It has a highly developed tourist industry, because it is a major religious center for Christianity, Islam, and Judaism and has many sites of interest. There are four main urban centers in the country: Tel Aviv, the largest metropolitan area of the country; Jerusalem, the capital and second largest city; Haifa, the major port and third largest city; and Beer Sheeba in the south, the fourth largest city. Each city has one or two major universities, of which there are seven in the country. Until 1967 Jerusalem was divided into an Eastern (Arab-Jordanian) section and a Western (Jewish-Israeli) section. After the June 1967 war the city was "reunited" and put under one administration under Israeli sovereignty. However, the population of the city and the culture of the city still reflect the former division. East Jerusalem is Arab and West Jerusalem, including the new areas to the north and south, is Jewish.

Police work was studied in the cities of Haifa and Jerusalem. Haifa is on the northern coast of Israel. It is known as the "workers" city. It has traditionally been a center of industry and the major port. The population has become more diverse over the past several years with the growth of institutions of higher education. There has also been a substantial Arab population in Haifa, approximately 6%, living in various areas of the city since before Independence. Jerusalem is in the east-central section of Israel, in the mountains. It was surrounded by Jordanian-administered territory until 1967, including the eastern section of the city, with the old city and its religious monuments and centers. Although the city is now united, there was little but commercial intercourse between the Jewish and Arab sections on the city through the early 1970s.

POLICE
History

The area now known as Israel has a history of thousands of years. For centuries prior to the First World War the area was ruled by the Ottoman Empire. After the war and the area was mandated to the British by the League of Nations. Although the British kept many of the laws of the Ottoman Empire in force, they completely reorganized the police. It was this reorganized system that was inherited by the founders of the State of Israel. The Israeli police force was created on May 14, 1948, by the provisional government of the newly-proclaimed state. Power was given to the ministers of the government to appoint officers and forces and use laws that had been extant under the just terminated British mandate. The effect was to transfer whole to the new state the inherited system of law and policing, with the exception

Israeli mounted police. (Courtesy Consulate General of Israel in New York.)

of laws that are inimical or antithetical to the basic concepts of the Jewish community (Yishuv). The purpose of the newly created force was to maintain law and order. This took place when the newly created state was in a state of war with the neighboring nations.

There were at the time of independence about 900 Jews in the mandate force, who along with recruits formed the new Israeli police force. The organization and structure of the new police force were based on the British Police Order of 1925. With some minor changes, this order is still the basis for the organization of police in Israel.

The formation of a police force for the area of Palestine began several years earlier. Shortly after the British took control of the area from the Turks it became evident that a policing organization was necessary. The initial force was composed entirely of persons recruited in England for service in the new colony. In April 1922, shortly after serious Arab violence against Jewish settlers,

. . . 650 British gendarmes . . . stepped on to the dusty little jetty near Haifa Railway Yards. They were the first Westerners, *embodied for exclusive service in Palestine and nowhere else*, to land since St. John of Acre fell to the Crescent in May, AD 1291. We were the first armed Christians sworn to no other service than to guard the borders of Palestine and to maintain peace within them, since the Knights Templar stole away in midnight's darkness from Castle Pilgrim.[1,p.5]

The exclusively British character of the force was to change almost completely within a few years. By 1926 the force was largely Palestinian (both Jewish and Arab). In that year the force was put on a legal basis. The British Police Order was promulgated and thereby instituted a permanent public security force, in which there were 120 British officers and 1800 Palestinian policemen.[1,p.124] As conflict between the two groups claiming the land increased, the British presence in the force was raised. In 1929 civil disorders again occurred, which led to the reinforcement of the force with large numbers of British officers and men. There continued to be a substantial number of both Jews and Arabs in the force, however. The British personnel constituted the command and a majority of the officers. They were primarily administrators and directors of operations, whereas police drawn from the native population primarily constituted the rank and file of the force (at the end of World War II approximately one third were Jewish and the rest Arab and Druze).

According to informants among the Israeli police the vast majority of the Jewish police in the mandate force had been closely identified with the underground independence movement. (As one police official who had lived through that time said, no Jewish policeman who did not cooperate with the underground lived very long.) These were the police who formed the Israeli Police Force at its inception. A few had unsavory records as collaborators and grafters and were discharged from the force when the Israeli government took over the police. Thus, from the outset and before, the police in Israel have been identified with the national and social aspirations of the majority of the population.

Organization

The British had organized the mandate police as a unitary force. It was run from a central headquarters in Jerusalem. The colony was further divided for police purposes into districts and subdistricts, each with a headquarters. Finally there were operations substations. The same organization with allowances for changed boundaries was continued under Israeli operation.

The Israeli police continues to be a national force. The districting of the country follows the pattern set by the British. There are three districts, north, south, and central; fifteen subdistricts; and two separate units, Haifa Port and Lod (Ben Gurion) Airport. The subdistricts cover discrete sections of the country. Larger urban areas such as Jerusalem, Tel Aviv, and Haifa form separate subdistricts. Within the subdistricts there are police substations, making police generally accessible to the population.

Ranking

There are fifteen ranks in the Israeli police force, divided into four levels, as follows:

Senior officers:	Head Superintendent (Rav Pakad)
	Assistant Commander (S'gan Nitzav)
	Associate Commander (Nitzav Mishneh)
	Deputy Commander (Tat Nitzav)
	Commander (Nitzav)
	Inspector General (Rav Nitzav)
Officers:	Subinspector (Mefakeakh Mishneh)
	Inspector (Mefakeakh)
	Superintendent (Pakad)
Noncommissioned officers:	Sergeant (Samal Rishon)
	Sergeant Major (Rav Samal)
	Head Sergeant Major (Rav Samal Rishon)
Constables:	Constable (Shoter)
	Head Constable (Rav Shoter)
	Corporal (Samal Sheni)

It is possible to enter the Israeli police force at any of the four levels, depending on education and experience (primarily in the armed forces). Between each level there is a training period at a police institution.

Qualifications for constable include 10 years of schooling. Officers must have at least a secondary education, and some university education is required for higher levels of the officers corps. Army experience when appropriate to police tasks is considered important as well.

Schooling

Four levels of schooling are given by the Israeli police force. Recruits at the base level are trained for 6 months. For promotion to sergeant one must attend sergeant's school for several months. Training for secondary school graduates (Officers Academy) is for 10 months. The Senior Officers Academy is coordinated with a university. Students study law as well as police material and receive university credit equal to about two semesters, which can be applied to further studies. Many of these students go on to become lawyers.

There are also special courses for police personnel specializing in particular areas of police work such as traffic, drugs, investigations, intelligence, and other special subjects. Graduates of these courses are assigned to the branch of the police dealing with relevant work. In addition veterans with special armed forces experience and training receive credit for such training when appointed to the police force. For example, a person who had been a lieutenant in the army with special training in intelligence work might be appointed directly as an inspector (mefakeakh) in the intelligence division of the police force.

Manpower

There were about 14,000 men and women in the Israeli police force in 1977. This was an increase from about 1900 at the end of 1948 and from 3500 in 1950. During a period (1950 to 1977) when the population was increasing approximately 250%, the strength of the police force increased 400%.[2,p.10] Police per population has increased during the same time period about 50%, from 2.5 per 1000 population to 3.8 per 1000 population. However, one cannot be lulled by these figures into assuming that there are enough police to do the work. With the increase in population and the international situation the problems with which police must deal have increased greatly. Police have been given the task of dealing with internal security problems since 1973, thus increasing their responsibilities. A small but significant proportion of the police force is made up of non-Jewish personnel. These come from the Christian, Arab, and Druze communities almost entirely. Until 1967 their percentage in the force remained at about 7%, with a low of 5% in 1950. Since the 1967 war there has been an increase to about 11.75% of the force, an increase of 135% from 1950. These police are deployed almost entirely in non-Jewish precincts, urban and rural, and in the border patrol.[2,p.12] Women have been part of the force from the inception of the state. They accounted for between 6% and 8% of the force from 1948 to 1967. After 1967 there was a continuous increase. In 1975 women comprised 15.7% and in 1977, 16.8% of the strength of the force.[2,p.11]

Women

In 1979 about 17% of all police and 8% of uniformed police were women. The most common duty assigned to women officers is traffic control; however, women also are involved in other aspects of police work. They are not completely integrated into the police force and are not regularly seen participating in patrol work. They are often assigned to those jobs in which women are supposed to be good, such as juvenile and family work and clerical work. An interesting cultural impact is the

Israeli policewoman directing traffic. (Courtesy Consulate General of Israel in New York.)

effect on Arab men stopped by a woman police officer for infraction of traffic regulations. It is difficult for many Arab men to deal with women in authority positions. It
is probably equally difficult for many Jewish men, particularly those from more male
supremist traditions. The society is dedicated to equality of women, however.
Woman have a similar role in the army. All women except those with religious ob-
jections are drafted, but they are not assigned to combat positions. In general the
position of women in the Israeli police is that of protected partners.[2,p.12]

The increase in women members of the force is explained by Hovav: There was
a need for more surveillance in the country, a lack of male recruits, and enlargement

of both central and district headquarters, "and more women were needed to serve in traffic units because of the increase in the country's motorization."[2,p.12] Hovav goes on to make some interesting comments on the role of women in the force. He reports a study that indicated the women in the force had a higher basic intelligence level than the men. Whether this is connected with reported friction between the men and women is not clear. It is clear that women had a difficult time being accepted by both their male colleagues and society as a whole in the role of police. At this point it is said that "Policewomen have been accepted by society and in the force, and are even looked upon as 'challenging.' Thus the force can be more choosy in selecting women than men."[2,p.12] In 1973, 65% of policewomen served in nonoperational functions, half of them in national headquarters.

Voluntary police

Until the October 1973 War there were a few special situations in which volunteers were deputized to perform special police duties. These included guarding government offices or establishments. Following the war the "civil guard" volunteer organization became an autonomous part of the force. This is related to the upsurge of terrorist activities and was designed "as a continuation of the volunteer movement to help . . . patrolling of public and deserted areas at night against terrorism and sabotage."[6,p.14] The civil guard is composed primarily of men who have completed their service obligations and thus are permanent residents over 53 with no service responsibilities. In 1979 there were about 108,000 people in the civil guard; they could be found in most public buildings and patrolling certain areas at night and in schools. The bringing of this large organization into the police force has not been a trouble-free union.[2,p.14]

Function

Although in Israel the police are seen primarily as law enforcement agents, the emphasis is on prevention, on the order of Rowan's concept. It is recognized that the police are only part of the means for preventing crime and that the social institutions of the society—legislative, medical, and services—are the primary means. As described in police material, the police are seen as one of a group of cooperating social institutions:

Only a small part of the means for crime prevention are in the hands of the police. Most of its activities in the field of prevention are designed first of all to check crime. The means for crime prevention in its broad sense are in the hands of the legislative, the social . . . the medical institutions.[3]

Beyond the concept of prevention, Israeli police are seen as helpers and service givers to the general population. The service function of the Israeli police is considered an important function equal to that of crime prevention and peacekeeping. Patrolling is seen as a means of responding to the population's needs for help of all sorts:

The activity of the patrol force and its achievements in preventing crime, in securing the public order and in giving various services, can be but partly evaluated statistically. The many thousands of cases dealt with and the services given by its men are not being recorded.[3]

The function of the police is probably greatly influenced by the attitude that the whole of the Jewish nation is one large family, partners in the building and defending of the newly reborn state. There is little evidence that police are seen as adversaries.[2,p.29] However, this might be changing. In the late 1970s, incidents of "police brutality" and corruption began to be published and were noted as a problem in the society.[2,p.28] See also Nyrop, p. 29.

The general function of the police in Israel follows the British model. Problems of internal security, however, play a much more important part in general police work because of the ever present tensions with the surrounding countries and the Arab independence movement. There is a need for constant vigilance against terrorist activities, calling for a high level of cooperation between the police and the general population. It is still possible to say that the Israeli police parallel the British police. They are unarmed, except for special units, and dependent for success on their ability to work cooperatively with the people.

Coast guard function. Until 1978 there was a marine patrol unit performing duties similar to those of the United States Coast Guard. They patrolled the coast lines, Mediterranean, Kinneret (Sea of Galilee), and Gulf of Eilat (Aqaba) and still perform some of these functions. However, in 1978, as a result of terrorist attacks from the sea, defense patrolling of the coastlines was assumed by the Israel Defense Force (IDF), or the armed forces.[4,p.289]

Analysis of tasks

Information about the content of police work was gathered through transcriptions of the incident summaries that are part of the daily log sheets. The logs are maintained in the central police station of each police district. Data were gathered for the week of November 24-30, 1971. Incidence was calculated on a monthly basis, multiplying the figures for a week by 4.4 (Table 7-1).

During the sample week the police in Haifa were involved in 524 incidents, an equivalent monthly rate of 10.6 per 1000 population; police in Jerusalem were involved in 586 incidents, an equivalent monthly rate of 12 per 1000 population (Figs. 5 and 6). The largest part of police work was devoted to support activities in both cities, over one third in Haifa and almost one half in Jerusalem. Law enforcement activities accounted for one sixth of police work in Jerusalem and slightly less in Haifa. Traffic-related incidents made up less than a tenth of incidents in Haifa and almost a sixth in Jerusalem. Other interstitial activities covered a wide range of tasks. Those in the patrol category accounted for over a fifth of the police tasks in Haifa and less than a tenth in Jerusalem, whereas miscellaneous tasks, primarily lost and found and delivery of messages, accounted for over a sixth in Haifa and somewhat less in Jerusalem. A special activity of the police in Haifa is delivery of

Table 7-1. Police tasks in Israel (November 24-31, 1971)

	Haifa (population 217,100)			Jerusalem (population 291,700)		
	Number	Percent	Incidence per 1000 per month	Number	Percent	Incidence per 1000 per month
Support						
Arbitration-mediation						
Public institutions	12	2.3	0.24	17	2.9	0.35
Businesses	19	3.6	0.39	23	3.9	0.47
Streets and terminals				18	3.1	0.37
Neighbors	7	1.3	0.14	34	5.8	0.69
Family	3	0.6	0.06	22	3.8	0.45
Residential area	46	8.8	0.93			
Animals	1			3		0.06
Unspecified	49	9.4	0.99	35	6.0	0.71
SUBTOTAL	137	26.1	2.78	152	25.9	3.10
Withdrawn or unfounded				42	7.2	0.86
Criminal file opened	7	1.3	0.14	34	5.8	0.69
TOTAL A-M	144	27.5	2.92	228	38.9	4.66
Service						
Assistance, nonspecified	38	7.3	0.77	6	1.0	0.12
Lost child	3		0.06	11	1.9	0.22
Older adults	3		0.06			
Disturbed persons				2		0.04
Notification of death				2		0.04
Person lying in street	3		0.06			
Injured persons	1		0.02	2		0.04
Mental patients				9	1.5	0.18
Suicide attempts	1		0.02	2		0.04
Drunks	2		0.04	6	1.0	0.12
Ill persons	1		0.02	2		0.04
SUBTOTAL	52	9.9	1.05	42	7.2	0.86
TOTAL	196	37.4	3.97	270	46.1	5.51
Law enforcement						
Criminal						
Theft	18	3.4	0.36	24	4.1	
Thief	4		0.08	17	2.9	
SUBTOTAL	22	4.2	0.45	41	7.0	0.84
Fraud in bank or hotel	1			2		
TOTAL CRIMINAL	23	4.4	0.47	43	7.3	0.88
Security						
Suspect articles	9	1.7	0.18	16	2.7	0.49
Sapper-ammunition or weapons	2		0.04	4	0.7	0.08
Shots or explosions	2		0.04	4	0.7	0.08
Suspect persons, nonsecurity						
Released or settled	24	4.6		9	1.5	0.18
Not found	2		0.04	10	1.7	0.20
Custody	12	2.3	0.24	8	1.4	0.16
SUBTOTAL	51	9.7	1.03	51	8.7	1.04
Morals						
Rape				2		0.04
Gambling	1			1		
Indecent act or exposure	2		0.04	1		
SUBTOTAL	3	0.6	0.06	4	0.07	0.08
TOTAL	77	14.7	1.56	98	16.7	2.00

Table 7-1. Police tasks in Israel (November 24-31, 1971)—cont'd

	Haifa (population 217,100)			Jerusalem (population 291,700)		
	Number	Per-cent	Incidence per 1000 per month	Number	Per-cent	Incidence per 1000 per month
Traffic						
Vehicular accidents	32	6.1	0.65	65	11.1	1.33
Traffic complaints	15	2.9	0.30	23	3.9	0.47
TOTAL	47	9.0	0.95	88	15.0	1.80
Patrol						
Patrol	56					
Alarms	8			9		
Windows, doors, lights in shops	4			5		
Property damage	22			12		
Court orders executed	9			4		
Court orders withdrawn or delayed	1			6		
Religious problems				6		
Public demonstrations, disturbances				5		
Pamphlets				2		
Arrest or detain	10			1		
TOTAL	110	21.0	2.23	50	8.5	1.02
Miscellaneous						
Fire	1			1		
Found things, nonvehicular	21			40		
Found vehicles	9			28		
Wireless message	40					
Written message	8					
Other	15			11		
TOTAL	94	17.9	1.91	80	13.7	1.63
TOTAL	524	100.0	10.62	586	100.0	11.96

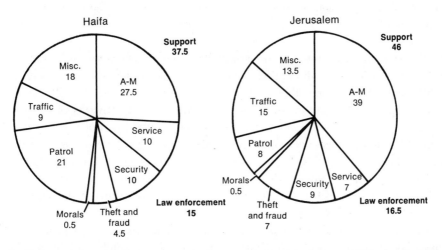

Fig. 5. Police work in Israel: percent distribution and incidence per 1000 population per month.

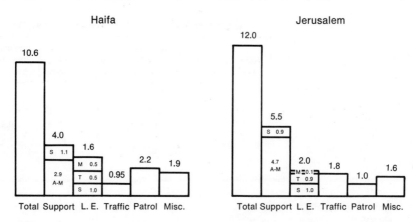

Fig. 6. Police work in Israel: incidence per 1000 population per month.

messages, both radio and written. This seems to be a tradition in Haifa and is not found in Jerusalem or in the other countries studied. In general police work in Israel is composed of elements similar to those found elsewhere, with support activities being the largest element. The specific types of activities found in each category are discussed on the following pages.

Law enforcement (social control). Law enforcement or social control activities in Israel have an additional component to those found in other countries. Because of the smallness of the country and the campaign being waged against it by its neighbors, there is an involvement in security issues in Israel not found elsewhere. These are divided into two types of activities: those dealing with people and those dealing with articles. In both cases there often are more reports of suspect persons or articles than in fact exist. However, in a society where the danger is very real, with attempts often made against civilian targets either with bombs, booby traps, or other dangerous articles, and where infiltration of hostile persons is not unknown, the public is constantly on the lookout for such things and often reports them to the police. The theory is that it is better to be wrong than sorry. Security-related incidents accounted for more than half of all law enforcement incidents, with a monthly rate of slightly more than one per thousand population in each city.

The aspect of law enforcement dealing with criminal activities of the general population has a very low incidence in Israel and is a small part of police work. The range of incidents is also very small, all incidents during the period studied related to theft, thieves, or fraud. In Haifa 4.4% of all incidents were of this nature, a rate of 0.47, of which three fourths (18 of 23) were reports of thefts. In Jerusalem 7.3% of all incidents were of this nature, with a rate almost twice that of Haifa, 0.88 per thousand. Almost all were involved with thieves or reports of theft.

Another element in law enforcement work in Israel is involved in morals incidents. These are practically nonexistent, both proportionately and by incidence. There was one gambling incident and two indecent acts or exposures in Haifa and two reported rapes, one gambling incident, and one indecent act in Jerusalem.

Social control activities of the law enforcement type numbered 77 during the week in Haifa, 14.7% of the total with an incidence of 1.6 per thousand population. In Jerusalem it was slightly higher: 98 incidents, 16.7% of the total, with a rate of 2 per thousand.

Support (social integration). In both Haifa and Jerusalem during the week studied the largest proportion of incidents involved support or social integration activities. Most were related to arbitration-mediation, and the remainder covered a large range of helping situations of people in need. In Haifa there were 196 incidents, 37.4% of the total, for a rate of 4 per thousand population. In Jerusalem there were 270 incidents, 46% of the total, an incidence of 5.5 per thousand.

Arbitration-mediation accounted for three fourths of the support activities in Haifa and five sixths of these activities in Jerusalem. In Haifa there was an incidence of 2.9 per thousand for arbitration-mediation incidents; in Jerusalem the incidence was 4.7 per thousand. Arbitration-mediation incidents occurred in public institutions, places of business, streets, transportation terminals, and residential areas and involved strangers, neighbors, family members, customers, and business persons; only one incident in Haifa and three in Jerusalem involved animals. In Jerusalem a large number of the complaints almost one fifth of the total, were withdrawn or unfounded on investigation. In a few of the conflicts criminal files were opened but charges were usually dropped. The calls to police for assistance in these types of incidents indicate a tendency toward hyperbole. Many of the complaints were for criminal trespass, attempted murder, criminal assault, and such. When investigated they almost always were noted as being disputes or arguments and were settled. There are very few incidents of actual violence, and most of the violence is verbal in these situations. One might credit the tension of a society under constant attack and the large number of immigrants from many different cultures and cultural levels for the high incidence of arbitration-mediation incidents. The hyperbole may be part of the cultural equipment for dealing with stress and survival under adverse conditions. The police certainly treat it with patience and understanding.

Service activities, although not as numerous as arbitration activities, also cover a wide range of tasks. Although in a number of incidents the assistance requested was not specified, most incidents did specify assistance required. Service activities were involved in 10% of the total in Haifa and over 7% in Jerusalem. Incidence was 1 per thousand in Haifa and 0.9 per thousand in Jerusalem. Activities included services to people in need—lost children, older adults, disturbed persons, persons lying in the street, injured persons, mental patients, suicide attempts, drunks, and ill persons —and notification of deaths. There was a generally even scattering of these incidents, with only a few per week. In Jerusalem, however, police assisted 11 lost children and nine mental patients during the course of the week. Service activities are thus an important, albeit not overwhelming, part of police tasks, covering a wide range of problems, almost all of people in need.

Interstitial activities. Interstitial activities include many different tasks in Israel,

as elsewhere, such as traffic and vehicular responsibilities. Israel has a high vehicular accident rate. This is particularly true of Jerusalem, which had an incidence
of accidents twice that of Haifa during the week of the study. The patrol activities
of the police are also similar to those in other countries and include answering
alarms, checking on windows or doors reported open or lights on in closed businesses
or public institutions, demonstrations, stopping of pamphlets being distributed
without approval, executing court orders, and arresting or detaining people. In
Jerusalem the police were involved in religious demonstrations during the period
under study. The remainder of police tasks were categorized as miscellaneous and
were involved with fires, lost and found articles and vehicles, and a number of single
incidents. In Haifa, as noted, the police were active in delivering both radio and
written messages to families. There is no police involvement in licenses and other
administrative matters as found in some countries. The interstitial activities, however, are a significant part of police work and involve police in daily contact with
numerous citizens.

   Police and social integration. In a study of socioecologic factors correlated with
police activities,[5] a direct relationship was suggested between police activities, both
support and law enforcement, and factors relating to social integration. In this study
it was found that those items associated with single-parent families headed by women
were most consistently related to the support function of police. There is also a
direct relationship between law enforcement and support functions of the police.
Thus it is found that in that city in which there are indications of lower social integration the police are most active in support and law enforcement activities.[5]

Problems

   The Israeli police face two totally unrelated problems. One is the difficulty of
providing security to the general population against terrorist attacks. The other is
the difficulty in recruiting sufficient personnel. A third area that may at times prove
problematic is the sense of family that pervades the Jewish population. This translates into a familiarity with police that is unknown to other countries.

   The security problem is all-pervasive in Israel. Unfortunately, police play a major
role in security precautions and disposal of suspect objects. Because prevention of
terrorist activities is very difficult, it produces a strain between the general population and the police. In some ways it binds the police and people together in that
both are involved in a life-and-death struggle to protect each other. The provision
of protection is not solely a police task but is organized by the police, and when it
fails police feel a sense of failure and guilt. There is often a chance for heroics in in-
tercepting a terrorist act, and this is without doubt the most dangerous and difficult
aspect of police work in the country.

   As in other countries with a wide range of job possibilities, police work is not one
of the preferred careers. Police work does not have a very high status, but neither
does it have a low status. Because it is not a traditional Jewish field, there is little

to induce young people to enter the police forces. An informant in the service suggested that if police work were to stress the social service aspects it would be easier to recruit new members to the force. Whatever the solution, there is some difficulty in keeping the Israeli police service up to strength.

The third problem is ironic. There is a sense of familiarity and thereby slight lack of respect for authority in Israel that is difficult to describe. There is a strong sense that the Jewish Israelis are almost members of the same family. They are very contentious but very protective of each other. It is not uncommon to see civilians arguing with police and army personnel about traffic and other infractions. The authorities, on the other hand, behave in a somewhat indulgent, protective parent manner toward the public. It is not uncommon for a driver to argue with great emotion when being given a ticket for a driving offense and the police officer to respond either with humor or by not giving the citation. Thus the strong sense of relationship also breeds a somewhat disrespectful attitude toward authority and its representatives. Fortunately there is a very low rate of actual lawbreaking to contend with, and that not of a serious nature (unless one wants to assert that the high traffic accident rate and attendant injuries are indeed serious). This issue may not be an actual problem, but it does have a potential for problematic results.

SUMMARY

The Israeli police force is a direct descendant of the Palestinian public security force organized by the British in the 1920s during their mandate over Palestine. The force was initially developed in response to conflict between Arabs and Jews and Arab resistance to Jewish settlement and development. As a solution to the conflict a decision was made to partition the country in 1948 under United Nations aegis. The resulting Jewish state is Israel. Arab neighbors have not until very recently, after four wars, been willing to accept the legitimacy of the Jewish state. In May 1948, on declaration of independence for the Jewish state of Israel, the Jewish components of the Palestinian force and the organizational structure were made the Israeli police force.

The force was and continues to be organized on a national basis, responsible to the national government. There are three districts, north, south, and central; subdistricts, and separate units for the main port and airport. Subdistricts, when appropriate, cover reasonable geographic areas, with urban areas being separate subdistricts, although political boundaries are not necessarily congruent with subdistrict boundaries. Police stations are spread throughout the country.

Women are part of the police force. However, they are assigned primarily to traffic control and situations dealing with juveniles and women. They are in essence protected partners in the force.

The Israeli police are seen as one of a group of cooperating social institutions. Their primary responsibility is preventive law enforcement and patrol. They also have a very important security role. Police are to be helpful to the population as well.

The actual function of police in Israel is similar to that found elsewhere. In a selected month police are involved in more than 10 incidents per thousand population. Between a third and half of police activities are support activities, primarily arbitration-mediation of a wide range of conflicts and disputes. Various services to people in need make up between 15% and 30% of support activities. Law enforcement activities account for about 15% of total police work, with over half of these related to security or suspect situations. Morals-related activities account for less than 0.1% of all police work. Incidents involving physical violence are practically nonexistent, other than in security situations. The rest of police work is made up of patrol, traffic, and some miscellaneous activities such as lost and found articles and delivery of messages. Both law enforcement and support activities are directly related to the level of social need within the community. Police in Israel function primarily as a social integration agency and also as a social control agency.

The problems of the police in Israel are not related to each other. One is the difficulty in recruitment and understaffing. Another is the difficulty of protecting the public against terrorism. For this task the police need and have the total cooperation of the public. There is also a third area that might prove problematic, the somewhat familiar relationship of public and police. This makes for a lack of the community-police relations problems found elsewhere. It also makes enforcement of civil regulations such as traffic and "minor" rules somewhat ineffective.

In general the police in Israel are involved in the building of a country, seen by its major group as a refuge from a hostile world and an expression of their national aspirations. They are in this way "ours" more than any other police force studied. The people, although possibly annoyed when dealing with the bureaucracy and regulations, have a feeling of "owning" their institutions, which reflects both the good and bad elements in the national life.

References

1. Duff, V.: Bailing with a teaspoon, London, 1953, Long Publishers.
2. Hovav, M., and Amir, M.: Israel police: history and analysis. In Police studies, 2:2 (5-31), New York, 1979, John Jay Press.
3. Israeli Police: Annual reports, Jerusalem, 1969 and 1970, Israel Police Publications Section.
4. Nyrop, R. F., editor: Israel: a country study, ed. 2, Washington, D.C., 1979, U.S. Government Printing Office.
5. Shane, P. G.: The social function of a civil agency, unpublished thesis, Baltimore, 1975, The Johns Hopkins University.

Chapter 8

The Netherlands

The Kingdom of the Netherlands (Holland) is in the northeastern corner of the European continent. It is bounded by Germany on the east, Belgium on the south, and the North Sea on the west and north. The country has an area of 36,160 sq km (14,125 sq mi) and a population of about 14 million. The language of the country is Dutch (Nederlandse or Duits), a Germanic language. In the southeastern part of the country the population is predominantly Roman Catholic; in the western and northern parts of the country the population is predominantly Protestant of Calvinist or Lutheran leanings. In the past religion had a very important role in the life of the country, but since World War II the religious divisions have become less important. Otherwise the country has had a long history of religious tolerance for non-Catholics and played host to many dissenters and oppressed religious groups from other parts of Europe and England. Much of the land has been reclaimed from salt marshes and low-lying coastal areas and is below sea level.

HISTORY

The Netherlands came under the influence of the Roman empire under Julius Caesar. It then became part of Charlemagne's empire, which dissolved in 814. Since then it has experienced Germanic, Spanish, French, English, and Scandinavian influences. In the late fifteenth century it came under Hapsburg domination and in the early 1500s, through various successions, became part of the Spanish Hapsburg dominion. In the middle of the sixteenth century resistance to Spanish and Catholic domination developed into rebellion. A confederation of states in the nothern and eastern areas of modern Holland was formed in 1579 in the Union of Utrecht, instituting a Republic that lasted until 1795.

During this period there was a constant struggle between the power of the states and the central authority as well as with other European powers. For a short period in the eighteenth century the Netherlands had a "golden age," during which it developed a large empire and strong naval and mercantile interests. By 1795 and the Napoleonic conquest, the fortunes of the country had fallen greatly. At the defeat of Napoleon and the institution of the Kingdom of Orange the issue of form of government was settled in favor of central authority. The Kingdom of Orange included the Belgian Netherlands (until then under Hapsburg rule) and Luxembourg until the 1838 Treaty of Separation resulting from Belgian resistance to Dutch rule.

119

There have been some further changes in the borders of the country since then, but the boundaries of modern Holland essentially date from that treaty. The Netherlands was neutral in World War I, which led to some conflict with Belgium after the war. In the Second World War the country was overrun by the Germans and suffered from great destruction in the resistance to the German occupation and during the liberation. Since 1946 the country has experienced general tranquility, increased prosperity, and dissolution of the empire. It has absorbed refugees of various racial backgrounds from various parts of the dissolved empire, primarily from Indonesia and the West Indies, and has attained one of the highest standards of living in the world.

Recently the Netherlands divested itself of the remains of its colonial empire, or is in the process of doing so, and most former colonies are either independent or autonomous within the kingdom. Only two areas are still within the kingdom but outside of the Netherlands proper: Surinam and the Netherlands Antilles in the Caribbean.

ECONOMY

The economy of the Netherlands is quite varied. There is a strong mercantile tradition, although the country is highly industrialized. Agriculture, primarily a small landholding industry, is important and diversified. About 80% of the arable land is in holdings of less than 20 hectares (80 acres), while almost one third of that is in holdings of less than 2.5 hectares (10 acres). Fishing is also a major industry. About 10% of the population is engaged in agriculture and fishing. Because the Netherlands is the outlet to the sea for the Rhine, Meuse (Maas), and Schelde rivers, there is a large shipping industry, with Rotterdam the major port. Manufacturing and extraction of raw materials are the sources of many jobs and are also quite diversified. There are 12 universities spread throughout the country and a well-developed service structure including health, social welfare, and education. The Netherlands is a member of two major economic blocks, the Benelux group including Belgium, the Netherlands, and Luxembourg and the Common Market of Western Europe.

CULTURE

The major difference between cultures in the Netherlands is religious background. Approximately one third of the population, in the southeast, is predominantly of Catholic background, and the remaining two-thirds, in the west and north, are predominantly of Protestant (Calvinist and Lutheran) background. For much of the country the River Rhine divides the two. The Protestant part of the country rebelled successfully against the Spanish in the sixteenth century, whereas the Catholic part of the country was under Spanish rule until the French occupation. During these intervening years the religious and cultural differences became deeply engrained. There were also economic differences until recent years, with the north and east being much more highly developed and affluent. Other cultural differences are not related to religion. There have been periodic separatist movements in the north (Friesland), and the language of the area is somewhat different from the Dutch spoken in the west. The delta area of the southwest also has strong cultural traditions that are somewhat different from those elsewhere. Thus within this rather small country there is a great deal of cultural diversity.

POLITICS

The Netherlands is a hereditary constitutional monarchy. There is also a strong democratic tradition. The constitution was originally promulgated in 1814 on the defeat of Napoleon but has since been revised. Under the constitution the monarch is the executive of the nation, with a cabinet of ministers. The legislative function is jointly exercised by the Crown and the parliament (states-general), which has two chambers. One chamber has 78 members elected for terms of 6 years by the provincial legislatures. The other chamber has 150 members elected for 4-year terms under direct popular franchise by proportional representation. All citizens over 18 years of age have the right to vote.

There is a council of ministers, the president of which is similar to a prime minister. The members of the council are chosen by the political party or coalition of parties that has the majority in the parliament. The council of ministers exercises executive authority for the Crown. There is also a state council chaired and appointed by the Crown, which must be consulted on some executive and all legislative matters.

Each municipality has a popularly elected mayor (burgomeister) and town council. There are also provincial legislatures elected by popular suffrage and proportional representation. The Crown appoints a commissioner of each province, representing the executive authority within the province.

POLICE

Police work was studied in the cities of Groningen in the north and Nijmegen in the southeast. They are middle-sized cities and centers for the surrounding country. Both are university centers. Nijmegen, in the area of rolling, hilly land that constitutes the southeastern part of the country, has a population of 150,000 (1970 census). It is a river port on the main branch of the Rhine and was a major crossing point for allied troops in the Second World War. One of the bridges over the river was left intact during the German retreat and became famous as a military subject. The city is very close to the German border and has traditionally had close relations with the German side of the coridor as well as its Dutch hinterland. The population in this part of the country is predominantly Roman Catholic. One of the cultural traditions that affect police work is the pre-Lenten carnival celebrated in the Catholic part of the country, during which the population is released from the day-to-day social inhibitions of the rest of the year. The police claim that their tasks are different during this time of year.

Groningen, in Friesland in the north, has a population of 165,000 (1971). Although an inland city, it is only a short distance from the north coast of the country. The area was a center of Protestant development, and the population is predominantly Protestant. In 1971, however, 48.5% of the population registered as having no religion. It is in a section of the country that was reclaimed from the sea centuries ago. Geographically the area is flat and combed with drainage canals. Much of the area is marshy, with many polders (land reclaimed from the sea). The University of Groningen is a major industry of the town and a major university of the Netherlands. The university has introduced an element of diversity into the city. In the 1971 census, 10% of the population was recorded as being full-time university students, many from other parts of the country and from outside the country. Although the city is industrialized, there is much agriculture in the surrounding countryside.

History

The specific character of the police in the Netherlands has been influenced by diverse historic elements. There are native Dutch elements, French accretions, English and Spanish influences, and the influences of several wars and major social changes. In aggregate they produced the police system of the modern Netherlands.

The concept of a paid police force in the Netherlands dates from the end of the eighteenth century. Prior to 1795 policing was performed by officials with different titles but similar duties in rural and urban areas. In the urban areas was found the sheriff (schout) and in the rural areas (platteland) was found the bailiff (baljuw). These were strictly local officials carrying out the executive, judicial, and law enforcement functions. The system is similar to that which existed in Britain during the same time. These officials were loosely responsible to the national authorities but maintained a great deal of autonomy. The beginnings of the development of police forces took place when the French invaded the Netherlands in 1795.

In that year the French under Napoleon Bonaparte occupied the Netherlands and organized a police force. The force was organized similarly to that in France. It was under central government direction and control. Under the central organization there were provincial directors of police. Preventive and repressive aspects of law enforcement were theoretically separated. Prior to the French occupation the concept of municipal and local police was discussed by various elements in society. It was a discussion similar to that which was occurring in Britain. In 1789 the Bergasse report to the Constituent Assembly suggested that the British idea be adopted. It proposed a system of police forces organized by municipalities.[6,p.7] The French occupation put the discussion to rest, and work was begun to fashion a national police force.

The original organization of police was apparently unsatisfactory. In 1801 the police were reorganized under the regulations of the Departement Holland. The office of the sheriff was recognized and reestablished. Police forces were put under the direction of the schout for local affairs, and he was deprived of his position as head of the court. Repressive and preventive, administrative, judicial, and executive powers were again united. This still did not seem to work, and in 1807 the executive function was given to the mayors and town councils and security (veiligsheid) police were instituted. This system lasted for a few more years, even though the Netherlands was annexed to the French empire in 1810.

Things did not remain stable for long. In 1813 Dutch sovereignty was reestablished, but under a monarch. The police were not immediately affected by this change, and police regulations and organization remained the same for a short while. Security was a primary concern at the time because of the Napoleonic war and its Jacobin (Republican) supporters within the country.[6,p.27] The organization of the police was still unsatisfactory. Regularly reorganization studies were conducted. The story becomes rather confusing as the struggle between national control and local autonomy continues. In 1818 control of the police was removed from provincial commissioners general. The police were placed under local control, but supervision was retained by the public minister or attorney general (openbare minister) for the courts and police through the provincial general prosecutors (procureurs general). This quickly changed, and in 1819 the police were put under the supervision of the criminal prosecutors (procureurs crimineel). The struggle continued, and in 1822 the Ministry of Justice published regulations governing police forces in large cities. These regulations did not clarify matters, because the city councils still were not given power over the police. There was an attempt to differentiate between local (plaatslijke) and national (regterlijke) police. In addition the Royal Militia (Koninklijke Marechausee) was formed, which became the foundation of the national police. Changes continued to take place in the assignment of responsibility for policing on both national and local levels.

During these reorganizations the roles of the Ministries of Justice and Interior (Binnenlandse Zaken) were never clarified, which remained a problem into the modern era. In 1836 the powers of local officials, mayors, and councils were further enhanced but not finalized. In 1842 policing powers were given to the Ministry of Justice and removed from the Ministry of the Interior by royal decree. Still the issue was not resolved. Further reorganization took place, and in December 1851 the national police (rijkspolitie) was instituted, with wide powers and jurisdiction. But in June of the same year the municipal police (gemeentepolitie) had been decreed in the municipal law. Under this act responsibility for public order, welfare, and health was delegated to the municipalities under supervision of the Ministry of Interior. In the years that followed there were additional reports and minor adjustments. None of these was sufficient to resolve the conflicts and ambiguities inherent in the system. The latest change prior to the Second World War was made in 1935. Regulations and organizational models were updated, but issues were not resolved.

The Second World War had a major effect on police, as it did on the whole of Dutch life. In some ways there were similarities to the French occupation, when the police were seen as collaborators and servants of the occupation. Although many Dutch police played important roles in the underground anti-German movement, the police in general appeared to the population at large as creatures of the Germans, doing their bidding. Dutch police publicly enforced the hated German laws. They arrested Jews and resistance elements, they searched houses and stopped people for violations of the pass and curfew laws,[3] while the Dutch people were in massive active and passive resistance to the occupation.

The experience of the Second World War led to a major reappraisal of police organization after reestablishment of independence. In 1945 a major commission was created to study the police organization within the country and make recommendations for reorganization and rebuilding of the police. The report of the commission was given in 1948. In the meantime the police law of 1945 was promulgated. This, it was hoped, would redevelop the police on a new basis.[3,p.119] The Royal Militia was relieved of all police duties, thus demilitarizing the concept of police. Unfortunately the police continued to wear the old military-style uniforms. As a result of the commission's report, in 1948 new regulations were made delineating the roles of the national and municipal police. Their supervision was placed, respectively, under the Ministries of Justice and Interior.[1,5] As can be seen, the 150-year-old confusion between the ministries was not resolved, but police work was given a more civilian, separate role.

In 1957 the last of the reorganizations took place. It was designed to resolve the conflicts and disputes between the various authorities and to clarify police organization within the country. The basic principle of the reorganization was that there should be as much local control of the police as possible.

Under this reorganization every municipality should have a police force responsible to the local authorities. In some cases municipalities are too small to do this effectively, and a force of the national police is assigned to cover policing activities for that municipality. All police forces are under national regulations, so there is uniformity with regard to rank, salary, uniforms, qualifications, training, examinations, and other such details. Costs for police are also paid for by the central government, directly in the cases where there are national police and through subsidies to the municipalities for the municipal police. The strength of the forces is also set by government regulation through the Ministry of Interior.

Under these regulations the police have three main chains of command for each of the three assigned functions. Law enforcement is under the Ministry of Justice through the attorney general and regional attorneys general for all police forces. Administration is in the hands of the local authorities, who are responsible to the Ministries of Justice and Interior, the latter setting the permissible size of each municipal police force. The national police are administered by the Ministry of Justice and the municipal mayor. Peace and order are the responsibility of the local authorities, except under certain conditions when they are under the Ministry of Interior. Internal organization of municipal police forces is determined by the local chief of police, who is nominated by the Crown under approval of the Ministries of Justice and Interior.[2,pp.46-47] The regulations under which the choices are made as to which municipalities have municipal police and which have national police are discussed later. It is obvious from the above that there still remains much confusion as to lines of authority and responsibility. The problems of local autonomy and national suzerainty have not yet been resolved.

New legislation for police organization has been suggested and is to be drawn up. The suggestion was made after serious disturbance took place in 1967 in Amsterdam. Until this legislation is passed no new police forces are to be organized. Reformation of police law is thought to be seriously necessary. Public hearings have been held, and in 1972 a commission was formed to study the matter. In October 1975 the commission presented its report. Through 1976 no action had been taken, although it was agreed that lines of authority and police organization were still confused and conflictual. The fruition of this latest attempt should take some time.

The police currently are operating throughout the country under the legislation and regulations promulgated in 1957.

Organization and ranking

National police. The national police force is a single force with subdivisions throughout the country. It is under the direct management of an inspector general attached to the Ministry of Justice. Assisting the inspector general are five regional inspectors. The ranking system of the state police is very similar to that of the military, as follows:

Commissioned officers:	Inspector General (Inspecteur Generaal)
	Colonel (Kolonel)
	Lieutenant Colonel (Luitenant Kolonel)
	Major (Majoor)
	Captain (Kapitein)
	Lieutenant (Luitenant)
Noncommissioned officers:	Adjutant (Adjudant)
	Top Sergeant (Opperwachmeester)
	First Sergeant (Wachtmeester 1e Klas)
	Sergeant (Wachtmeester)

The last two correspond to trooper ranks in the state police in the United States.

The state police force has a strength of about 8000. They serve in 736 municipalities that have no local forces, mainly rural, having a combined population of about 5 million persons.[4,p.2] For purposes of detachment there are 23 police districts divided into 327 groups that cover several sections or posts. Posts may be staffed by any number of persons, from one to a small force.

Special branches of the national police that serve special transportation sections are the River Police, organized into four districts, 18 groups and posts; the aviation Branch; and the Highway Police. In the national police each municipality served has a group commander with responsibilities similar to those of the municipal chief of police. Here again the unclear division of responsibility for police work becomes evident. The group commanders are responsible to the municipal mayor for the maintenance of public peace and order; however, they are responsible to the attorney general in the Ministry of Justice as deputy attorneys. The municipal councils have no influence on the policy of the national police.

Municipal police. The Police Act of 1957 gives responsibility to the mayor for the maintenance of public peace and order in each municipality, without sharply defining the powers. Under the same act every city of 25,000 or more is to have a police force directly responsible to the local authorities. Some cities with populations of less than 25,000 also have municipal police forces. One such is Harlingen, a city of about 12,000 population. Harlingen is an old seaport with a historic right to maintain a police force. The Harlingen force has 12 members. However, Harlingen is an exception.

Dutch waterways police helping injured man.

The size of the municipal forces varies greatly. The largest, with 2300 police, is in Amsterdam, a city of about 900,000 population. In 1972 there were 122 municipal police forces with a total strength of 16,000 covering 130 municipalities and approximately 8 million population. Of the 122 municipal forces, 80 have fewer than 60 members. Very few approach the size of the Amsterdam police force.

The lines of authority for the municipal police are several. Each force has a chief (hoofdcommisaris). Theoretically the mayor alone is responsible for the function of the local police. The chief is directly responsible to the mayor for the administrative and peace-and-order aspects of the job. Responsibility for the law enforcement aspects is to the Ministry of Justice. The chief has a great deal of autonomy: "The internal organization of the police force, and the amount and standard of its equipment, is determined by the Police Chief."[2,p.47] Although the central government bears the costs of the municipal police, there are no inspection powers or powers regarding fulfillment of the police task. The local council approves the police budget but has no direct influence on the function of the police. It thus appears that by function and operation the municipal forces are quite independent.

Cooperative relationships exist between both municipal and national police in neighboring jurisdictions and across the country. Officials are often at least acquaintances from training programs and meetings. Chiefs of police know each other and expedite cooperative relationships between their forces. Coordination is found in law enforcement and maintenance of peace and order. It is most evident in traffic

Dutch police talking to mother and children in amusement center.

tasks. Traffic regions have been developed in the busiest sections of the country. In these regions municipal and national police cooperate closely under a single command to supervise traffic throughroutes. Cooperation is natural in cases where problems are too large for the local police to handle. In these situations the nearest police force, whether municipal or national, may be asked for assistance. In special cases there is also the possibility of assistance from the Royal Militia. Assistance is normal in investigations of crime when needed. Centralized services available to all Dutch forces, such as Interpol, are situated in The Hague, the capital.[2,p.49] Thus, even though there are separate forces in each municipality, there are means for providing coverage to the whole country on a unified basis.

The relationship between the police and the population has changed greatly since the Second World War. The scars of that experience seem to have healed. Police generally are respected by and give respect to the public. In general neither the government of the country nor the police are seen as repressive. They are not generally viewed as the enemy, but whether they are yet thought of as friends is not clear. They have attained a generally positive relationship with the public. Part of this might come from the development of auxiliary or volunteer police.

The internal organization of the municipal forces is the same throughout the country and is set by the central authorities. Each force has the following ranks:

Commissioned officers:	Chief of Police (Hoofdcommissaris)
	Deputy Chief (Commissaris)
	Head Inspector (Hoofdinspecteur)
	Inspector (Inspecteur)
Noncommissioned officers:	Adjutant
	Brigadier
	Head Patrol Person (Hoofdagent)
	Patrol Person (Agent)

As can be seen, the ranking system of municipal forces is not based on the military model. Adjutant and brigadier are the only titles that remind one of the military. They correspond to sergeants in the United States.

Auxiliary police. In addition to national and municipal police, there are auxiliary police, volunteers who have received training, wear police uniforms, and carry arms as the regular police do. They are mobilized when the regular police "have to be enlisted for other duties in exceptional circumstances, e.g., times of war or emergency." Auxiliaries work with both municipal and national police. They are a link to the general public for many police forces.

Duties

The duties of the police in the Netherlands are stated in the Police Act as keeping the peace and giving assistance to people who need help. Under these two main responsibilities three further charges are given emphasis: sustaining law and order, investigation of crime and its prevention, and traffic control. The maintenance of law and order is the specific responsibility of the mayor of each municipality, assisted by either the national or municipal police assigned to that jurisdiction. Each province has a commissioner representing the Crown to supervise the mayors. Police, in general, are given the power to investigate "all punishable offenses and actions within the area they are supposed to cover."[4,p.3] Their powers are extended to other jurisdictions only when they have been assigned specifically to provide assistance to the force or group operating in that area.

Police forces may have a number of specialized units. Within the municipal police there may be united or special departments for aliens, juveniles, vice, traffic, law enforcement, and administration. The national police, aside from the special water, air, and traffic branches, has special departments for administration, criminal investigation, and juveniles. Within the Police Directorate of the Ministry of Justice there are special experts on such things as drugs, fingerprinting, forgery, photography, transport of prostitutes or other traffic in human beings, thefts of vehicles, and international crime. There are also both physical and medical forensic laboratories. Within the Justice Department and serving both national and municipal police are a Police Communications Department, a Police Technical Department, and a Supplies Department.

Women

Women, although formally eligible for police work and guaranteed equal assignments and pay, are not completely accepted in police work. Many chiefs of police do not accept women into their forces. Those forces with women are generally found in the larger municipalities in the urban areas. When police forces do appoint women they are subject to the same standards and training as men. However, most women start in the uniformed branch in patrol car work. In 1972 women were admitted to training to become sergeants for executive work in the traffic and youth affairs segments of police work. This was the initial breakthrough for women in police work. It is the opinion of observers that the primary impetus for the acceptance of women into the larger forces is lack of enough male applicants. It is still felt that women have special talents for use in the youth and vice squads, and outside of traffic details they are generally found in these two areas of police work. Women also have begun working in the CID units and horse patrol units. However slowly, they are making inroads into uniformed police work in the Netherlands, primarily in larger cities in somewhat protected fields or special women's work.[4,p.3;7]

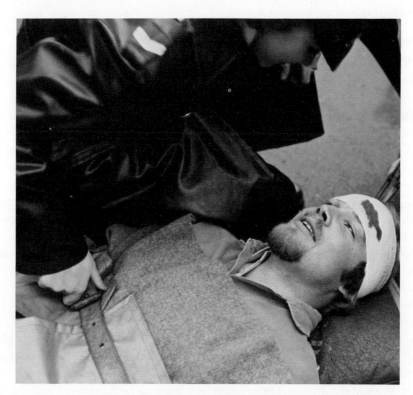

Dutch policewoman comforting injured man.

Training

The National Training Centre for Commissioned Police Officers at Hilversum has a 3-year course for training both national and municipal police officers. Continuing education courses of both a generalized and special nature are given by the Training Center for Commissioned Police officers at Heelsum. Training for noncommissioned officers is given in courses of 1 year at seven schools for municipal recruits and at the Corps Training School at Arnhem for the national police. General educational and specialized courses are also given at these facilities. Educational standards are high for officers and noncommissioned officers. Officers have university level education and noncommissioned officers have secondary schooling prior to entering the training institutes.

Police work

Data were collected by the research and planning departments of the police forces of two cities, Groningen and Nijmegen. Police activities are entered in logs and then abstracted to monthly report forms that generally are uniform throughout the country. The two directors of research and planning communicated with each other to ensure consistency of data between the cities. The reports on which the data are based were for the month of February 1972. Data are examined in two ways.

National Training Centre for Commissioned Police Officers at Hilversum.

First, incidents are grouped in categories. There is one minor deviation in that public order is separated into subcategories, arbitration-mediation and the other public order (Fig. 7). Second, the original data are grouped into six classifications to correspond with the data from other countries (Fig. 8). In the analysis of police work the distribution of police work tasks is examined and then some comparisons are made between the two cities (Table 8-1). Data for the uniformed police are examined in depth (Table 8-2), with a summary about the work of the Recherche police (Criminal Investigations Department) in Groningen.

The work of the Recherche police of Groningen shows a very different distribution of tasks. As expected, their work is heavily concentrated in the area of crime. During the month of February 1972 the Recherche police dealt with 485 incidents, of which 382, or 78.8%, were criminal matters. Of interest, however, another 50 incidents, or 10%, were service or mediation activities, the major ones involving missing and runaway persons (14 incidents) and annoyances and inconveniences (20

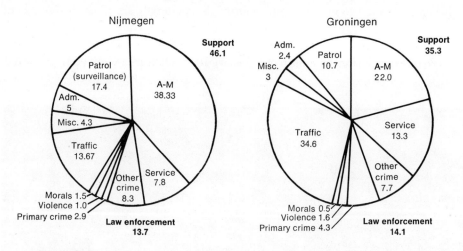

Fig. 7. Police work in the Netherlands: percent distribution, February 1972.

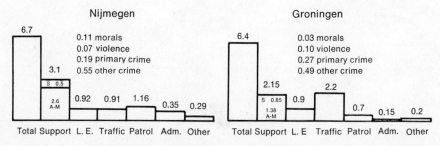

Fig. 8. Police work in the Netherlands: incidence per 1000 population per month, February 1972.

Table 8-1. Summary of uniformed police work distribution in the Netherlands by categories

	Groningen			Nijmegen		
	Num- ber	Per- cent	Incidence per 1000 population per month	Num- ber	Per- cent	Incidence per 1000 population per month
Support						
Arbitration-mediation (part of Public Order)	232	22.0	1.28	384	38.33	2.56
Service	140	13.3	0.85	78	7.78	0.52
TOTAL	372	35.3	2.25	462	46.11	3.08
Law enforcement						
Violence	17	1.61	0.10	10	1.0	0.7
Primary crime	45	4.27	0.27	29	2.89	0.19
Other criminal matters	81	7.69	0.49	83	8.28	0.55
Morals	5	0.48	0.03	16	1.60	0.11
TOTAL	148	14.06	0.90	138	13.77	0.92
Patrol (surveillance)						
Remainder of Public Order: morals	11	1.0	0.07	6	0.60	0.04
Remainder of Public Order: other	11	1.0	0.07	41	4.09	0.27
Public safety	59	5.5	0.36	50	4.99	0.33
Protection of property	32	3.0	0.20	77	7.68	0.51
TOTAL	113	10.7	0.68	174	17.37	1.15
Administration						
Regulations	15	1.45	0.09			
Public health	9	0.87	0.05	45	4.49	0.33
Economic matters	1	0.01	0.01	3	0.30	0.02
TOTAL	25	2.33	0.15	48	4.79	0.35
Miscellaneous	31	2.94	0.19	43	4.29	0.29
Traffic	364	34.57	2.21	137	13.67	0.91
TOTAL	1053	100.00	6.38	1002	100.00	6.68

Table 8-2. Distribution of police work in the Netherlands by activities*

| | Groningen (pop. 165,000) | | | | Nijmegen (pop. 150,000) | | |
| | Recherche | Uniformed | | | | | |
	Number	Number	Percent	Incidence per 1000 population	Number	Percent	Incidence per 1000 population
Support							
Arbitration-mediation (part of Public Order)							
Mediation and assistance		17	1.5	0.103	40	3.9	0.267
Domestic quarrels		39	3.6	0.236	34	3.3	0.227
Problems between neighbors		11	1.0	0.067	18	1.8	0.120
Disturbance in eating places	7				27	2.6	0.180
Disturbance in sports events					1		
Disturbance in the streets		12	1.1	0.073	11	1.10	0.073
Disturbance of quiet and night		15	1.4	0.091	1		
Disturbance of juveniles		91	8.5	0.552	96	9.4	0.640
Playing soccer in street		1			59	5.8	0.393
Noise		9	0.8	0.055	25	2.4	0.167
Annoyances and inconveniences		20	1.9	0.121	42	4.1	0.280
Trouble with animals		17	1.6	0.103	30	2.9	0.200
SUBTOTAL	7	232	22.0	1.406	384	38.3	2.56
Service							
Assistance		4	0.4		18	1.8	0.120
Strangers					1	0.1	0.007
SUBTOTAL		4	0.4	0.024	19	1.9	0.127
Social concerns							
Mentally ill	3	7	0.7	0.042	2		
Protection of children	1	1			1		
Accidentally injured persons (includes physically and mentally ill)	2	59	5.5	0.358	12	1.2	0.080
Drunks		17	1.5	0.103	18	1.8	0.120
Missing or runaway persons	14	4			16	1.6	0.107
Natural deaths	2	3					
Truants							
Other	1	45	4.2	0.273	10	1.0	0.067
SUBTOTAL	23	136	12.9	0.776	59	5.8	0.393
TOTAL	30	372	35.3	2.254	462	46.2	3.080
Law enforcement: morality							
Morality							
Public morality: sex							
Rape	2						
Assault	1	1			4		
Immorality with minors	3				2		
Exhibitionism	3	1			5		
Voyeurism	5	3			2		
Streetwalkers					3		
Other sex infractions	1						
SUBTOTAL	15	5	0.5	0.031	16	1.6	0.107

*Percents and incidence rates have been rounded off, so totals may not equal 100%.

† (V) violence; (P) primary crime; (O) other crime.

‡ Comprised over 60% of public safety.

Table 8-2. Distribution of police work in the Netherlands by activities—cont'd

	Groningen (pop. 165,000)				Nijmegen (pop. 150,000)		
	Recherche	Uniformed					
	Number	Number	Percent	Incidence per 1000 population	Number	Percent	Incidence per 1000 population
Law enforcement: morality—cont'd							
Criminal‡							
Murder (V)	3	1			0		
Suicide (V)	1	3			1		
Woundings (V)	23	13	1.2	0.079	9	0.9	0.060
Threats against life (O)		7	0.7	0.042	11	1.1	0.073
Theft (P)	151	15	1.4	0.091	28	2.8	0.187
Burglary (P)	89	22	2.1	0.133	1		
Trespassing (O)	1	1					
Robbery (P)	4	4					
Pickpocket (O)					1		
Auto theft (P)	15	4					
Joyriding (O)		1			3		
Bicycle theft (O)	7	3			3		
Invasion of privacy (O)	1	1					
Destruction of property (O)	30	57	5.3	0.345	51	5.1	0.340
Door-to-door sales rackets (O)	11	1					
Fencing of stolen goods (O)					2		
Other criminal matters (O)	46	10	0.9	0.061	12	1.2	0.080
SUBTOTAL	382	143	13.6	0.867	122	12.2	0.81
TOTAL	396	148	14.1	0.897	138	13.8	0.92
Administrative							
Public health							
Dumping and burning garbage		6			19	1.9	0.127
Sewage and water		3			2		
Parks and ponds					3		
Housing issues					2		
Annoyance regulations					1		
Dilapidated cars					18	1.8	0.120
SUBTOTAL		9	0.8	0.055	45	4.4	0.33
Registration of persons staying overnight		15	1.4	0.091			
Economic matters and work conditions							
Work regulations					1		
Industrial accidents	(1)	1					
Business closure and blue laws					2		
SUBTOTAL	(1)	16	1.5	0.097	3	0.3	
TOTAL		25	2.3	0.152	48	4.7	0.35
Patrol (surveillance)							
Public morality: other							
Cruelty to animals		3					
Hurt or dead animals		7	0.7	0.042	1		
Hurt or dead birds					1		
Drug regulations and use					4		
Drinking regulations		1					
SUBTOTAL		11	1.0	0.07	6	0.6	0.040

Continued.

Table 8-2. Distribution of police work in the Netherlands by activities—cont'd

| | Groningen (pop. 165,000) | | | | Nijmegen (pop. 150,000) | | |
| | Recherche | Uniformed | | | | | |
	Number	Number	Percent	Incidence per 1000 population	Number	Percent	Incidence per 1000 population
Patrol (surveillance)—cont'd							
Remainder of Public Order							
Infringements of ordinances		5	0.5	0.031	8	0.7	0.053
Illegal poster	1				8	0.7	0.053
Restoring order		1			9	0.9	0.060
Weapons laws					2		
Firearms laws					2		
Unlicensed solicitation		1			2		
Other	_	4	_	_	10	1.0	0.067
SUBTOTAL	1	11	1.0	0.067	41	4.0	0.113
Public safety							
Supervision on dangerous ice		8			7		
Drowning					1		
Floods		1					
Fires‡	(1)	36	3.4	0.218	31	3.0	0.207
Explosives and war materials	(1)				3		
Airguns		2			8	0.8	0.053
Other	_	12	1.1		_		
SUBTOTAL	(2)	59	5.5	0.358	50	4.9	0.333
Protection of property	(17)	32	3.0	0.194	77	7.5	0.513
TOTAL		113	10.7	0.68	174	17.4	1.16
Miscellaneous	(17)	31	2.9	0.188	43	4.2	0.287
Traffic		364	34.6	2.206	137	13.4	0.913
TOTAL		1053	100.0	6.38	1002	100.00	6.680

incidents). However, their work in social concerns was not limited to these areas. There also were incidents involving the mentally ill, child protection, accidentally injured persons, and others. The remainder of the Recherche police activities consisted of diverse surveillance (patrol) incidents.

Analysis of tasks

The police have a very wide range of involvement in the life of Dutch municipalities. In the two cities examined, there were 6.3 to 6.7 incidents of all kinds per thousand per month. In Groningen there were 1053 incidents during the month studied and in Nijmegen 1,002 incidents. The work is examined in essentially the same categories as in the other countries, except that there are some types of activities not included in police work elsewhere. These are essentially in the area of

Dutch police helping sick woman.

patrol and an additional subcategory, administrative, for the benefit of this analysis. This latter was not a large part of the police involvement during the month studied. Police reports in the Netherlands contain 10 separate categories of police work. These are public order (containing subcategories that have been put in patrol and arbitration-mediation categories for this analysis), public morality (containing subcategories assigned to law enforcement and patrol for this analysis), social concerns, public health, public safety, economic matters and work conditions, traffic, criminal matters, protection of property, and miscellaneous.

The most significant elements of police work in these two cities during the month in which it was studied were support activities, traffic activities, law enforcement, and patrol. In both cities the law enforcement activities made up about 13% of the total, and the patrol activities about the same. Support activities were accounted for from one third to nearly one half, and traffic more than one third in Groningen and less than one sixth in Nijmegen. It is clear that the largest part of the police job is involved in support and interstitial activities in both cities.

Police work was specifically divided between categories as follows. Criminal matters in Groningen numbered 143 incidents, 14% of total, an incidence of 0.87

per 1000 population; in Nijmegen there were 122 incidents, 12.2% of total, a 0.81 per 1000 incidence. Criminal morals totaled five incidents in Groningen, 0.5% of total, an incidence of 0.03 per 1000; in Nijmegen there were 16 incidents, 1.6% of total, 0.11 per 1000 incidence. Arbitration-mediation involved 232 incidents in Groningen, 22% of total, an incidence of 1.4 per 1000; in Nijmegen 384 incidents, 38.3% of total, 2.6 per 1000. Service or social concerns numbered 140 incidents in Groningen, 13.3% of total, and 0.9 per 1000; in Nijmegen 78 incidents, 7.8%, and 0.5 per 1000. Traffic constituted 364 incidents, 35% of the total in Groningen, but only 137 incidents, 13.7%, in Nijmegen. Patrol work constituted 11.0% in Gronigen and 17% in Nijmegen. This was composed of incidents in the categories of public order and morality, protection of property, and public safety. Administrative was about 2.5% of the total in Groningen and 5% in Nijmegen. It included public health and economic matters and work conditions. Miscellaneous was 3% in Gronin-gen and 4.3% in Nijmegen.

Law enforcement (social control). Law enforcement activities are divided into two categories: criminal matters (Recherche) and morality. In both Groningen and Nijmegen approximately 13% of the police incidents were criminal matters and 1% morals. There was no separation of serious crime from that of less serious crime in the reports. Matters included in the original Recherche are (approximately in order of magnitude, greatest first), destruction of property (about 40% of criminal inci-dents in both cities), theft, woundings, burglary, threats against life, and a scat-tering of incidents of murder, suicide, trespassing, robbery, auto theft, joyriding, bicycle theft, invasion of privacy, door-to-door rackets, fencing of stolen goods, and others. The incidence of criminal matters was about the same in both cities: 0.9 per 1000 population per month. Morality incidents were scattered among the fol-lowing: assault, immorality with minors, exhibitionism, voyeurism, and street walkers.

Crimes of violence, including murder, suicide, and woundings, made up between 1% and 1.7% of the total. They accounted for about 12% of all crimes in Groningen and 17% of all crimes in Nijmegen. Assault, not well defined but nonetheless prob-ably violent, was involved in 20% of all morals cases in Groningen and 25% of the same in Nijmegen. There were no rapes reported in either city during this period. There were an additional few incidents involving threats against life without any injury. The incidence of violence is low but still significant in both cities.

Part of the reason for the low incidence of criminal matters in the uniformed police files is that there is a specialized bureau (Recherche police) in the municipal police forces in both cities that deals with similar situations but many more of them. For example, in Groningen the Recherche bureau dealt with triple the number of morality incidents and two and one half times as many criminal incidents as the uniformed police during the month. The majority of these incidents were theft and burglary, including auto and bicycle theft. Woundings and destruction of property were next, followed by a scattering of the other categories. It can thus be seen that the role of the uniformed, or regular police, is minimized in dealing with incidents of criminal matters by the specialized unit's existence.

Support (social integration). Support activities are divided into two categories, similar to those in other countries, that is, arbitration-mediation and a range of service activities, most of which are reported under the classification of social concerns. There are striking differences between the two cities in occurrence of the many different types of incidents within these categories and in the occurrence of the subcategories as well. However, the types of incidents found in both cities are the same. In general, 20.5% of the incidents in Groningen were arbitration-mediation and 13.5% service or social concerns. In Nijmegen 38% were arbitration-mediation and 8% were service incidents. The types of incidents with which police were concerned in arbitration-mediation incidents are general mediations and assistance, domestic quarrels (over 3.5% in both cities), problems between neighbors, disturbances in various places and of juveniles playing soccer in the street, noise annoyance, general annoyances and inconveniences, and trouble with animals. Nijmegen had a much greater incidence of problems with soccer, noise, and general annoyances than did Groningen. The incidence of arbitration-mediation activities was 1.3 per 1000 in Groningen and 2.5 per 1000 in Nijmegen for the month.

The service or social concerns incidents of the two cities again were of the same type but differing in number. There were a relatively large number of incidents with accidentally injured persons (including physically and mentally ill), drunks, and in Nijmegen missing and runaway persons. The police involvement with the mentally ill and accidentally injured was much greater in Groningen (five times greater in number and four times greater in incidence). The Recherche police in Groningen also dealt with social concerns, primarily, however, with runaway or missing persons. Other types of incidents included mental illness, protection of children, natural death, and others not specified. The incidence of service activities was 0.9 per 1000 per month in Groningen and 0.52 per 1000 per month in Nijmegen.

The total of support incidents for the two cities was 352 in Groningen and 462 in Nijmegen. This is almost one half the monthly incidents in Nijmegen (46%) and one third the monthly incidents in Groningen (34%). The incidence was three per 1000 per month in Nijmegen and two per 1000 per month in Groningen. In Nijmegen this was the largest single aspect of police work. In Groningen it was a close second to traffic work.

Interstitial. The responsibilities of the police in interstitial activities is much broader than that found in the other countries studied, at least insofar as the police reports indicate. This area has been divided into several subcategories, one of which, administrative, is not found in the other countries. This reflects the involvement of the Dutch police in matters of public health and economic and work conditions, although these make up a very small proportion of the incidents in which the police are involved. Just a list of the categories in which the Dutch police have responsibilities gives an idea of the wide range of their involvement. There are matters they consider related to public safety and those that involve protection of property, aside from a whole range of incidents in the categories of public order and morality that are more likely to be related to general overseeing of the quality of life, both human and nonhuman. The kinds of things that Dutch police become involved in relating to patrol work, under their heading of public order, are infringements of ordinances, illegal posters, restoring order, demonstrations and strikes, unlicensed solicitations, and laws having to do with regulation of weapons and firearms. Under the rubric of public morality they are expected to deal with issues relating to hurt or abused animals and birds, regulation of drugs and their use, alcohol, gambling, and cinema. Public safety concerns include supervision of dangerous ice, drownings, explosions, fires, explosives and war material, and airguns. Under protection of property is found trespassing, alarms, unclaimed vehicles, lost and found, runaway cattle, and poaching. Miscellaneous matters include trailers and houseboats, suspect persons, escaped prisoners, and civil matters. The public health concerns with which police are involved that are administrative in nature are dumping and burning of garbage, sewage and flooding, parks, green zones and ponds, prohibited swimming, housing issues, air pollution, cattle regulations, meat inspection regulations, regulations about goods, annoyances, and dilapidated cars. The other administrative type of activities are related to economic matters and work conditions, including residency laws, clearance sales, measurement standards, work regulations, industrial accidents, blue laws, and others. It should be remembered that the actual involvement in these matters is not extensive in terms of actual incidents. There were no incidents relating to gambling or cinema regulations, nor demonstrations, strikes, hand-weapons, air pollution, cattle regulations, meat inspection regulations, regulation of goods, explosions, residency laws, clearance sales, measurements standards, trespassing, runaway cattle, trailers or houseboats, or poaching during the month in either city. Many of the other activities had from one to five incidents during the month. A few activities had more than five incidents. There were over 30 fires in each of the cities, and dangerous ice had to be supervised seven or eight times. There were 15 ownerless vehicles and found articles in Groningen and 42 in Nijmegen, and 18 dilapidated cars in Nijmegen. Nijmegen seems to have had a particular problem with the dumping and burning of garbage during the month, there having been 19 incidents to six in Groningen of that type. Groningen had 15 incidents of registration of overnight guests. Nijmegen had eight infringements of ordinances, eight illegal posters, and nine incidents of restoring order. Groningen had 10 incidents of abused or hurt animals, while Nijmegen had one during the month. Administrative activities included 48 incidents, 4.8% of total in Nijmegen, and 25 incidents, 2.4% of total in Groningen. Patrol activities numbered 174 incidents, or 17.4% of total in Nijmegen, and 113 incidents, 11% of total, in Groningen. Miscellaneous had 43 incidents, 4.3% of total in Nijmegen, and 31 incidents, 3% of total in Groningen. It can easily be seen that the interstitial areas of police work, although over 26% of the total in Nijmegen and about 16% in Groningen, is spread over a large assortment of tasks that in many ways are unique to the police in the Netherlands.

Comparison between cities

Criminal matters and public morality take up between 14% and 16% of police work, less than one incident per 1000 population during the month. Although the other categories vary the major law enforcement activities are about the same in both cities in terms of proportion of police work and incidence per 1000 population. A more detailed examination of the data shows some further interesting differences and similarities between the two cities' police forces. The data are examined by categories, starting with criminal matters and public morality. In both cities the largest single criminal matter the police deal with is destruction of property. In both cases it was 42% to 44% of the criminal matters and over 5% of the total incidents. Other similarities were the very low rates of most crimes dealth with by the uniformed police (footnote Recherche). In both cities the uniformed police deal with very few or no murders, suicides, assaults, trespassing, robbery, pickpockets, auto thefts, joyriding, bicycle thefts, invasion of privacy, sales rackets, and fencing of stolen goods. Other criminal matters dealt with by both the Recherche and the uniformed police in Groningen included woundings, theft, burglary, and destruction of property. The only difference between the two cities is that there was only one burglary incident in which the Nijmegen uniformed police were involved, whereas there were 22 in Groningen. Nijmegen police dealt with more sexual matters, such as immorality with minors, exhibitionism, voyeurs, and street walkers, while the Groningen police were minimally involved (five incidents, 5% of total). The total of morality matters was small in either case. Public order other than mediation-arbitration, small in both cities, was less than one third the amount in Groningen as in Nijmegen, approximately 1% as opposed to 3.5%. In problems of public safety the majority of incidents were involved with fires, 61% in Groningen and 66% in Nijmegen; another area of involvement was the supervision of dangerous ice. In the category of protection of property the major item in both cities was abandoned cars and found articles, 50% in Groningen and 55% in Nijmegen. This total category took up more than twice as much police work in Nijmegen (77 incidents) than in Groningen (32 incidents). In the miscellaneous category the major item in both cities was persons suspected of holdups, although in Groningen it was essentially the only item in this category (29 of 31 incidents) and in Nijmegen it was slightly more than half the incidents (23 of 43 incidents).

A major category of work in both cities was the combined support categories. There are two major classifications of incidents in the police reports that contain these types of incidents. The arbitration and mediation activities generally are in the public order category, whereas the service activities are primarily in the social concerns category, with a few under public order. There are some scattered service activities reported under other categories as well, but these generally do not include any large number of incidents. In the public order classification there is a mediation and assistance subclassification. There are, in addition, subclassifications of domestic quarrels, problems with neighbors, annoyances and inconveniences, noise annoyance, disturbances in eating places, at sports events, and in the street, disturbances of quiet and the night and by juveniles playing soccer in the street. In the service areas and social concerns are work with mentally ill persons, child protection, accidentally injured persons (including physically and mentally ill), drunks, missing and runaway persons, and other things. The other category was one third of the classification of Groningen and one sixth in Nijmegen. As was seen in the summary, this category of activities contains many more incidents in Groningen (139) than in Nijmegen (59). The reverse is true in arbitration-mediation, with 354 incidents in Nijmegen and 195 in Groningen. There are four activities included in public order that I believe belong in the service classification. These are registration of people staying overnight, strangers, trouble with animals, and other assistance.

There are some interesting differences and similarities between the two cities in the tasks, which might be related to culture or police and public responses to stimuli. There are about the same number of juvenile disturbances in both cities, about 9% of the incidents; slightly over 3.5% of the incidents are domestic quarrels in both cities; about 1.2% are street quarrels; and slightly under 2% are drunks. There are almost no child protective incidents in either city, no truants nor work with strangers, or disturbances in sports events. In Groningen there does not seem to be many incidents dealing with soccer in the streets or with missing and runaway persons. However, there seem to be more complaints and disturbances of quiet and the night, registration of overnighters, and accidentally inured people in Groningen. The sociological and socioecological causes of the similarities and differences are at this point unknown. It is known, however, that there are some significant cultural differences between the populations in the two cities, and yet there are obviously many similarities.

In the analysis of police work using the same categories of police work as used in the other countries, some differences in figures are found. These are the products of the slightly different categorization of tasks for the study than for the general usage. As mentioned above, I found that some items included in other categories by the Dutch police are defined as support activities in the other countries; at the same time there were law enforcement activities included in other categories also. To help in some comparison with the other countries, the same six categories were developed and items were classified regardless of the classification made by the Dutch police.

Raw data were categorized into six categories from the 131 subclassifications:
Law Enforcement
    Crime: all incidents of all breaking except those in morals cases
    Morals: sex, psychoactive drugs, and alcohol

Support

    Arbitration-mediation

    Service

Preventive patrol (surveillance)

Traffic

In the other countries the law enforcement activities are not separated into crime and morality subdivisions. Otherwise the same general classifications of police work are found in the other countries. Table 8-2 shows the distribution of police work in numbers of incidents, percentage of police work, and incidence per thousand population during February 1972.

It has already been seen that the uniformed police in both cities dealt with about the same number of incidents during the month. Several differences are seen immediately. One is the much higher involvement of the Groningen police in traffic incidents, more than twice as much as in Nijmegen. Surveillance is also twice as high in Nijmegen. Incidence of service activities is smaller than arbitration-mediation in both cities, but higher in Groningen by a good third. Criminal matters are about the same in both cities and in number of incidents and percentage of total police work. When the data are examined without including vehicular incidents, the proportion of support work is about the same in both cities, about 55% of non-traffic work, whereas the proportion of law enforcement activities is higher in Groningen (27%) than in Nijmegen (20%). Of course, the incidence remains the same in both analyses. A major relationship that can be deduced from these figures is that the rate of support activities does not vary with the rate of law enforcement activities.

In summary, the uniformed police in these two cities in the Netherlands are significantly involved in support, law enforcement, patrol, and traffic activities. Among the patrol activities are some that are peculiar to the Dutch police because of historical developments. There are some significant differences between the two forces, but it is not descernible whether these reflect police record keeping, differences in police priorities (the traffic differences), cultural differences, or a combination of these and other factors. In both cities the ratio of incidence of support to law enforcement activities is about two or three to one, whereas the percentages vary in somewhat the same relationship. In Nijmegen support activities are almost 50% of police work, whereas in Groningen support and traffic activities together make up slightly more than 70% of police work, being about equal in imprtance in terms of incidence and number of incidents. There are thus some interesting similarities and differences between police work in the two cities.

Problems

The major problem faced by the Dutch police is the still unresolved relationship between local and national responsibility for policing. This issue was discussed at some length earlier in the chapter. The organizational split between national and municipal police and the sharing of responsibilities between Ministries of Justice and Interior is seen as unsatisfactory and is subject to further revision. Whether, in fact, this untidy organization has any real effect on the function of the Dutch police is not clear.

There is still concern about the bifurcated police system within the ranks of professionals and the civil authorities. The two ministries, Interior and Justice, are to submit some proposals for rectifying the shortcomings in the structure of the police system in the near future. The sharing of control between the two ministries may be the most difficult thing to rectify. It is probable that there will be an attempt to merge national and municipal police forces into one force, thus solving the problem of the very small forces.

The Dutch also share a problem with police in a number of other countries, that is, the problem of maintaining full strength in police forces. The problems of recruitment and understaffing are found in the Netherlands in a number of forces. This may in part be the result of the large numbers of alternatives available to the population for employment and careers. Whatever the cause, it does not have a serious effect on the ability of the police to serve the public and may be leading them to improve efficiency and technology.

SUMMARY

The organization of the Dutch police is complex. Various authorities control different aspects of the police job. The history of the Dutch police, with multiple influences on the development of the forces, has led to this situation. There has been a constant tension between forces, leading to greater local autonomy and those leading to centralized control, between the Ministries of Justice and Interior for influence over police work. Part of this is a product of the broad mandate that police have in the Netherlands. These tensions have been addressed by the Dutch authorities almost continuously since the early nineteenth century. The tensions have not yet been resolved, and there is to be new police legislation resulting from the latest commission studying police work. Through it all the Dutch police have developed a respecting and respectful relationship with the public and a high level of professionalism.

Modern police forces in the Netherlands were first formed during the French occupation in 1795. Previously there had been local officials with many functions, including policing. The forces founded at that time were institutionalized when the country regained independence 20 years later under a monarchy. Since then there has been tension between the concepts of local autonomy, strengthened by British philosophy, and national control. Further, the national control has been divided between the Ministries of Interior and Justice. Currently there are locally autonomous forces in all municipalities with populations of 25,000 or more and in a few with smaller populations. There is a national force for the rest of the country, with local units responsible to the local authorities. The national authorities exert

POLICE REPORT CATEGORIES IN THE NETHERLANDS*

Public order

Infringements of ordinances (S)
Illegal posters (S)
Restoring order (S)
Demonstrations (S)
Strikes (S)
Laws against weapons (S)
Laws against firearms (S)
Undesirable handweapons (S)
Mediations and assistance (S & M)
Domestic arguments (A & M)
Neighbor problems (A & M)
Disturbances in bars and restaurants
  (A & M)
Discord at sports events (A & M)
Disturbances on the street (A & M)
People staying overnight (A & M)
Other assistance (HS)
Annoyances and inconveniences (A & M)
Disturbance of quiet and night (A & M)
Noise annoyance (A & M)
Juvenile disturbances (A & M)
Playing soccer in the street (A & M)
Trouble with animals (HS)
Strangers (HS)
Unlicensed solicitations (S)
Other (S)

Public morality

Rape (Z)
Assaults (Z)
Immorality with minors (Z)
Exhibitionism (Z)
Voyeurism (Z)
Street walkers (Z)
Homosexuality (Z)
Pornography (Z)
Other sex problems (Z)
Cruelty and torment to animals (HS)
Injured or dead animals (HS)
Laws against hurting birds (HS)
Opium regulations (HS)
Drinking regulations (S)
Gambling regulations (S)
Cinema regulations (S)

Social concerns

Mentally ill (HS)
Protection of children (HS)
Injured persons including physically and
  mentally disturbed (HS)
Drunks (HS)
Lost and runaway persons (HS)
Natural death (HS)
Truants (HS)
Other (HS)

Public health

Dumping and burning of garbage (HS)
Sewage and flooding (HS)
Parks, green zones, and ponds (HS)
Prohibited swimming (HS)
Housing issues (HS)
Air pollution (HS)
Cattle regulations (HS)
Meat inspection regulations (HS)
Goods regulations (HS)
Annoyance regulations (HS)
Dilapidated cars (HS)

Public safety

Supervision of dangerous ice (S)
Drownings (HS)
Floods (S)
Explosions (S)
Fires (S)
Explosives and war material (S)
Airguns (S)
Other (S)

Economic matters and work conditions

Residency laws (S)
Clearance sales (S)
Measurement standards (S)
Work regulations (S)
Industrial accidents (S)
Business closure or blue laws (S)
Other (S)

*A & M, arbitration and mediation; HS, helping service; S, patrol (surveillance); R, crime (recherche); Z, morals (Zedelijkheid).

Continued.

POLICE REPORT CATEGORIES IN THE NETHERLANDS—cont'd

Criminal matters

Murder (R)
Suicide (R)
Woundings (R)
Public assault (R)
Threats against life (R)
Theft (R)
Bank robbery (R)
Burglary (R)
Trespass (R)
Robbery (R)
Pickpocket (R)
Auto theft (R)
Joyriding (R)
Bicycle theft (R)
Invasion of privacy (R)
Destruction of property (R)
Door to door sales rackets (R)
Other criminal matters (R)

Protection of property

Prohibited entrance
Alarms
Unclaimed vehicles and lost and found
Runaway cattle
Poaching
Other

Traffic

Regulations, drunk driving
Regulation 28
Regulation 30
Regulation 36
Total collision
Other accident regulations
Other regulations
Street fixtures, signs, lights
Potholes
Salting and cindering roads
Traffic jams
Escorting dignitaries
Parking problems (driveways)
Rail travel
Water travel
Air travel
Air disasters
Throwing objects out of airplanes

Other

Trailers and houseboats
Suspects
Escaped prisoners
Suspicious persons
Civil matters

standardizing and minimal levels, powers, setting strength of forces, and other basic standards. There is cooperation between forces. There are also auxiliary police, trained uniformed volunteers who relieve regular police when necessary. Women are officers in some forces in larger municipalities but generally in restricted positions. Although there are separate forces in each municipality, there are means for providing coverage to the country on a unified basis.

The duties of the police are to keep the peace and to provide assistance to people in need of help. Three further charges are given emphasis: sustaining law and order, prevention and investigation of crime, and traffic control.

Police are trained for a minimum of 1 year in government-run training schools. There are also special schools for officers' training and continuing education for officers. Noncommissioned officers must have a secondary school education, and officers a university level education.

Police were involved in an average of 6.5 incidents per thousand population per month in both cities studied. Support activities constituted from one third to nearly one half of all incidents, being predominantly arbitration-mediation activities. Service activities constituted about 10% of the total and predominantly dealt with people in need of help. In the Netherlands these activities are called social concerns. Law enforcement took up about 17% of the total, of which morals situations were few. Incidents involving injury or death were somewhat more numerous but still low. The involvement of the uniformed, general police with law enforcement activities and violence is minimized by the existence of active criminal investigations units; thus it is not possible to discuss the level of violence or criminal activity in these cities from general police data.

A special factor in Dutch police work is the involvement of police in a variety of activities not found in the other police forces (see box, pp. 145 and 146). These deal with situations of public safety, public health, protection of property, economic matters, and a range of other miscellaneous tasks. Although there is a wide range of these activities, they do not account for a very high percentage of the work of the police.

The police of the Netherlands and the government of the country still are not satisfied with the national organization of police services, although it was reorganized in 1967. The split between national and municipal police, between the Ministries of Justice and Interior, is seen as problematic. At this writing there are to be proposals submitted for another reorganization. A simpler and more universal problem faced by the Dutch police is the difficulty in recruiting qualified persons and maintaining authorized strength in the various forces. Neither of the problems seems to seriously affect the function and standards of the Dutch police, both of which are high.

REFERENCES

1. Commissie ter Bestudering van het Politie-vraagstuk: Report presented by joint request of the Ministries of Justice and Interior, October 1, 1948, The Hague, 1948, Staatsdrukkerij and Uitgeverijbedrijf.
2. A comparative study of police systems in the Netherlands, England and the UAR, 1968, pp. 46-47.
3. Fijnant, C.: The rebuilding of the Dutch police, Neth. J. Criminol. 18(3):119-130; 18(5):320-334, 1976.
4. Kingdom of the Netherlands, Ministry of Foreign Affairs: Police, civil defense, fire services: 5, The Hague, 1973-1974, Netherlands Government Printing Office.
5. Perrick, F.: The postwar foundations of the municipal police in the Netherlands, 1976.
6. Van Der Burg, F. H.: Preventive justice and local police dissertation, University of Utrecht, March 22, 1961.
7. Van Reenen, P.: specialist in Dutch police work, private communication, 1979.

Chapter 9

The United States

The United States of America shares the North American continent with Canada and Mexico. The continental United States is bounded on the east by the North Atlantic Ocean; on the south by the Caribbean Sea, Gulf of Mexico, and Mexico; on the west by the Pacific Ocean, and on the north by Canada and the Arctic Sea. The continental United States has an area of 9,250,000 sq km (3,608,700 sq mi) and consists of 49 states. Hawaii, an archipelago in the mid-Pacific Ocean, became the fiftieth state in 1959. There also are island territories with various political relationships with the national system, both in the Caribbean and Pacific. When discussing the United States, only information about the 50 states is included.

In 1979 the population of the United States reached 220 million people. In both population and area it is the fourth largest country in the world. Its population is slightly smaller than that of the Soviet Union. In size it is slightly smaller than China or Canada, slightly larger than Brazil or Australia. The size and diversity of the country has been a major factor in the development of its national character and led to the development of regionalism.

HISTORY AND CULTURE

The original inhabitants of the country, Amerindians, migrated from Asia some tens of thousands of years ago. They had tribal social systems and a large number of lingual and cultural groups distributed territorially throughout the continent. When the area that now constitutes the United States was definitively rediscovered by Europeans in the late fifteenth century, there were between several hundred thousand and 3 million inhabitants. To the original inhabitants were then added over a period of 500 years many millions of people of European, African, and Asian stocks. European powers colonized the "new" world. This colonization was rather slow to start and was first attempted in the south and southwestern parts of the country by Hispanic colonizers from Spain and Mexico. The predominant colonization began in the seventeenth century with British and northwestern European settlements and settlers along the East Coast. The first settlers were British (English, Irish, Scottish, and Welsh), Dutch, French, German, and Scandinavian, with smaller numbers of southern and eastern Europeans as well. The British influence came to dominate, and from it comes the national language, English, and political and cultural patterns. Blacks were brought from Africa and the Caribbean, first

148

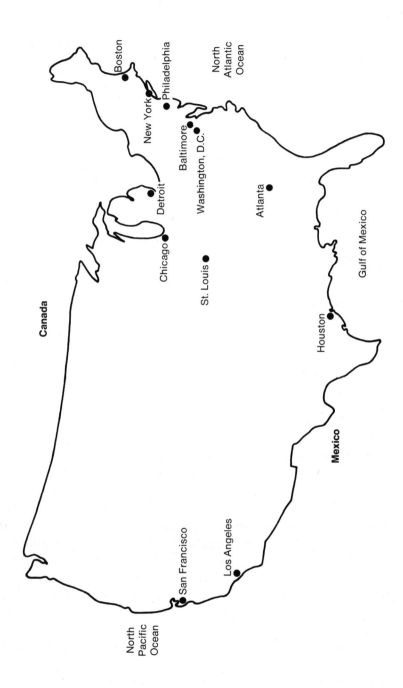

as servants and shortly thereafter as slaves. Slavery became a major institution, particularly in the southern regions, and has had many effects on the national condition.

The original settlers were predominantly Christian, Protestants primarily, but there were also Roman Catholics. There was also a very small Jewish element. Somewhat later in the nineteenth century a migration from Asia began, and the flow from southern and eastern Europe and the Middle East became heavier. The immigration patterns have changed somewhat during the twentieth century. Although the traditional countries of origin have continued sending immigrants, more and more of the immigrant population has come from Asia and Latin America.

After much controversy, particularly between the French and British, the British gained suzerainty over most of the area, particularly the 13 colonies that later founded the United States. In the 1770s these colonies revolted against the crown of England and in 1776 declared themselves independent states. It took several years before the states agreed on a form of governance. With the adoption of the Constitution in 1788 and its enforcement in 1789, the country became a federation of states. There were several controversies with Britain in the years that followed before independence was finally secured. There then began a process of stabilizing the relationships between the states. This culminated in civil war in the 1860s, which resulted in a strengthened union of states under the dominance of the industrialized and urbanized northern region of the country. It also resulted in the abolition of slavery.

From independence on there has been expansion of the country geographically across the continent, adding states along the way. Population has increased greatly through natural increase and a high rate of immigration. In 1790 the population of the nation, which hugged the eastern coast, was about 4 million. Many of the Amerindians had died or moved to the west. Immigration remained uncontrolled until the end of the nineteenth century when restrictions on Asian immigration were first enacted. With the great increase in immigration from southern and eastern Europe at the end of the nineteenth century and beginning of the twentieth century and the apparent stabilization of the size of the country, immigration was severely restricted with national quotas in the early 1920s. These laws were designed to slow immigration down and maintain the northwest European nature of the population. Immigration since then has been held to a few hundred thousand per year. Immigration laws have been changed several times in the third quarter of the century to remove some of the ethnic and racial biases and make the country more hospitable to victims of oppression. It has also changed from a predominantly rural immigration to that of predominantly urbanized people.

There is a large population of mixed ancestry sociologically designated as black (about 12% of the total population), primarily concentrated in the South and in metropolitan regions. There is a remnant Amerindian population of a few million, many residing on reservations in rural areas and others living in metropolitan areas.

There is also a growing Hispanic minority, estimated to soon be the largest minority group in the country, as well as growing minorities from various Asian countries and racial groups. The largest single group is still made up of descendants of colonists and later immigrants from the British Isles and northwestern Europe, although in an increasingly diverse population this group may constitute less than half of the total population and in some areas is a small minority. Intermarrying between the various ethnic and racial groups has produced a large population of mixed ancestry. Although there are identifiable ethnic and racial cultural groups, almost all of the population of the United States has integrated enough that they share many cultural attributes. Major cultural differences are mainly attributable to regional differences. There are definite cultural and economic regions of the country, although boundaries are somewhat fluid.

ECONOMY

The economy of the United States is among the most diverse and successful in the world. The country has become one of the superpowers in the world, both politically and economically, during the past 60 years. Although there have been some reverses in the past few years, the United States is still considered the wealthiest country in the world, with a great deal of heavy industry, light industry, and possibly the most successful agriculture in the world. It is a major exporter of basic foodstuffs for the world markets. The country is very rich in natural resources, having great forests, mineral resources, ports, water, and a very diverse though temperate climate.

POLITICS

The country has a federated, democratic, republican form of government. The national government is divided into three generally independent branches: executive, legislative, and judicial. These branches are supposed to provide checks and balances on each other to prevent the development of any undue power in any one of them and forestall the growth of autocracy. The executive branch consists of a popularly elected president, vice president, and various secretaries headed and represented in the president's cabinet by an appointed secretary (appointed by the president and confirmed independently by the legislative branch). The president is elected for a term of 4 years and by constitutional limitation can serve only two terms. The legislative branch is composed of two houses of Congress. Both are filled by popularly elected members. The Senate contains 100 members, two for each state, elected for 6 years. The House of Representatives contains 435 members, elected from districts of approximately equal population, for 2-year terms. Both the president and the members of Congress are generally members of one of the two major parties. The judiciary is largely appointed, theoretically nonpartisan, and headed by a Supreme Court with nine members appointed for life. State governments are similar in form and division of powers, as are local governments. Policing responsibilities and powers are found in branches of the executive aspects of government throughout the system. They are in theory and largely in practice independent of the political process, although abuses of this principle are not unknown.

POLICE

The city in which the content of police work was studied for this book is Baltimore, Maryland. Baltimore city is a political entity of 91 sq mi situated in the Chesapeake Bay area of the middle Atlantic region on the east coast of the country. Maryland was the only colony settled predominantly by English Catholics during the early colonial era. The city, with an excellent port, quickly became a major center of commerce and industry. In 1970, with a population of more than 905,000, it was the sixth largest city in the United States. By the late 1970s it was seventh in population. It is predominantly an industrial and port city, being the third largest port on the east coast.

The population is ethnically and racially mixed, similar to that of other older cities. Most of the ethnic groups of which American society is formed are represented. In 1970 approximately 45% of the population was black, concentrated in the older and poorer areas of the city. The metropolitan area of 2 million population had a more balanced population distribution. The black population has increased rapidly since World War Two with a major immigration from the rural south. It has been accompanied by a movement of predominantly middle-class white population to the suburbs.

Although the city is in the middle Atlantic region of the country, historically Baltimore and Maryland have had ties with the southeastern region of the United States, not the least of which was the institution of slavery. It is considered one of the "border" states, sharing many of the values of the "old" South. Although it did not join the Confederate rebellion during the Civil War, there were many sympathizers. The city also has many ties with, and resembles, the two nearest large cities: Washington, D.C., 90 km (50 mi) to the southwest, and Philadelphia, 160 km (100 mi) to the northeast. With the movement of population as the result of industrial developments and other social changes, the city has become more and more similar in both culture and problems to the other cities of the northeastern and northern industrial belt.

The municipal police department is part of the executive branch of the city government. It is responsible to the mayor, with little regulation or control exerted by other levels of government or branches of government. The police are appointed under civil service regulations, under provisions meant to ensure merit selection and promotion. The city has been divided into nine police districts, each of which has many precincts with separate station houses. The districts are divided into beats. Boundaries of districts and precincts are uniquely defined and not congruent with those used by other municipal or governmental agencies. For example, there are 201 census tracts within the city limits. The boundaries of these tracts and those of police districts are rarely and only serendipitously congruent. The same is true of health districts, mental health catchment areas, congressional districts, and so forth. The police are thus an independent municipal agency with only informal ties to other municipal agencies and neighboring police departments, similar in organization, problems, history, and function to other urban police departments in the United States.

History

Policing took place in the United States from the beginning of European settlement in the seventeenth century. The form was brought from Britain with the settlers. Remnants of these earlier forms of policing are found in the sheriffs of the rural areas and many counties. In a few areas of the country, settled by German, French, and Spanish settlers, the forms of early policing resembled those of the home country. Through the seventeenth and eighteenth centuries while the country was still a colony, the British influence was predominant. As in Britain, there was a great reluctance to allow the government to assume any major policing powers for fear of tyranny. Added to this were the special conditions of life in America. A very weak and permeable class system, excepting slavery, and a strong distrust for the aristocratic heritage of the Old World, mitigated against the development of military-like discipline and command. The dispersed and isolated nature of American settlements and farms strengthened the strong commitment to localism and self-defense. One needs to remember that the country was essentially a wilderness only intermittently settled, with very poor communications until well into the nineteenth century, to understand the strongly federal nature of the society.[3] It was not until approximately 65 years after the Revolution that organized police forces appeared. The first police force in the United States was organized in New York City in 1845, sixteen years after the Metropolitan Police of London. This new force was consciously patterned on the new London police organization. Although the United States was made up of a population culturally diverse in origin, the British influence was still the strongest. The Boston police were organized after this, following the model of New York. This same model was adopted by the other urban areas of the country rapidly thereafter. With the conditions existing in the United States—large immigrant populations, the deeply engrained localism, expanding frontiers, rapid growth both urban and industrial, particularly after the Civil War of the early 1860s—the American forces developed in slightly different directions than did the British. By the Civil War there had been, essentially, a transformation of police work in the urban areas of the United States from the watch committee to police forces. These police forces, molded on the concepts of territoriality and preventive work, were uniformed, hierarchic, and semimilitary.[10,p.12]

The initial impetus for the development of police forces was much the same in both the United States and Britian. In the mid-nineteenth century the United States was going through a period of major growth, both in population from immigration and in industrialization and urbanization. Large numbers of immigrants were entering the country, primarily from northwestern Europe's peasantry and urban lower classes. The industrial development of the country was based on the cheap labor these immigrants provided. In the cities there were large areas in which poverty and poor living conditions were rife. Added to this was the nativistic, antiimmigrant impulses of the working classes who had previously established themselves. The poverty and social changes, coupled with exploitation and poor conditions, spawned civil disruption and disorder. The availability of hard spirits probably did not make matters easier. The local watch committees were found to be corruptible and ineffective, as they had in Britain. There were recurrent riots, either against or by immigrants. The open frontier probably kept conditions from reaching the depths of dissolution of public order found in London and other industrial cities of Britain. Coincidentally, the rise of the middle classes fueled reformist political currents. These were aimed at increasing participation in the running of society by the bourgeoisie. These elements were strongest in the cities. In the United States these had to be combined with a severe distrust of government and centralized power inherited from those who had fled the autocratic societies of Europe and reinforced by the isolation and independence of settlements. This strengthened the drive for local autonomy in policing and has led to the almost total absence of centralized supervision or influence over general civil police forces in the United States.

Initially American police were unarmed, as were their British models. With the frontier nature of the society and other social forces, this changed rapidly. Revolvers were added to the uniform of the New York police in 1858 in the aftermath of major rioting. In the 1880s the police of Boston were armed. This completed a virtually complete change from unarmed to armed police throughout the nation's urban areas. Rural police traditionally had been armed, as had much of the population. Since the introduction of arms into the police uniform, police in the United States are generally considered out of uniform without their revolvers. In many cities today they are even required to carry a gun while off duty.[4]

In the early days of police forces it was considered sufficient for police to be burly men. Qualifications for entrance into many a force in the United States were that the person be big, strong, healthy, white, and male until well into the twentieth century.[1] (In the late 1970s Philadelphia was under court order to integrate nonwhites, hispanics, and women into its police force, under strong resistance, particularly to women, from the political powers.) Other qualifications were minimal. Often the police were recruited from the ranks of newly arrived immigrants. Since Irish immigrants almost always could speak English and many settled in cities, police work came to be dominated by the Irish in many places. The initiation of a recruit into the ranks of the police was rather haphazard. The exception was uniform requirements, though these were not too high either. In most places uniforms had to be supplied by the police themselves. "The rookie was given a gun and a nightstick; a badge was pinned on his gray uniform and he donned his coal-scuttle hat and was sent on his rounds."[2,p.41] Since size and strength were considered to be the major determinants, training was not too extensive. Most of it was on-the-job training. It usually consisted of being paired with an experienced policeman and being advised to use common sense.[2,p.41] In the earliest days police were appointed for 1 year at a time. This left police open to political control, and often the personnel of the police force changed with a change in political control of city hall. This was not conducive to high standards and morale nor morals. It is not a surprise that not long after the inception of police forces, efforts toward reform and raising professional standards began to be made.

By the early 1900s, police work was being approached from a more professional point of view. Police and their allies demanded and received greater job security, freedom from political pressure, and professional status. Appointments were slowly made more permanent. Uniforms were developed and provided by the government. Civil service status was achieved in most places. By the 1920s one-year status, political appointments, and inadequate uniforms were generally gone. Most urban police were fully civil service tenured and wore distinctive uniforms provided by their forces.[4,p.17] Police training had also made great strides. Before the 1920s police were rarely trained in formal training facilities. The number of such facilities was negligible. During the 1920s this situation changed. It became expected that police receive specialized police training. Local jurisdictions developed facilities to train their police recruits and provide continuing training in police matters for people already on the job. At present "all cities of over 500,000 population, together with a few score of smaller cities, have their own training establishments."[12,p.132] Most of these are police academies. It is not to be inferred that progress toward these conditions was continuous or uneventful.

The progress being made toward professionalization was temporarily halted during Prohibition. This was a dismal experience for the American police. Many of the gains that had been made in terms of status, training, and professionalization in general were lost and were not regained until the end of the World War II. Society tended to place the blame for the upsurge of disorder and the breakdown in law and order on the police. The problems were seen to stem from inadequate policing rather than social conditions and inappropriate laws. The Wickersham Report of 1931 put the onus on the police for the increase in criminal activity during Prohibition. The demand grew for measures that would stop the lawlessness quickly. Scapegoats were sought. A cry for improved "crook catching" became dominant in the society.[4,p.72] The discretionary element present in the watchman tradition was negated by the demand to stop crime. The rigid legalistic approach to law enforcement that gained ascendance during that time seemed to be coupled with a demand for change away from professional standards. A discussion of the changes of the time is not really germane. Suffice it to say that many of the features such as political independence, civil service status, and tenure came under attack. Harvard's James Q. Wilson said at that time, "If the job of the police is to catch crooks then the police have a technical, ministerial responsibility in which discretion plays little part."[4,p.73] With the repeal of Prohibition, the depression, and then the war, the situation changed again.

Since the Second World War the development of police forces in the United States has been toward continuing the trends found in the pre-Prohibition era. Police forces have reintroduced civil service standards in the hiring and promotion of personnel. Unionization or its equivalent has become widespread (the Fraternal Order of Police or Patrolman's Benevolent Associations). Training programs have continued to improve. Many forces encourage personnel to work part-time toward degrees in higher education.

Concurrent with the trend to increased professionalization has been professionalization of equipment or mechanization. As with other areas of modern American life, technology has come into its own. Computers are common in modern urban American police forces, both for research and planning purposes and for service purposes. Mechanization has taken place in other areas as well. It has led to a situation in which the police of the United States are the most highly mechanized police in the world. "Man for man, American city police forces have more mechanical aids and other equipment at their command than those of any other nation."[12,p.111] This has not necessarily led to greater competence in police work. There are times when it might seem that dependence on equipment might even be detrimental to the practice of police work. It cannot be suggested "that the confident claims of those who sell police equipment or the optimistic hope of those who buy it, are often realized. Indeed, many urban police forces in this country are actually burdened with equipment."[12,p.114] There is ongoing discussion in many areas of police work as to whether it might not be better for police to return to the foot patrol and personal contact with the public rather than depend on armaments and machinery, which may lead to further alienation.

Operations

The general pattern of organization of policing in the United States parallels that of the governmental structure. Responsibility for policing is placed in the executive or administrative branches of government at all levels. For reasons discussed previously, there is a greater emphasis on local autonomy for this aspect of governance than for many others. The primary responsibility for day-to-day civil police operations lies almost entirely with local government. Although the state and federal governments exert pressure on local police operations through legislation and supplemental funding, local governments for the most part control their own agencies. There are, however, specialized police agencies at every level of government in the country, generally without coordination and at times with overlapping jurisdictions. The welter of agencies with policing responsibilities has been a subject of concern, and it will be seen that some attempts have been made to rationalize the situation.

At the federal level policing responsibilities, primarily those of a specific law enforcement nature, can be found in over 100 different agencies, each having juris-diction over violations of federal statutes only. The agencies are found in several of the national departments (similar to ministries). There are four separate agencies within the Department of Interior and several in the Department of Justice. The Federal Bureau of Investigation (FBI) in the Department of Justice is probably the best known and has the widest jurisdiction of all federal policing agencies. The FBI, with primary jurisdiction over general federal laws, is investigative in nature and provides technical assistance to local and state governments. The Justice Depart-ment currently also houses the Drug Enforcement Agency (DEA) and the Immi-gration and Naturalization Service–Border Patrol. The Treasury Department has agencies that enforce federal statutes, including the Secret Service, the Alcohol, Tobacco, and Firearms Division of the Internal Revenue Service (IRS), and the Customs Bureau. The Coast Guard is under the Department of Transportation. The Central Intelligence Agency (CIA) serves certain quasipolicing functions for the State Department. Most of these agencies have limited jurisdiction and function independently without formal central coordination or direction.

In early 1978 the federal administration after some study proposed a reorgani-zation of police functions within the several governmental departments to try and reduce some of the duplication and disorganization. A single agency for manage-ment of the country's borders was proposed, to be part of the Treasury Department. This would be formed through the transfer of major sections of the Immigration and Naturalization Service, including the Border Patrol, from the Justice Depart-ment to the Treasury Department, to be merged with the Customs Service. Si-multaneously there would be a transfer of major sections of the Bureau of Alcohol, Tobacco, and Firearms from the Treasury Department to the Justice Department, along with the Drug Enforcement Agency and the FBI. The aim was to "provide for a more coherent and effective police of border control . . . and to provide more uni-form standards and policies in criminal enforcement."[7]

These proposals resulted from a team instituted to study the effectiveness of governmental organization on the federal level by President Jimmy Carter in 1977-1978. One of the problems they considered most serious was the multiplicitous and uncoordinated federal law enforcement maze. According to daily newspaper accounts of the report, there was claimed to be untold waste of money and energy because of the lack of coordination of the varied federal law enforcement programs and agencies. "More than one hundred federal agencies spend five billion dollars a year on law enforcement responsibilities, but no one has authority to coordi-nate their activities."[14] Substantial duplication of work was suggested as well. The problem had become particularly acute in the 1970s. The report called the growth in federal law enforcement agencies and programs during this decade "meteoric." "Interestingly enough, over one-third of the one hundred thirteen agencies sur-veyed did not exist at the beginning of 1970."[14] This situation, though extreme on the federal level, is found on both the state and local levels as well.

Every state except Hawaii has a statewide enforcement agency primarily responsible for control of highway traffic. Other duties may include statewide criminal jurisdiction and general law enforcement of unincorporated areas. This agency may be called the State Police, the Highway Patrol or the Department of Public Safety. In addition many states have a variety of specialized programs and agencies for criminal activities. There are many differences between the states in this area.

What the public generally understands as policing is organized and controlled on the local level. General policing is the prerogative of local government throughout the United States. Because of this, large police forces are local and primarily urban. There are, however, municipal, township, and county police spread throughout the country. Much of the nonurban areas of the country are served by small, quite localized police, often poorly equipped and poorly trained. There has been some movement to consolidation of local suburban and rural governments into county governments. In these cases there has also been consolidation of local police. These counties represent a distinct minority. A significant example of such consolidation is found in Maryland in Baltimore County and others throughout the state. In recent years there have been some increase in the number of such counties, but there is much popular resistance to such consolidation. Within the same jurisdiction one can find a similar though not as extreme situation as that found in the federal government, with different police forces organized for specific tasks or jurisdiction within the locality. Throughout the country there is little coordination or central standardization of police from one locality to another, within or between states and counties. The federal government does have some influence, primarily consultative, through various mechanisms and funding. There is often, however, de facto cooperation between police forces and an amazing similarity in public appearance of forces across the country. It is apparent that, nothwithstanding the local control and bona fide differences, the various local police forces are more similar than different. Major differences are probably between larger urban-suburban and smaller town-rural police forces.

There is not, therefore, a police system in the United States, or even sets of police systems within the sense of that terminology. Bruce Smith mentioned the difficulty of discussing a police "system" in the country. "Our so-called police systems are mere collections of police unities having some similarity of authority, organization or jurisdiction; but they lack any systematic relationship to each other."[12,p.20] In many localities there are sheriffs and their system operating parallel to a modern police forces with all the latest paraphernalia. Sheriffs being the traditional county police official, this exists in many areas where a city and county have coterminous or overlapping borders. For example, New York City with five counties within its borders has citywide police forces, and each county has a sheriff and force. Philadelphia has a similar situation, being a city and county coterminously, and there are both city police and a sheriff's office. Within the city there also may be several police forces operating under city auspices, the general civil police and police servicing specialized branches or functions of city government. In New York

City the general policing is the responsibility of the city police, but there are also transit police (primarily for rapid transit) for the Transit Authority and housing police in the public housing projects for the Housing Authority. In Philadelphia until recently there was a separate park district police force, merged in the early 1970s with the city police, and currently there are housing police in the Housing Authority projects and talk of setting up a transit police force for the rapid transit system. Chicago until recently had separate park district police, merged with the city police in the 1960s.

Not all policing in the United States is done by publicly organized and supported police forces. Adding to the welter of police forces are the private police forces. These are often organized and run by large private corporations and institutions or hired by them. Universities often have campus or college police forces, usually functioning in an area nominally under the jurisdiction of a local public police force. There are privately organized security forces that supply guards and policelike services to private institutions, businesses, and residences for a fee. It is difficult to find order or a system within this conglomeration of varying jurisdictions and forces.

Many of the specialized police forces have developed in response to legislation or regulation of particular situations or as an aid to other governmental functions. The largest local forces have come into existence with the rise of great urban centers of the nation. More recently there has been a great growth in police forces in response to the challenge of modern superhighways and the increase in automotive traffic throughout the nation and in less populated areas. The increase in organized criminal activity that was coincident with Prohibition, during which alcohol was prohibited during the 1920s and early 1930s, appeared to make specialized police necessary. The resurgence of such organized criminal activity during the past 20 years and the increased responsibility for federal criminal jurisdictions have reinforced these currents.[12,p.20] The development of special major local services, such as housing, transit, and parks, with the specialized problems intendent on these services, led to other police developments. The federal system and the popular fear of governmental power have been instrumental in the development of the multitudinous police structures that operate throughout the United States.

It has been estimated that there are upward of 40,000 separate and largely autonomous police forces within the United States. Many have overlapping jurisdictions, as has been seen. The range is wide in the number of people employed, the types of training and equipment available, and the guiding philosophy. The differences relate primarily to size and wealth of the jurisdiction of which they are a part and the local political conditions. In terms of numbers of forces, the vast majority throughout the country consist of less than five people working part-time. Many police are not even paid regular salaries but are reimbursed on a fee-for-service basis. Many of the police in the small forces are not subject to any qualifying standards, either physical or mental. One observer characterizes them as "wholly untrained and largely unsupervised, [they] are ill-equipped and under-disciplined."[12,p.22]

The police described above, though representing a majority of the police forces of the country, do not represent the majority of police in the United States. Most of the police in the nation are part of the large forces found in the cities, counties, and states. These forces often demand much from their police, including prior and continuous education. They are highly supervised and have the most modern equipment. John Jay College, part of the respected City University of New York, is devoted to studies in police work and criminal justice. Most cities have special police academies for training personnel and also have made special arrangements with local institutes of higher education to help and encourage police to receive further education. Several forces either require a university legal degree or are moving toward such a requirement for members of their police forces, especially officers. In some forces officers are given salary differentials for educational attainment and some promotions require specific education above the minimum requirements.

In many police forces there are special sections for special problem areas, despite the general police philosophy that officers are to be generalists rather than specialists. It has been noted that there is a feeling that somehow the officers in special squads are somehow lesser police, particularly if the squad deals with an area other than crime. These special squads vary from city to city. There may be a special investigations unit, vice squad, juvenile unit, or homicide unit, and in some cities there have been organized in the past few years special rape units. The officers assigned to these units usually are plainclothes, or nonuniformed, officers. These officers are often given special assignments or participate in cases found to have special requirements. For example, the homicide unit is usually called when a dead person is found by regular officers. The names of the units are not the same in all jurisdictions, nor is their functioning.

Ranking

The line command of the general uniformed police extends to the special units as well. In some places all police are called officers, while the ranking officers are called officials. An example of the chain of command is that found in the Washington, D.C., police department,[1,p.119] from the lowest rank up: patrolperson–officer, sergeant (in charge of a squad), lieutenant (in charge of a platoon), captain (in charge of a section–station house), inspector (in charge of a district), deputy chief, assistant chief, and chief (responsible to the mayor).

Though the organization is modeled after the military, there are some essential differences in functioning. A major difference is the solitary nature of police work. Soldiers usually function as a group; police usually work alone. They cover their beat or other assignment in ones and twos, occasionally at special occurrences operating with larger numbers of police. Thus the sergeant does not lead the officer into battle, as in the military. In police work the sergeant sometimes meets the officers at an incident and when the officers report to the station house at the beginning and end of a tour of duty. This means that the sergeant has to take the officers' word for the occurrences during their tour of duty. Second, officers are required to keep records of their activities, quite unlike the military. Third, the officers are not operating in a war zone but in an area of their own country with and against their fellow citizens.

Women

Women have been working in police forces in any numbers since shortly after the Second World War. However, until recently they were assigned primarily to the juvenile units and worked primarily as paraprofessional social workers. Though a number of forces have integrated women into the regular uniformed work force, there is much resistance to this.

Women were integrated into the Washington, D.C., police department in the early 1970s. They had been working in the police department in the juvenile units for a number of years prior to that. Until 1972, however, they did not wear uniforms, patrol, or work outside of regular 9:00 AM to 5:00 PM hours. In 1972 women were admitted to all aspects of police work on an equal basis with men. They then were uniformed, armed, and given the same working conditions and assignments as men.[1,p.267] In Philadelphia women were hired by court order in 1977 and in San Francisco in 1979, when the court ordered that 20% of new recruits be women. Other cities opened up general policing to women earlier than Washington, and some have not yet. Of interest, the jobs that were thought unsuitable for women in one city were being performed perfectly satisfactorily by women in another. Often the very city that kept women from a job that was being performed in another city would assign them work that was interdicted in the first. The pattern as of this writing is that slowly and unevenly women are finding police work more and more open to them on an equal basis with men. A breakthrough was made in 1980 in Philadelphia. The new police commissioner of the city "issued an order that, for the first time in the department's history, makes every position open to women."[13] This was one of the first things Commissioner Solomon did upon his appointment. This action may speed up full integration of women into police work throughout the country.

Volunteer police

There are volunteer police in some jurisdictions. The pattern is quite varied throughout the country. In some places the volunteer police function is organized by community groups. Often their jurisdiction does not cover areas coterminous with the police jurisdiction. For example, there are Town-Watch groups operating in some sections of Philadelphia. Although supported in noneconomic ways by the police department through the precinct houses and personnel, the groups are organized by local community organizations and block committees. The Town-Watch concept involved organizing the residents of a particular area to be alert to any possible problems and act as the eyes and ears of the police. They are also used to help educate citizens in ways to reduce the crime susceptibility of the area. In some areas of Brooklyn, N.Y. (a borough of New York City) local patrol groups have been organized. These are usually a product of fear of street crime. In some instances they have successfully brought different ethnic groups together for mutual protection. In other areas they have been seen as hostile moves by one ethnic group against another, often in racial terms. None of these groups are uniformed, armed, or part of the police system. In some cities there are volunteer, or auxiliary, police who wear uniforms and are organized as part of the police force. In Jersey City, New Jersey, there is such a program. It is largely composed of young people, some of whom are interested in becoming police when finished with their education. In New York City there has been an auxiliary mounted police to help patrol Central Park. The major fact that can be stated about volunteer police in the United States is that there is no general pattern. Organization and the auspices under which they are organized are highly idiosyncratic, varying with local conditions and history.

Function

Police in the United States fulfill two major functions within society. These are social control and support (an aspect of social integration). The actual function of the police force of Baltimore during the two 2-week periods in 1971 are examined to provide an idea of the proportions of police work devoted to each function and to the range of activities with which police are occupied. The social control function is generally carried out through law enforcement tasks. The support or integrative function is generally carried out through those activities that are mediatory or responsive to service needs. Other activities, somewhat interstitial in nature, are traffic and patrol work and the arbitration of conflict. Since the vast majority of conflicts are civil in nature and result in some mediatory activity rather than criminal action, they have been assigned to the integrative function for the purposes of this discussion. On the following pages the content and relative involvement of the Baltimore police in each type of activity are discussed separately after a general discussion.

Analysis of tasks

Police in Baltimore handled a total of 16,549 calls during the first 2 weeks of February in 1971 (Figs. 9 and 10). This is an incidence of 18.29 per 1000 population, or an equivalent monthly rate of 40.23 per 1000. Of these slightly less than one fourth were related to social control or law enforcement, about evenly divided between the more serious and less serious crimes, and had an equivalent monthly rate of 5.42 per 1000 population. Social integration activities composed about 40% of all calls, with an equivalent monthly incidence of 16 per 1000 population. Of this about three fourths were service calls and one fourth were arbitration-mediation calls. Traffic and vehicular incidents made up about one sixth of the total, and various

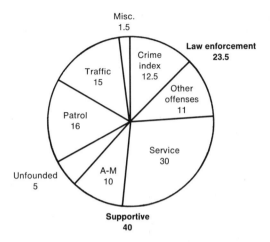

Fig. 9. Police work in the United States: percent distribution, Baltimore, Md., February 1-15, 1971.

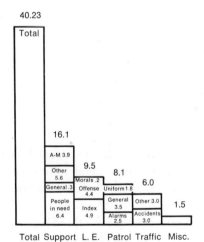

Fig. 10. Police work in the United States: incidence per 1000 population, Baltimore, Md., February 1971.

patrol and other activities another sixth. There were also a rather large number of unfounded calls, almost 5% of the total, an equivalent monthly incidence of 1.84 per 1000 population. It is evident that almost twice as many calls are related to what we have called support activities as to law enforcement activities (Tables 9-1 to 9-3).

Law enforcement (social control). Social control activities are reported in two categories: index crimes and other offenses (Table 9-4). *Index crimes* are those that the FBI requests police departments to report, which are then published and at times used to compare crime conditions in different cities. These are generally the crimes considered most serious. The 12 types of crimes included in this category include four categories of assault (common, cutting, shooting, and aggravated [with a weapon]), purse snatching, four categories of holdup (bank, taxicab, service station, and other]), yoking, breaking and entering, and auto theft. During the periods examined index crimes were about 12.5% of incidents in which police were involved. This varied from district to district only slightly. The greater variation was in incidence per 1000 population. For the city as a whole, the incidence was 6.73 per 1000 for 2 weeks. This varied from 3.7 per 1000 in one district to 11.9 per 1000 in another (the central city district). In the other districts the variation was much less: from 5.8 to 7.7 per 1000. Only three of the 12 subcategories contained over 0.6% of total incidents. These were breaking and entering, 3.7%; common assault, 3.5%; and auto theft, 1.9%. During the second 2-week period the figures are quite similar: breaking and entering, 4.4%; common assault, 3.3%; and auto theft, 1.8%; with all other subcategories 0.8% or less. This is not to say that these incidents are unimportant, for each has the potential for serious distress and human complications (Tables 9-5 to 9-7).

Crimes involving violence are included in the categories of assault. The serious crimes involving violence are assaults in which someone was either cut with a knife or shot. These were 0.8% of the total, 6.7% of index crimes, with a monthly incidence of 0.33 per 1000 population. All assaults were 4.8% of the total incidents, 39.4% of index crimes, with a monthly incidence of 1.93 per 1000 population. There were no reported murders during either time period. One would assume that some of the murders, if there were any, would be included in the cutting or shooting incidents. Though the threat of violence is high, almost 40% of all major crime incidents, the actual wounding by weapons of some kind was not very high, one sixth of all assault incidents.

Other offenses include nine subcategories: three types of larceny (reported, from automobile, and bicycle), armed person, sex offense, indecent exposure, false pretenses, destruction of property, and gambling. During the two 2-week periods similar patterns are discernible. In one period destruction of property comprised 4% of total calls; reported larceny, 3.3% and larceny from auto 2.6%. During the other period destruction of property comprised 4.1%; reported larceny, 3.2%; and larceny from auto 2.6% of total calls. During this second period armed persons were 1.2% of total. In sum, the other offenses category comprised around 12% of the

Text continued on p. 170.

Table 9-1. Distribution of police activities: Baltimore (pop. 905,000), February 1-15, 1971*

	Number	Percent	Incidence per 1000 (2 wk)	Incidence per 1000 (mo)
Law enforcement				
Index	2020	12.2	2.23	4.91
Other	1794	10.8	1.98	4.36
SUBTOTAL	3814	23.0	4.21	9.27
Morals	59	0.4	0.07	0.14
TOTAL	3873	23.4	4.28	9.41
Support				
Services				
Person in need	2614	15.8	2.89	6.35
General service	119	0.7	0.13	0.29
Other	2296	13.9	2.54	5.58
SUBTOTAL	5029	30.4	5.56	12.22
Arbitration-Mediation	1580	9.6	1.75	3.84
TOTAL	6609	39.9	7.30	16.06
Patrol				
Alarms	1043	6.3	1.15	2.54
Gone on arrival	1423	8.6	1.57	3.46
Other	124	0.7		0.30
SUBTOTAL	2590	15.7	2.86	6.30
Unfounded	758	4.6	0.84	1.84
TOTAL	3348	20.2	3.70	8.14
Traffic and vehicular				
Accidents				
No injury	973	5.9		
Injury	270	1.7		
Fatality	2	0.01		
SUBTOTAL	1245	7.5	1.38	3.04
Parking complaint	663	4.0		
Investigation of auto	564	3.4		
TOTAL	2472	14.9	2.73	6.01
Miscellaneous				
Lost property	184	1.1		
Recovered property	60	0.4		
TOTAL	244	1.5	0.26	0.59
TOTAL	16,546	100.0	19.65	43.25

*Percents and incidence rates have been rounded off so totals may not equal 100%.

Table 9-2. Classification of "other calls" incidents, Baltimore, February 1-15, 1971

	Number	Percent	Percent other calls
Support			
Arbitration-mediation			
Family	506	3.1	
Juvenile	899	5.4	
Street	86	0.5	
Animal	43	0.3	
Vehicle	46	0.3	
SUBTOTAL	1580	9.6	12.5
Person in need			
Disorderly	1363	8.2	
Suspect	184	1.1	
Intoxicated	242	1.5	
Injured	192	1.2	
Sick	321	1.9	
Missing	250	1.5	
In street	62	0.4	
SUBTOTAL	2614	15.8	20.6
General service			
Sanitation	11	0.1	
Street obstruction	32	0.2	
Storm damage	5	0.03	
Dog bite	71	0.4	
SUBTOTAL	119	0.73	0.9
Other	2296	13.9	18.1
TOTAL	6609	40.03	52.1
Patrol			
Gone on arrival	1423	8.6	
Warrant	108	0.7	
Assisting officer	16	0.1	
Holdup	44	0.3	
Fire	373	2.3	
Silent	263	1.6	
Audible	92	0.6	
ADT	237	1.4	
NPC	34	0.2	
TOTAL	2590	15.8	20.4
Unfounded	758	4.6	6.0
Traffic			
Accidents			
No injury	973	5.9	
Person injured	270	1.7	
Fatality	2	0.01	
SUBTOTAL	1245	7.61	9.8
Parking complaint	663	4.0	
Investigation of auto	564	3.4	
TOTAL	2472	15.01	19.5
Miscellaneous			
Lost property	184	1.1	
Received property	60	0.4	
TOTAL	244	1.5	1.9
TOTAL	12,673	76.94	100.0

Table 9-3. Distribution of "other calls," Baltimore, November 16-31, 1971

	Baltimore—incidents		
	Number	**Percent other calls**	**Percent total police work**
Support			
Arbitration-mediation			
Family disturbance	634	4.58	
Juvenile disturbance	1789	12.98	
Street disturbance	223	1.61	
Animal disturbance	89	0.64	
Vehicle disturbance	74	0.53	
SUBTOTAL	2809	20.34	13.10
Services			
Disorderly person	2065	14.90	
Suspect person	553	3.99	
Intoxicated person	219	1.58	
Injured person	172	1.24	
Sick person	446	3.22	
Missing person	272	1.96	
Person in street	134	0.97	
Dog bite	100	0.72	
Storm damage	7	0.05	
Sanitation	12	0.09	
Street obstruction	53	0.38	
Other	2991	21.59	
	7024	50.63	32.48
TOTAL	9833	70.97	45.59
Norm enforcement			
Traffic and Vehicular			
Parking complaint	1027	7.41	
Investigate auto	824	5.92	
SUBTOTAL	1851	13.36	8.54
Preventive patrol			
Assist officer	29	.21	
Holdup alarm	70	.51	
Fire alarm	455	3.28	
Silent alarm	398	2.87	
Audible alarm	134	0.97	
ADT alarm	267	1.93	
NPC alarm	9	0.06	
Gone on arrival	233	1.68	
Wanted on warrant	144	1.04	
SUBTOTAL	1739	12.55	8.02
Miscellaneous			
Lost property	276	1.99	
Received property	163	1.18	
SUBTOTAL	439	3.17	2.02
TOTAL	13,862	100.00	64.17

Table 9-4. Distribution of total calls, Baltimore, November 16-31, 1971

	Number	Percent
Index crimes		
Assault, common	721	3.3
Assault, cutting	74	0.3
Assault, shooting	72	0.3
Assault, aggravated (weapon)	86	0.4
Purse snatching	122	0.6
Holdup, bank	0	0.0
Holdup, taxicab	10	0.0
Holdup, service station	15	0.1
Holdup, other	158	0.7
Yoking	183	0.8
B & E (Breaking & Entering)	951	4.4
Auto Theft	398	1.8
TOTAL	2,790	12.7
Other offenses		
Larceny report	701	3.2
Larceny from auto	564	2.6
Larceny of bicycle	55	0.3
Armed person	260	1.2
Sex offense	57	0.3
Indecent exposure	14	0.1
False pretense	67	0.3
Destruction of property	891	4.1
Gambling	47	0.2
TOTAL	2,656	12.3
TOTAL INDEX CRIMES AND OTHER OFFENSES	5,446	25.0
Other calls		
Parking complaint	1,027	4.7
Investigate auto	824	3.8
Disorderly person	2,065	9.5
Suspicious person	553	2.6
Intoxicated person	219	1.0
Injured person	172	0.8
Sick person	446	2.1
Missing person	272	1.3
Person in street	134	0.6
Wanted on warrant	144	0.7
Dog bite	100	0.5
Lost property	276	1.3
Received property	163	0.8
Storm damage	7	0.0
Assist officer	29	0.1
Family disturbance	634	2.9
Juvenile disturbance	1,798	8.3
Street disturbance	223	1.0
Animal disturbance	89	0.4
Vehicle disturbance	74	0.3
Holdup alarm	70	0.3
Fire alarm	455	2.1
Silent alarm	398	1.8
Audible alarm	134	0.6
ADT alarm	267	1.2

Table 9-4. Distribution of total calls, Baltimore, November 16-31, 1971—cont'd

	Number	Percent
Other calls—cont'd		
NPC alarm	9	0.0
Sanitation	12	0.1
Street obstruction	53	0.2
Gone on arrival	233	1.1
Other	2,991	13.8
TOTAL	13,871	63.93
Accidents		
Auto accident	1,432	6.6
Accident, personal injury	243	1.1
Accident, fatal	3	0.0
TOTAL	1,678	7.73
Unfounded	703	3.2
TOTAL	21,698	100.00

Table 9-5. Police activities, Baltimore, February 16-28, 1972

District	Number of incidents		
	Total	Index crimes–other offenses	Other calls*
1	3,528	829	2,371
2	2,257	543	1,477
3	3,060	679	2,113
4	2,652	639	1,763
5	2,737	792	1,688
6	2,953	732	1,881
7	3,363	680	2,423
8	2,631	665	1,705
9	2,745	507	1,910
TOTAL	25,926	6,066	17,331

*Excluding unfounded.

Table 9-6. Proportion of index crimes–other offenses versus other calls

District	Index crimes–other offenses		Other calls*	
	Number	Percent	Number	Percent
1	829	23.5	2,371	67.2
2	543	24.1	1,477	65.4
3	679	22.2	2,113	69.1
4	639	24.1	1,753	66.1
5	792	28.9	1,688	61.7
6	732	24.8	1,881	63.7
7	680	20.2	2,423	72 0
8	665	25.3	1,705	64.8
9	507	18.5	1,910	69.6
TOTAL	6,066	23.4	17,321	66.8

*Excluding unfounded.

Table 9-7. Incidence of police activities in index crimes–other offenses versus other calls for 2 weeks

District	Index crimes–other offenses		Other calls*	
	Number	Incidence per 1000 population	Number	Incidence per 1000 population
1	829	11.90	2,371	34.03
2	543	6.41	1,477	17.44
3	679	6.70	2,113	20.84
4	639	5.83	1,753	16.10
5	792	7.73	1,688	16.47
6	732	7.10	1,881	18.25
7	680	7.73	2,423	23.83
8	665	7.10	1,705	22.08
9	507	3.72	1,910	11.71
TOTAL	6,066	6.73	17,321	18.93

*Excluding unfounded.

total during these two periods. Thus about 25% of the incidents with which police officers were involved during these 2-week periods were law enforcement, social control activities.

Interstitial activities such as traffic, miscellaneous, and general patrol activities occupied about 35% of the incidents during these two periods. These activities might be characterized as maintenance of order as well. The *traffic* activities are included in five different subcategories. There are three accident categories: those without damage, those with personal injuries, and those in which there was a fatality. Of the 1245 accidents that occurred during one 2-week period, only two resulted in fatalities, and over 20% had injuries. The remainder of the traffic activities were parking complaints and investigation of autos. The latter was in connection with suspicion of some other type of wrongdoing, that is, stolen auto or some other suspect activity. The miscellaneous activities were related to lost and found property and included only 1.5% to 3% of the reported incidents during either of the 2-week periods. The *patrol* category included almost 20% of activities, but half of these were calls in which there was no caller when police arrived (called gone on arrival). Most of the other patrol incidents were alarms investigated. There were six different types of alarm calls, including two in which premises are wired directly to police stations for police response. The remainder were serving warrants and a few cases of assisting an officer. The latter was only 0.1% of the total, 16 incidents in one of the 2-week periods, 0.2% of the total, 29 incidents in the other. Thus, aside from traffic activities and responding to alarms, often false, police in Baltimore are not overly involved in the patrol aspect of police work.

Support (social integration). Supportive activities of the police take two forms: arbitration-mediation and services. Together these incidents comprised the largest group of activities performed by police in Baltimore in both of the time periods.

In both periods incidents of this nature made up 40% to 45% of the total incidents. Of support incidents about 25% were arbitration-mediation, while about 75% were general service incidents. These are reported in the generalized category of *other calls*, which includes interstitial activities such as patrol and traffic. A breakdown of the calls in this category shows that between 55% and 70% are what we have defined as *support* activities (Tables 9-3 and 9-4).

Arbitration-mediation activities cover a range of interactions making up between 9.5% and 13% of all incidents. In both periods over 50% of arbitration-mediation incidents involved juvenile disturbances, and approximately another 25% involved family disturbances. This translates to between 5.5% and 8.5% of total incidents being juvenile disturbances and 3% of total incidents being family disturbances. Other arbitration-mediation incidents are categorized as those taking place in the street, between 0.5% and 1% of total incidents; dealing with animals, 0.3% to 0.4% of total incidents; and those involving vehicles, 0.3% of total incidents. It is thus seen that arbitration-mediation activities are focused on those involving juveniles and family crises. These do not appear to be the wide range of arbitration-mediation activities in Baltimore that is found in other places. This may also have something to do with reporting. Police may be less likely to call other situations disturbances, though one is hard put to find another category such incidents would fit into.

Service incidents cover a wide range of activities and interactions, making up over 30% of all incidents during the two periods. Police often claim that they have regular clients who call them on weekends and holidays. The service category has been divided into two subgroups. One involves people in need. This includes incidents involving disorderly people, between 8.5% and 9.5% of total incidents; suspicious persons, between 1% and 2.5% of total incidents; intoxicated people, between 1% and 1.5% of total; injured, about 1% of total; sick, about 2% of total; missing persons, about 1.5% of total; and persons in street, about 0.5% of total. Together these incidents make up between 16% and 18% of the total activities of the police in these two periods. Another group of activities that can be called general service activities include dog bite, sanitation, street obstruction, storm damage, and the general other category, including approximately another 15% of police work during these two periods. One peculiarity of the data was that there was a much higher rate of "gone at arrival" calls in February than there were in November. These may be related to the cold weather in Baltimore during February.

General discussion

Police in Baltimore are involved in incidents that fulfill two social functions: social control and social integration–support. The specifically social control activities are law enforcement incidents that fall into two categories: index crimes, about 12.5% of total police work; and other offenses, about 12% of total police work. The social integration–support activities also fall into two general categories: arbitration-mediation, about 10% to 13% of total police work; and supportive services, over

Table 9-8. Police Districts, Baltimore City 1971

Number	Name	Area (sq mi)	Population	Number of police assigned	Police per 1000 population
1	Central	3.45	59,847	311	5.2
2	Southwestern	10.20	84,694	188	2.2
3	Southern	12.02	101.375	228	2.2
4	Northern	13.36	109,527	191	1.8
5	Northwestern	10.82	102,489	205	2.2
6	Western	2.61	103,045	238	2.3
7	Southeastern	7.96	101,691	221	2.2
8	Eastern	2.75	77,208	217	2.8
9	Northeastern	17.43	161,666	194	1.2
TOTAL LAND		80.60	901,420	1993	3.3
TOTAL WATER		13.21			

30% of total police work. There are also a number of incidents that are interstitial between control and support, such as patrol, traffic, and lost and found. Together these make up about 30% of police work. It can be seen that the largest percentage of work was in integration activities of police in Baltimore during the two 2-week periods for which data were examined; next were the interstitial activities, and then the control activities.

There are, of course, variations from one police district to another in the percentages and incidence rates of the various categories of police work. Tables 9-5 to 9-7 give the figures for one of the 2-week periods. In comparing police work from one district to another it was found that incidence rates are the best comparative figures. There is a rather wide range of incidence rates between districts, though the percentages stay similar throughout the city. The range of law enforcement activities is from 3.72 to 11.9 incidents per 1000 population. There is a citywide rate of 6.73 incidents per 1000 population. The incidence of support activities range from about 7 to 25 per 1000, with a citywide rate of 13 per 1000. There was a direct relationship between the incidence of support and law enforcement activities. In those districts with the lowest rate in one there was also the lowest rate in the other, and similarly for high rates. There is also a wide range of police per populations between districts, from 1.2 to 5.2 per 1000, averaging 3.3 per 1000 (Table 9-8). These vary, as do the work load of the districts, through police department design. Thus more police are assigned per population where there is a heavier per population work load.

Socioecological analysis

Baltimore police districts vary in area, population size, and characteristics. The areas of the districts range from 2.6 to 17.4 sq mi. The ethnic and socioeconomic characteristics of the populations vary also. Four of the police districts have a black majority. The city can almost be said to be two cities, a predominantly black and a predominantly white city.

A study of socioecological correlates of police work in Baltimore found that it was helpful to analyze police work in black and white subsets as well as for the city as a whole. In general, high correlations were found between police activities, both support and control and social need factors. This suggests that the incidence of police work in Baltimore increases with the level of social need. In predominantly white districts there was a high correlation between support activities and factors relating to disorganized families and males. In black districts high correlations were found between support activities and factors related to transiency and disorganized males. The implications are that there are differing socioecological variables that indicate weakness in the support system in different communities. The results of this study indicate that in Baltimore there is a close relationship between social need, a measure of social integration, and the incidence of police work, both support and law enforcement.[11]

The results of the study suggest that police work does not occur serendipitously. There are social factors that provide the conditions for variations in incidence of activities for which police are called. These appear to be connected to the socioeconomic conditions and social integration of communities and social areas. Police work would thus appear to be one indication of and response to the social conditions of communities. Police have known this for a long time, but it is often ignored in discussions of police work. It seems clear that police fulfill a multiple role in society, one that cannot be denigrated by either the public or police.

Problems

The problems faced by the police in the United States are generally interrelated. Many of them follow from the complete local autonomy of general policing. Problems include a wide disparity in quality and standards between forces, training, recruitment, and retention of personnel, police morale, relationship between police and community, and the development of popular self-protection movements. There is another major problem in police organization in the United States, that is, the multiplicity of agencies and bureaus with policing powers and responsibilities on all levels of government. Each is discussed briefly.

Local autonomy, though in and of itself not a negative thing, has led to some very negative developments in American police organization. The concept of local autonomy is extremely well developed and sacrosanct in American political life. This is particularly true in regard to police powers. Though founded in the historic development of the nation, the concept as applied to policing has in some ways survived in a world that renders it somewhat archaic. It stems from the need for independent settlements to be self-sufficient and capable of immediate self-defense. These settlements were separated from all others except neighbors by wilderness and poor communications links. The conditions have obviously changed. Local police autonomy has come to mean that there is little standardization between forces. Working conditions, expertise, training, and even integrity vary greatly from one place to another. This is not necessarily the result of local autonomy nor are there only problematic results of local autonomy. There remain local problems of social control. However, the major social control problems of American society have become institutionalized and without respect to political boundaries. Unfortunately a further result of local autonomy is that there is little to prevent local systems from becoming involved in the political process or local corruption. In 1978 the police force of Chester, Pennsylvania, was involved in a major scandal of corruption intimately connected with corruption in the city government. In Paterson, New Jersey, a group of policemen were alleged to be involved in a slum housing scandal.[6] The problems of corruption probably may not be that widespread within the police system. However, the inadequate resources of many localities have led them to have poorly trained and equipped and paid police forces, while neighboring jurisdictions may have highly trained, paid, and well-equipped forces. There is a problem of extremely uneven policing standards and quality in the United States.

Related to this is the problem that many forces face in providing adequate training to their personnel. Considering the complex job that American police have and the wide range of interactions in which they are involved, the somewhat cursory training that many forces offer does not lead to the most effective functioning of the resources available. There is a movement among many of the larger forces and even some smaller ones around the country to require or strongly encourage increased educational levels. There is also development of more intensive training in some places, indicating that the problem is recognized. However, there are also evidence that these may not be addressing the training needs of police work. The Police Foundation in Washington, D.C., released a report in 1978 that indicated that police education as presently designed was not having the desired effects. It was stated that police education needs to be upgraded and improved greatly, that a coherent package needs to be developed that combines academic training in the social sciences and humanities with training in police academies around specific police skills and knowledge.[8] Unfortunately the concept of local autonomy militates against any wide-ranging solution to training needs.

Recruitment and retention of suitable personnel is also a problem in many forces. Forces throughout the country complain of being understaffed and having high turnover of personnel. This problem, of course, is part and parcel of other problems discussed here. Probably causally related to turnover and recruitment difficulties is the low level of morale among police personnel in many jurisdictions. In February 1979 the police in New Orleans conducted a bitter 2-week strike. This incidentally all but forced cancellation of Mardi Gras. The bitterness of police personnel expressed during the strike may have been an extreme manifestation of the frustration and alienation expressed and felt by many police throughout the country. There are probably many reasons for this phenomenon, but police report that they do not feel that they are being supported in their work by the general public and society in general. These expressions come from widely diverse sections of the country and not only from the major cities. Changes in expectations of what social institutions are about on the part of large sections of the population, the changed social positions of segments of the society (blacks, women, youth, other minorities), and the movement of the middle class out of the cities have all affected the stability of social norms and expectations, increasing the ambiguity of the police within the social system. This in turn has increased the uncertainty of police work and the frustrations and alienation felt by police personnel. The training of police has not kept pace with, nor prepared them, in most places, to deal with the changes. It is, of course, possible that there is no training that could prepare anyone for the changes in status and expectations current in the United States. Be that as it may, the feelings of alienation and frustration among police are very real.

On the other hand, not only police feel frustrated and alienated. Segments of the population feel a similar frustration with and alienation from the police. The cry of "kill the pigs (police)" may not be current as it was during the turbulence of the late 1960s. There are, however, significant segments of the population, particularly in the larger cities and among the poor and minorities, who feel that the police represent the enemy. Even among more favored segments of the population there are elements who have negative conceptions about police and police work. Most police forces in urban areas have community relations officers or units assigned to counter the negative community responses to police and their work. There have been a number of programs scattered among diverse forces to affect parts of the problem, either through training police, developing dialogue, or special programs to sensitize public and police to each other. The attempts have been sporadic and of limited lasting success. Social forces and the nature and organization of police forces work against any piecemeal solution to the problems of poor police-community relations.

An interesting recent development has been the growth of self-protection groups and private security organizations. The feelings of insecurity and danger that many people have, particularly in certain areas of the cities but elsewhere as well, are clearly stated by the self-protection movement. Some have called these groups vigilante groups. Most are an attempt of private citizens to combat what they see as a threat to their peaceful and safe way of life. Many of the groups work in cooperation with police forces. They usually arise from a perception that the police are not able to or simply are not doing an adequate job of protecting their persons and property. Though these groups may not be a problem per se and may actually be helping police, there is always a danger when private citizens organize and take the law into their own hands. The danger is of violence, injustice, and intergroup disharmony. The self-policing trend must be watched carefully so that it does not become a destructive force in the United States.

A final major problem of American policing is the multitude of agencies and levels of government involved. There has been some attempt at the federal level to at least address the problem during the late 1970s under President Carter's administration. However, the over 100 federal agencies and bureaus involved in some form of policing, added to agencies on the state, county, and local levels, actively encourage duplication, inefficiency, competition, and inadequate functioning of all police bodies within the country. One does not have to attack the tradition of local autonomy in police, and can indeed support much of it, to recognize that the multiplicity of police agencies is somewhat dysfunctional. Probabilities of effectively addressing the problem of multiplicity of number and levels of police agencies are not high.

Six major problems have been indicated within the American police structure. These problems are often interrelated. Local autonomy has resulted in a great disparity in standards and quality between police forces throughout the country. This disparity can be found in neighboring as well as widely dispersed forces. There are many questions about the level and kind of training that police receive as well as the educational level of police personnel. In addition many forces have problems of high turnover and understaffing. Morale is low in many forces and may contribute to the understaffing and turnover. Not only is there frustration and alienation among police personnel, but there is often a serious problem of community relations. Indicative of some of the social problems with which police have to deal and the public perception of police inadequacy is the growth of private, both voluntary and for hire, policing and protection organizations. A final major problem is the multiplicity of agencies and bureaus having policing powers and responsibilities on all levels of government.

Future trends

Currently the entire range of police concerns is under study at many levels, from local to federal, from public to private, in the United States. The Ford Foundation has a special subsidiary foundation called the Police Foundation. The Justice Department of the national government has instituted a division for the study of law enforcement and the administration of justice, which provides support to local police forces and to students of the police. The Department of Health, Education and Welfare also has several programs for the study of police activities and functions. In the American tradition it seems as though everyone is getting into the act. There are also commissions on the state and local levels throughout the country. These activities have been taking place since the early 1960s at least.

The questions that are raised indicate that there is some uncertainty about what role police are to take in society and how the problems of crime and social unrest are to be handled. As in most of the social sciences, the science of criminal justice is still rather theoretical. A major difficulty is that the police and the systems of which they are part are impinged on by many other factors—economic, psychological, social, political, and historical. Exactly what relationship each of these factors has to the others is unclear. In the introduction to the 1967 Task Force report on the police of the President's Commission on Law Enforcement and the Administration of Criminal Justice in the United States, the questions and uncertainties were stated succinctly. A theme that runs through this entire volume is the extent to which police work is limited by a lack of precise knowledge about crime and the means of controlling it.[9,p.3] This is followed by a plea for research and increased information that would clarify issues and improve police effectiveness. "Almost every chapter demonstrates, indeed documents the urgent need for research into every aspect of police work by the police and by scholars working with the police."[9,p.3]

This is not a call for simplistic and easy answers. The Task Force acknowledged that the issues are complex and that the work to be addressed is big. The Task Force report contains many hundreds of suggestions and recommendations for things to be done. "The complexity and the magnitude of the tasks of controlling crime and improving criminal justice is indicated by the more than two hundred specific recommendations and the many hundreds of suggestions for action, that this report contains."[9,p.291] The report ends with the statement, "If America is to meet the challenge . . . it must do more than it is doing now."[9,p.291]

The evaluation of which the 1967 Task Force is a part is the reevaluation of many aspects of American life that occurred at the same time. It is significant that the role of the police and a concern for more effective services by the police is part of the national reappraisal. The outcome of the reappraisal is still far from certain. The movement will of necessity be slow, particularly because the principle of local autonomy is involved. There has not been an observable realignment of police forces to move toward centralization outside of very few places. Some forces have changed uniforms toward less formal, less military style clothes. Women are taking an increasing place in police work. There has been movement toward inclusion of black and Hispanic people on forces. There are those who want police to become more involved in the solution of social problems and concern for those who are caught in the problems. They are opposed by those who believe in more stringent enforcement of the law and mandatory sentences. All of this is part of the national discussion about what the role of government and the institutions of society should take in dealing with social and individual problems. What effect this will have on the traditional conception of police as gunslingers and crime fighters is unknown. What is certain is that the role of police and their relationship to the rest of society is a matter of concern and is still evolving in the United States. Similar currents are found in the Netherlands, Britain, and other countries. The police in the United States still remain a highly fragmented and diverse institution. Power is still retained at the local level over most police work, and movement toward greater professionalism, higher educational standards and salaries, and more complicated equipment continue.

SUMMARY

Police in the United States are organized on many levels of government and under many different governmental jurisdictions and agencies. Some have specific regulatory responsibilities, and others broad policing responsibilities. The agencies responsible for general policing are organized in quasimilitary bureaucratic systems under local control and autonomy throughout the country. There are, however, many similarities in function, organization, and problems between police departments throughout the country. It is estimated that there are upward of 40,000 independent, autonomous local forces in the United States. These vary in size from a few part-time personnel to forces of several thousand. The large forces are found in large cities generally. These forces are departments of the local government and generally have a training academy and the latest equipment. During the 1970s many departments integrated women into regular police work.

Though many police forces have special, usually plainclothes, units to handle particular types of problems such as juvenile, rape, and vice, the large bulk of police work is handled by generalist uniformed patrol people assigned to specific sectors or beats. Police handle wide ranges of activities. In Baltimore about a quarter of the incidents in which police are involved are law enforcement taks, fulfilling a social control function. These are almost equally divided between more serious index crimes and other offenses. Crimes involving violence represent a small percentage of the total. Slightly less than half of the incidents are support activities, fulfilling a social integration function. One fourth of these are arbitration-mediation activities, primarily juvenile and family situations. The rest are various service activities, usually helping people in need. The remainder of police work is divided between patrol, traffic, and miscellaneous activities that combine control and integration functions. The incidence of both support and law enforcement activities between police districts varies directly with the social need of the districts. In those districts with high social need there are high support and law enforcement incidences.

There are a number of problems that afflict police work in the United States, though not all are found in all jurisdictions or necessarily together. General problems are uneven standards and quality between forces, adequate and appropriate training and educational levels, and the multiplicity of policing responsibilities and agencies on all levels of government. Problems that may be specific to some forces are understaffing and high turnover, morale among personnel, police-community relations, corruption, and the development of private voluntary and mercenary patrol and policing groups and organizations. The problems have been addressed by various official and nonofficial bodies, and solutions have been suggested. Attempts have been made to resolve some of the problems, but they will take a long time to resolve. At the same time there are many instances of high standards and superb performance found among police forces and personnel in the United States.

Uniformed generalist police are organized in almost all local political entities in the United States. They deal with the myriad problems and dislocations associated with life and the social changes associated with life in the areas in which they work. They provide, essentially, a measure of both social control and integration in the society.

REFERENCES

1. Abrecht, M. E.: The making of a woman cop, Wm. New York, 1976, William Morrow & Co., Inc.
2. Arm, W.: The policeman, New York, 1969, E. P. Dutton & Co., Inc.
3. Boorstin, D. J.: The Americans: the colonial experience, New York, 1958, Vintage Books, Random House, Inc.
4. Fleming, T.: The policeman's lot, American Heritage 21(2):4, 1970.
5. New Orleans police, *Philadelphia Inquirer* and *New York Times*, March 5, 1979, p. 1.
6. Paterson cops tied to arson, slumlord racket, *New York Post*, March 7, 1979, p. 18.
7. Plan to reorganize U.S. law enforcement studied, *New York Times*, May 24, 1978, p. 20.
8. Policy of encouraging policemen to attend college challenged, *New York Times*, November 28, 1978, p. A20.
9. President's Commission of Law Enforcement and the Administration of Justice, Task Force on the Police: Task force report: the police, Washington, D.C., 1967, U.S. Government Printing Office.
10. Rubinstein, J.: City police, New York, 1963, Farrar, Straus & Giroux, Inc.
11. Shane, P. G.: The social functions of a civil agency: the police, unpublished thesis, Baltimore, 1975, The Johns Hopkins University.
12. Smith, B.: Police systems in the United States, second revised edition, New York, 1960, Harper & Row, Publishers.
13. Solomon's judgment: now women can seek any job, *Philadelphia Inquirer*, January 10, 1980, p. 1.
14. Study: law enforcement in chaos, *Philadelphia Inquirer*, January 7, 1979, p. 7C.

PART THREE

PRESENT COMPARISONS AND FUTURE IMPLICATIONS

Chapter 10

Comparisons

Although there are major differences in the historical development and organization of police forces in the five countries, the function of the police in all countries is quite similar. There are, of course, cultural differences between the specific tasks with which the police are involved. However, the general functions that police seem to serve in all these societies are similar. In this chapter the differences and similarities of police development, history, organization, and function are examined as related to police forces in Britain, India, Israel, the Netherlands, and the United States.

HISTORY

The police forces represented developed from native and borrowed elements at the end of the eighteenth and beginning of the nineteenth centuries, except for Israel, which became part of the British Commonwealth after World War I. Major reorganization of all the forces except Israel's took place in the middle and late nineteenth century. This reorganization was the basis on which modern police forces in these countries are still functioning. In three of the societies the development of police forces was connected with colonialism and its impact on the colonial society. The forces in India and the Netherlands were originally organized by colonial authorities at the end of the eighteenth century. In both instances the national authorities took over the colonially organized forces on attainment of independence. In the Netherlands this happened only 20 years after the initial formation of the force. In India it took over 160 years. Israel experienced a similar development only over a century later. The Israeli force was initiated by the British in the early 1920s, and independence occurred in the mid-1940s. Both the British and American experiences were not connected to colonialism. The British forces were instituted in 1829 and thereafter, while the American forces began in 1845 and thereafter. The major element found in the development of these police forces was the conceptions of the British police philosophers relating to prevention and patrol.

ORGANIZATION

The way police forces are organized in all five societies is a result of the tensions between local autonomy and national aspirations and power. These tensions have been resolved in different ways in all five countries. There are the completely lo-

182

cally responsible and organizationally autonomous forces of the United States. A combination of local autonomy under national regulation is found in the Netherlands. The county forces of Britain are independent by statute but under strong influence of both the national legislature and the Home Office. In India there is a combination of state-run forces, with a national officers corps serving all states under national legislation. Israel is an example of a national police force with no local autonomy in principle, though the local authorities have influence, almost a reverse of the British and Dutch systems. Of course the population of Israel is equivalent to that of a large city in Britain, India, or the United States, and its size is equivalent to a state or county in these countries. Bases of organization thus run the gamut from independent local forces to one national force.

Within these remarkably different organizational systems the actual outcome in quite similar. Police forces in all five countries are organized in a pyramidal bureaucracy, quasimilitary in manner, under control of the civil authorities. In theory they are divorced from the political fervors of the society. Police are deployed in units in all five countries, centered in district posts or stations. The concept of the small subdistrict, called a sector or beat, which is assigned to particular police for patrolling, is also common in all countries. Police are kept visible and, it is hoped, accessible to the population through patrolling of these beats, either by foot or by vehicle (e.g., horse, bicycle, motorcycle, automobile). Police are also visible through distinctive uniforms (navy blue in all but India where they wear khaki). In all countries police are organized in a ranked pyramidal structure, with greater authority higher on the pyramid. The titles have some similarity to military titles. In all countries but India it is possible for police to progress in the ranking system and achieve high rank and authority. In India there is a bifurcated system. The officers corps is national and separately organized from the lower ranking state forces, in which they provide the administrative and directive elements. In all countries but the United States the ranking systems are the same for all forces. In the United States the function of local autonomy has produced a wide variation in ranking systems. Despite these differences most moderate and large systems operate essentially the same with slight differences in nomenclature.

Specialized units

In each country the police have specialized units. which vary from district to district responding to local conditions. Most of the forces have special criminal investigations units dealing with criminal activities. These units are usually brought into action after the general uniformed police do the initial investigation and reporting. In the United States there are in addition homicide units brought in when there is a death. The criminal investigations unit in other countries handles these situations. In all countries but India there are special units to assume responsibility when situations involve children and youth. In India these types of units exist, but rarely. In larger cities in the United States there are also vice squads responsible for morals situations (i.e., those dealing with sex, gambling, and narcotics). In Britain, Israel, and the Netherlands there are special traffic units throughout the country. In the United States these units are usually found in the state forces and deal generally with highway offences. Most traffic direction in the United is done by regular uniformed police. Thus though the police in all five countries are organized as general service systems, they have specialized units, depending on local conditions, most often criminal investigations units, bomb units (for disposing of bombs and other explosive devices), often juvenile units, traffic units, community relations units, and other special service units.

Women

Women police are in the process of being integrated into the forces in Britain, Israel, the Netherlands, and the United States and to a lesser degree in India. There is variation in the degree to which women have been integrated into forces in these countries. Where there is local autonomy the variations are between forces within the country as well. In some forces there has been a recent commitment to completely integrate women into police duties. In many forces this is resisted in fact if not in law. Wherever women have become active in police work this has happened almost exclusively since the Second World War and has accelerated during the past 20 years. In the United States some forces have been ordered by the courts to integrate women and minorities. There is still a strong feeling that women are able in the helping aspects of police work, but many traditionalists question their use in general police work. The tendency, however, is for women to become more integrated into police work as generalists, functioning with the men.

EQUIPMENT

The equipment of police is becoming more sophisticated in all countries, with obvious differences due to economic factors. Police in the United States, the Netherlands, and Britain generally have motor vehicles and modern radio equipment and computers. In Israel the process is not as far advanced as in the above countries, and in India the process is the least well developed. In the first four countries most people contact the police by telephone. There has been some move toward providing expensive and highly sophisticated equipment for control of hostile groups. This was particularly true in the United States during the later years of the Viet Nam War. The probability is that this tendency has been stopped in the United States and never really developed in the other countries. There is also a move toward demotorizing police in various urban areas of the United States, returning police to a more personal relationship with the people in the area patrolled.

Training

In all five countries police forces provide training for new recruits. The general pattern in Britain, Israel, and the United States is for police to enter at the lowest rank and work their way up in the system. In the Netherlands and the bifurcated system of India, people can enter the police forces above the bottom rank. Training for recruits is provided by the local authorities in Britain, India, and the United States. Training thus is on the county level in Britain, the state level in India, and the municipal or other local authority level in the United States. In Israel training is similar to that in the aforementioned three countries except that it is done by the national police service. All systems provide further training for officers. In the United States this is sometimes done in cooperation with a local college or university and sometimes by the local authority. In India the training of the officers corps is the responsibility of the Indian Police Service (IPS), with several regional training centers distributed around the country. The system in the Netherlands is somewhat more complicated. There is a national police academy at Apeldoorn with a 4-year course for officials. Municipal police officers are trained at six schools around the country. There are 1-year courses for primary forms of training and additional training courses for promotions. In Israel promotions between the four divisions of rank are accompanied by training. The system resembles that of the Netherlands.

The quality and intensity of training varies, particularly in the United States, and emphasis is on the law enforcement aspects of police work in general. In some places the training for police work is equivalent to postsecondary schooling; in other places training may essentially consist of a 3- or 4-month intensive initiation into the police culture. In all places there is a move toward intensifying and broadening the training of police officers and making promotions dependent, at least partially, on further education and training.

Duties

In all five countries the primary legal charge of police forces is the maintenance of law and order. In addition the police are to provide requested help to the public. This is generally subsumed under the concept of keeping the peace. The primary emphasis in all countries is on the maintenance of law and order, crime investigation and prevention, and traffic control. A major unstated duty is simply patrolling assigned sectors or beats. Thus a major duty of police in all countries is to be available in case of need of almost any kind.

In reality there are some differences in duties for police in the five countries. The specific kinds of activities in which police are involved are discussed in greater detail in the discussion of function of police; here only a brief general discussion is given. The major differences are in the addition of administrative tasks to the uniformed police tasks in both Britain and the Netherlands, greater in the Netherlands. What appears to be the province of the Department of Licenses and Inspections or equivalent in most American cities is partially handled by the police in both the Netherlands and Britain. In Britain the involvement is rather minimal. In the Netherlands, on the other hand, police have responsibilities in the area of public health, safety, and economic matters and working conditions that are not the province of police work in the other countries. The concept of public morality is also broader in theory in the Netherlands than in the other countries. In reality the police have apparently withdrawn from much of the work in these areas, at least on a day-to-day basis.

In all countries police are involved in several main categories of work. The area with the most widespread acceptance and sanction is that dealing with law enforcement, the investigation of possible crimes, the search for and apprehension of the culprit(s), and the initial processing of the case. There is a large category of relatively minor crimes in which police are involved as well as the major crimes. There is a residual involvement in morality issues in most countries. These are the areas of sexually related incidents, gambling, and narcotics and in India alcohol. In all of the countries except India this work is currently a very insignificant part of police work, though the police patrolling Times Square in New York and equivalent areas in other cities would probably deny this. In India incidents related to drugs and alcohol were among the most numerous law enforcement incidents.

The police in all countries are involved in a range of activities not directly related to law enforcement but often covered by regulations. Traffic control is the most generalized of these. In all countries police officers are the directors and controllers of traffic. They also are involved in vehicular accidents, which are common in all countries. Another major activity in which police are involved in all countries is patrolling. In Britain, Israel, the Netherlands, and the United States police are involved in monitoring the many alarms of different kinds in places of business and even in residences. These alarms seem to have a high rate of malfunction.

In addition, there is the support aspect of police duties, related to helping people under various circumstances. In all countries a significant part of police duties are involved with responding to requests for help. These requests are of two kinds: arbitration-mediation of conflicts and disputes and responding to people and animals in need. There are cultural differences affecting the distribution of these kinds of tasks in specific police forces and districts, but all the police forces deal with these types of incidents on a regular basis.

Function

Police perform two major social functions in all the countries: social control and social integration. The work of the police is often so close a mixture of these two functions that it is difficult to assign tasks to one or the other function. In this section the composition of police work in the five countries will be compared to see how they specifically carry out the two functions.

The social control function can be said to be the predominant function of law enforcement elements of police work. On the same scale the social integration function can be said to be the predominant function of the support elements of police work (i.e., arbitration-mediation and services). Those types of work that more nearly combine the two functions are the patrol and traffic elements and the administrative elements in those countries in which these are part of police duties. Table 10-1 indicates the percentage and monthly incidence per 1000 population distribution for the various categories of police work in all forces studied.

Social control. The social control function is most clearly represented by the law enforcement activities of the police. This represents less than 10% of total incidents in Britain, about 15% in Israel and the Netherlands, slightly less than 25% in the United States, and from 45% to 60% in India. In Britain, India, and the United States slightly more than half the nonmorals crime-related tasks are primary law enforcement, the more serious crimes. In Israel and the Netherlands slightly more than half of these tasks are the less serious crimes. In all countries the differences between the two generally are not great. Only in India do the morals-related law enforcement incidents constitute a major element in police work, in one case the largest single category, 40%, in the other 20%. This may be related to two variables. One is that there is a prohibition of alcohol in most of India, which would lead to a large amount of illegal alcohol (a major part of the morals situations). The other is that the general incidence of crime is so low that a similar rate of morals situations as exists in other countries examined would lead to a relatively high proportion of all crimes being morals related. In Britain there were no morals-related incidents, and in the other three countries they were almost insignificant.

In all cases the incidence of crimes involving violence (in which there was injury or death) was also very low. In Britain there was no separation of assaults resulting in injuries and without injuries. Assaults in Britain were about 0.7% of the total with an incidence of slightly under 0.1 per 1000 population. In the Netherlands the range of crimes resulting in injury was between 1% and 1.7% of the total, with an incidence of about 0.1 per 1000. In the United States there was a large number of assaults, about 4.5% of the total, with an incidence of almost two per 1000. However, those that resulted in injury constitute less than 1% of total incidents, a monthly incidence of 0.33 per 1000 population. In India, though the percentage of total police work that involved injured people was from 2.2% to 5% the monthly incidence was similar to that found in other countries, a low of 0.04 to 0.1 per 1000 population. Thus the incidence of crimes in which there is violence seems to be quite stable among these countries.

The total law enforcement rates were rather low for all the countries except the United States. The rate for law enforcement in Baltimore was almost 9.5 per 1000 per month. That in India was 1 to 1.3 per 1000 per month. In the other three countries the rates were from 0.2 to 0.65 per thousand per month. Thus, except for the United States, the incidence rate for law enforcement activities per month is one per 1000 population.

Social integration. The social integration function of police work is most clearly represented by the support activities of the police, both arbitration-mediation and services. In all the countries except the United States the arbitration-mediation element of support activities is larger than the service element. In India, Israel, and the Netherlands arbitration-mediation tasks are from twice to five times the service

Table 10-1. Comparative distribution, percent, and incidence per 1000 population

	Britain				India			
	Cheshire		Gloucestershire		Julundur		Ludhiana	
	Per-cent	In-cidence	Per-cent	In-cidence	Per-cent	In-cidence	Per-cent	In-cidence
Support								
Arbitration-mediation	16.3	1.08	14.0	1.84	28.2	0.62	18.7	0.40
Service	11.2	0.70	10.0	1.32	4.9	0.11	6.2	0.13
TOTAL SUPPORT	27.5	1.78	24.0	3.16	33.1	0.73	24.9	0.53
Law enforcement								
Primary law enforcement	6.3	0.48	4.7	0.62	14.1	0.31	11.4	0.24
Other law enforcement	3.5	0.27	2.3	.30	10.5	0.23	10.3	0.22
Morals	—	—	—	—	20.4	0.45	39.9	0.85
TOTAL LAW ENFORCEMENT	9.8	0.75	7.0	0.92	45.1	0.99	61.7	1.31
Traffic	16.4	1.08	19.3	2.56	4.9	0.11	3.6	0.08
Patrol	26.2	1.73	26.9	3.54	9.2	0.20	—	—
Administration	5.0	0.33	5.8	0.77	—	—	—	—
Miscellaneous	15.1	1.01	17.0	2.24	7.7	0.16	9.9	0.20
TOTAL	100.0	6.68	100.0	13.19	100.0	2.19	100.0	2.12

activities. In the United States, Baltimore service incidents are three times the arbitration-mediation incidents. The total of support activities is from one fourth to one half of the total incidents in all cases. In all countries but Britain the range of activities included in services is quite wide and includes most types of situations of people in need, including sick, injured, lost, old, disturbed, missing, drunk, and so forth. In Britain the only type of activity specified is missing and runaway people. Arbitration-mediation activities in all countries cover a wide range. These include family crises and disputes involving neighbors, business, and juvenile and are found in almost every setting. These include disputes in homes, in the street, in places of business, and in public places. Many of the service activities of police are probably not reflected in the data, since they take place while patrolling and are not recorded. It can be seen that in all cases the support aspect of police work is a major aspect of the work of the uniformed police.

Interstitial. There are many activities with which the police deal in all countries that are both control and integrative in function. These are the traffic, patrol, administrative, and miscellaneous activities. In all countries but India these activities together make up at least 35% of all police work and in some cases approach 60% of the total incidents with which police deal. In India they are from slightly less than 15% to 25% of the total. In all cases, therefore, they are a significant element of police work. Since the time spent patrolling is not counted in actuality, this becomes an even more important part of police work. The contact with the public per month

Israel				Netherlands				United States	
Haifa		Jerusalem		Nijmegen		Groningen		Baltimore	
Per-cent	In-cidence	Per-cent	In-cidence	Per-cent	In-cidence	Per-cent	In-cidence	Per-cent	In-cidence
27.5	2.92	38.9	4.66	38.3	2.56	22.0	1.40	9.6	3.85
9.9	1.05	7.2	0.86	7.8	0.52	13.3	0.85	30.4	12.23
37.4	3.97	46.1	5.51	46.1	3.08	35.3	2.25	39.9	16.06
4.4	0.47	7.3	0.88	5.0	0.33	6.7	0.42	12.3	4.91
9.7	1.03	8.7	1.04	7.2	0.48	7.2	0.45	10.8	4.36
0.6	0.06	0.7	0.08	1.6	0.11	0.5	0.03	0.4	0.07
14.7	1.56	16.7	2.0	13.8	0.92	14.1	0.90	23.5	9.42
9.0	0.95	15.0	1.80	13.7	0.91	34.6	2.21	14.9	6.01
21.0	2.23	8.5	1.02	17.4	1.16	10.7	0.68	20.2	8.14
—	—	—	—	4.8	0.35	2.3	0.15	—	—
17.9	1.91	13.7	1.63	4.3	0.29	2.9	0.19	1.5	0.59
100.0	10.62	100.0	11.96	100.0	6.68	100.0	6.38	100.0	40.22

made during these encounters probably greatly affects the concepts most people have of the police in the community. The range of activities involved in these encounters is wider even than that discussed above. Suffice it to say that there is a great similarity in these types of activities between all of the countries examined.

General function

There is a wide range of activities in which police are engaged in all of the countries discussed. What is probably not surprising is that there is an even wider range of incidence of police activities between the countries. This in itself is probably the most surprising difference between the police forces. For example, the total monthly incidence of police incidents in Baltimore was 40.2 per 1000 population. In India, on the other hand, it was less than 2.2 per 1000 population. The monthly incidence in the Netherlands was slightly more than 6 per 1000 population, in Israel between 10.5 and 12 per 1000 population, and in Britain between 6 and 13 per 1000 population. One might thus conclude that the police in the United States, at least in Baltimore, are more active than those in the other countries, and further that the police in Britain, Israel, and the Netherlands are about moderately active and those in India are relatively inactive. This means that the police in the United States have a much higher rate of contact with the public relating to incidents than do those in the other countries. The incidence rate per police person is probably quite similar.

Problems

The problems with which the police seem to be most concerned vary from country to country. There seem to be three main problem areas as seen by authorities: the general organizational relationship of police to governmental bodies, maintaining an adequately staffed police force in terms of quantity and even quality of recruitment, and the relationship of police with the public. In the Netherlands there has been continuous dissatisfaction with the organization of forces in relationship to governmental bodies. This has led to a continuous reassessment of this issue and readjustments. So far the authorities are still not satisfied with the split between municipal and national police and authority vested in the Ministries of Justice and Internal Affairs. Britain has similar problems, but the reorganization of 1967 seems to have resolved the problems for the time being. In the United States there does not seem to be much discussion of this issue, since local autonomy in police matters is very strongly embodied in the political ethos of the country. Of more concern is how to improve the quality of those forces that are not as highly trained and well organized and whether there needs to be greater standardization. This seems to be working itself out through borrowing and consultation between forces.

In Britain and Israel the problem most often discussed by police officials is the problem of maintaining the forces up to strength. Police work is not seen as a primary choice of occupation by enough of the population to keep forces fully staffed. This seems to be a problem in the Netherlands and the United States as well. The problems of understaffing and recruitment exists in those countries with generally adequate alternative employment opportunities.

The most serious problem facing the police in India is that of community relations. This is a problem also in the United States. In India police training material discusses the issue, but there does not appear to be any concerted effort to address this problem as of yet. In part the negative feelings on the part of the public toward the police stem from their identification with the colonial power in preindependence India. In part it is reinforced by the public's perception that police are unreasonably violent and are therefore dangerous. Whether this in fact is true is not clear, but it is the public perception. In the United States certain segments of the population have similar perceptions of and aversions to the police. In some cases it is based on reality, but the probability is that the situation in general has been exaggerated and totalized. The problem of community-police relations is particularly acute in India and the United States.

Police in India face several other problems as well. These are primarily technical and organizational problems, however. Communications and transport are major deficiencies in police work in India. The telephone is rudimentary in most of the country, particularly interurban, and there is a shortage of vehicles. Another area that might be problematic is the bifurcation between national officers corps and state police corps. One area in which this does prove somewhat problematic is in possibilities of lingual incompatability between officers and local population. In other words, the officer may not speak the local language.

There are a number of problems that are unique to the police of the United States. Along with those mentioned above, understaffing and community relations, police forces in the United States are faced with a host of serious problems, though not all universal or faced by any one force necessarily. They seem to stem from three sources: (1) the deep-rooted philosophy of local autonomy, (2) the major social changes and readjustments of status lines within the society, and (3) the multiplicity of policing agencies and levels. There are problems of morale, wide diversity in standards and quality, diversity in training quality and educational level, turnover, development of private voluntary and mercenary policing groups, and police-community relations.

It is seen that the problems that police forces face in the various countries are quite different, though there is overlap. All but India are experiencing recruitment and understaffing problems. The Netherlands is moving toward a reorganization and planned streamlining of police organization. Israeli police have a public in which familiarity sometimes seems to breed contempt. They are also faced with major problems of security due to hostile relations with neighboring countries and people not found in other countries. Indian police are faced with a community relations problem as well as deficiencies in communications links and transport. The bifurcation of national and state police services may also introduce problematic elements. In the United States the independence of local police forces leaves a wide disparity in quality, quantity, training, equipment, morale, and other factors. There are also the problems of multiplicity and duplication. The United States thus seems to have the most functional problems in terms of policing of any of the countries.

In many ways police are at the cutting edge of social change. The police forces examined were born and developed during times of social change and disorder. Times are again in a state of change and in some places disorder. The police are apparently going through major changes in some places parallel to the social changes. This is particularly evident in the United States, though it is true elsewhere as well. In Britain, after 150 years, the police are finally being given guns, though not yet as part of their uniforms. In the Netherlands there is to be a reorganization. In the United States the growth of the private, often voluntary, citizen patrolling groups is a major sign of change. Will these be institutionalized? One does not know. Numerous studies have called for changes in American policing organization, training, and practices. The shape of police work in the United States in the near future may be very different from what is now found. The police organization in the other four countries, though it may be somewhat altered, will probably remain the same for some time.

SUMMARY

The police forces in the five countries examined developed during periods of social stress and change. For all the forces except Israel's, major developments took place during the mid-nineteenth century, which has effectively shaped the forces since then. Israel's force had its genesis under colonial conditions during the period between the two world wars. The post–World War II period brought significant changes to most societies and police forces. In India and Israel there was the advent of independence and the reshaping of these forces to serve and support an independent nation. In Britain there was consolidation of forces at first, leading to the eventual formation of countywide forces. In the Netherlands reorganization was designed to strengthen municipal control and standardization throughout the country. In the United States the regrowth of professionalism and increasing demands for higher training and education, accompanied by major changes in society, movements of population, and increasing diminution of the centrality of cities to American life, affected police development.

Though the forces examined are responsible to different levels of government and are coordinated in different ways, from complete local autonomy to one national police force, the basic structures of all are similar. There is the pyramidal, quasimilitary bureaucracy, under civil control. Police are stationed in units throughout the country and its political subdivisions, down to the local community. They are assigned territories for patrolling, and they wear uniforms. There are generally nonspecialized units that carry the main burden of everyday policing. There are also support units specializing in various areas such as criminal, juvenile, and traffic.

Women play various roles in the police in these five countries. In the United States they are in the process of becoming integrated into all types of police work and at most levels, in many jurisdictions, often under court order. In Britain and Israel women police operated in semiprotected areas somewhat stereotypic in nature (i.e., juvenile, women, traffic, and office work). In the Netherlands there is a similar situation, though women are still generally integrated in police forces only in the larger urban areas. In India there are very few women in police work. Thus there is almost a progression from near exclusion to the drive toward total integration of women in police forces.

In all five countries the responsible authorities sponsor training for new police recruits and officers. In addition officers in Britain, India, Israel, and the Netherlands are expected to have university level education. Sometimes this education is sponsored by police authorities. In the United States there is movement toward requiring such higher education for police in general.

The duties of the police in all countries are rather similar. Uniformed general police are charged with the maintenance of law and order, prevention of crime, and provision of help to the general population. In both Britain and the Netherlands police additionally have responsibility for administrative tasks. In reality these tasks are not too great a part of the everyday duties of police.

The major part of police work in all but India is support activities, including services to people in need and arbitration-mediation of a vast range of conflicts and disputes. It is contended that this work is related to social integration and is part of the social integration function of police. Another major part of police work is patrolling and traffic control and incidents. These activities are both integrative and social control in function. The social control function of police is primarily carried out through law enforcement activities. These are about 10% to 20% of police work in all but India, in which violence occurred in no more than 10%. In India almost 50% of incidents in which police are involved are law enforcement in nature.

The integrative function of police varies widely. Though police are involved in these types of activities, the dominant activities are different from culture to culture. In all countries except the United States the arbitration-mediation activities are the majority of social support tasks.

Problems of police vary from country to country. In all but India there is a general problem of getting and keeping police personnel. Problems of understaffing and recruitment are common in the countries in which employment is not a major problem for upwardly mobile and educated people. In Britain police are moving to deal with social changes, toward a more heterogeneous society, with conflict between groups and growing violence. In India police suffer from the lack of tech- nologic support (i.e., telephones, radios, and cars) common in the other countries. In Israel police must deal with problems of security and terrorism. In the Netherlands there is a planned reorganization to further clarify the issues of local control, the dual system of local and national police, and the dual responsibilities of the ministries of Justice and Interior. In the United States police forces are faced with a host of problems, many related to local autonomy and the multiplicity of policing agencies.

Police at the cutting edge of social change are faced with many challenges in the years to come. They will be called on to deal with an increasingly changing world, in both values and expectations. The relationships between groups is changing as well, with formerly powerless groups demanding and gaining power. These conditions demand flexibility and understanding from the agencies of society and particularly so from police.

Chapter 11

Discussion and implications

The original instructions to the Metropolitan police forces stressed that
. . . every member of the force must remember that it is his duty to protect and
help members of the public, no less than to bring offenders to justice.[2,p.89]

There are several areas in which the material in this examination of police work
in five countries might have implications for future developments in police work.
One is the response to and preparation for support tasks by police forces and police
themselves. Another is the relationship between effective nontyrannical policing
and local autonomy. The questions arise whether the problems which arise in situations where police are locally autonomous are balanced by the protections for individual and group freedom and human rights afforded by such autonomy. Are
there indeed necessarily connections between governmental control of policing and
tyranny? These issues will be dealt with in turn.

The first issue is whether there is some natural balance between integrative
and control aspects of police work. Are there natural demands for supportive activities on the part of police that cannot be shifted? What should police do about
this aspect of police work? It is assumed that the law enforcement, traffic, and patrol aspects of police work are not at question. It is also assumed that the police are
currently performing these tasks with relative comfort and effectiveness. The big
question is, what are police doing when they intervene in interpersonal conflicts,
family crises, and so on, and when they respond to people in need? Are they really
helping? Do they often exacerbate the problem? Does it have to be dangerous?
Why indeed do people ask police for help and why do police perform these types
of tasks? Is police training adequate to enable police to positively respond to requests for help in these areas? Some of these issues will be discussed on the following
pages.

POSSIBLE REASONS FOR DEMAND FOR SUPPORTIVE POLICE ACTIVITIES

There are a number of possible reasons for the demand for police provision of
supportive services:

1. The police are always available and do not charge for service. Almost all other
   support agencies are available at set times during the day and week and often

cost money. The police are on duty 24 hours a day, seven days a week, every day of the year.

2. The police are generalists. People in distress do not have to diagnose problems and decide which specialist to call.
3. Police deal with any and all problems brought to their attention.
4. Police respond rapidly to immediate problems.
5. Police have transportation in Britain, Israel, the Netherlands, and the United States and not only go to scenes of difficulty but can also provide transportation to some other service agency if need be.
6. Police have authority by delegation and authorization. The police are the most accessible deliverers of short-term, acute, and unspecialized supportive services in industrialized urban settings.

From the viewpoint of a professional in the social support system, the data indicate that the police are an integral though not necessarily acknowledged part of the support system of society in the countries examined. Several professionals in the health and welfare service system have written about cooperative projects done with the police in the United States, Canada, and Britain.* These investigators have seen the police as natural allies of the human service delivery system.

The policing function was part of the management function of early government in England. Other functions previously included in the societal management function, such as health and welfare, have moved toward independence from the general management aspect of government in the modern era. The development of specially trained professionals and specializing agencies has been concomitant with the gain of independence from the management aspect of government. Independence from the governmental management functions has resulted in deemphasis on societal cost benefit evaluation and increased emphasis on the quality of service delivered. The move toward specially trained professionals in police forces has led in the same direction toward increased independence from the general management function of government. This has raised the question of what professional role police will assume in support functions.

Developments of police professionalization has led to conscious deliberation about the supportive police role. Police forces can continue either to rank supportive activities secondary to law enforcement activities or to change their perceptions of the support role. A change in priorities might lead either to greater emphasis or active rejection of support activities by police forces.

POSSIBLE REASONS FOR RESPONSE BY POLICE

There are alternative suggestions about the reasons for police performance of support activities. One suggestion is that police use such activities to fill spare time. This would be indicated if the support activities were inversely related to the norm

---

*References 1, 3, 4, 13, 15, 16.

enforcement activities of the police. This is not found to be a consistent pattern. It is not true in urban Britain, Israel, the Netherlands, and the United States but is true in rural Britain and very slightly so in India. This leads to the conclusion that there is in general no replacement of law enforcement activities by support activities.

A second suggestion is that the more available police there are, the more support activities they will perform. Rank order correlations were performed on Baltimore data, testing for correlations between the number of police per 1000 population and the incidence of both support and law enforcement activities.[11] Both aspects of police work were found to correlate with the number of police per 1000 population. There are two problems with this. One is that police are assigned more heavily to districts with high activity rates. The other is that, unfortunately, the number of police per 1000 population does not necessarily indicate the number of working police available to respond to incidents. A study done in New York City and Kansas City shows that only a small proportion of working policemen are available on the streets at any one time. In New York City, with a police force of 31,000 persons, only 1000 are available for response to calls at any one time.[12] (With 31,000 police personnel on three shifts, there would be only 10,000 per shift. Subtract from this officials, those working in the central office, 7-day weeks with 5-day tours of duty, sick days, vacations, and personnel on special duty as well as in special units. One can begin to see how few people really are available for any period of time on a regular basis.) Thus it is difficult to show from the overall police per population ratio what the actual availability of police are for response to calls for assistance of any kind.

The correlation between the police per population ratio found is not a reliable statement of the number of available police at any one time. The only conclusion that can be drawn from the direct rank order correlation between police per 1000 population and the incidence of supportive and law enforcement police activities found is that more police work is done in areas with a higher assigned police per population ratio. However, no conclusions as to causality can be drawn from this information. It can mean that more police are assigned in areas where there are the highest demands for police activity. This is suggested by police officials. It could mean inversely that having the high police to population ratio causes the high activity level of the police. This could be either through being more available for response to calls for help or through the manufacture of incidents to provide work for the higher number of police. Thus there are no definite findings in the research to support or reject the hypothesis that it is the number of police per population that influences the amount of support police activities.

One fact is clear. In all countries studied the findings indicate that police work includes major elements of support activities, including arbitration-mediation activities, and a large variety of human service activities. Support police activities are correlated with social need.

From the origins of the English police forces it was intended that the police perform support activities. This has not become less important in the intervening years, as has been seen. Other commentators also have noted an increase in the importance of support police activities over the years:

Rising expectations, population growth, and urbanization exert ever greater pressures on the embattled police agencies. One thing is certain: the pressures on the police can only increase in the years ahead. Continued erosion of the authority of the schools, the churches and the family and other institutions of social control leaves the law enforcement agencies to deal alone with some of society's deepest problems. [10, p. 171]

The police will have to respond to the pressures, whether due to erosion of social control or to an increase for need of societal inputs into the support system.

Some investigators suggest that police training be oriented to reflect the importance of the support role that they play. Expanding the training of police to include greater emphasis on the social, psychological, and physical needs of people is suggested in a number of studies written by and for the police. In one of the popular books recently written about the subject in the United States the following statement is made:

In the personal view I had, I found complex and sometimes confused individuals grappling first hand with the sickness of society while the rest of us theorize about prevention and cure. [14]

Policemen are not loath to get involved with the "sickness of society." Yet it is often noted that the police are not sufficiently trained to handle problems of a social, economic, or other non-law-enforcement nature.

Inadequacy of training often leads to aggravation of problem situations rather than solutions to such situations:

In a three year study of the New York City Police Department the author, in reviewing "critical incidents" involving police and citizens, was initially struck by the extent to which the handling of relatively minor incidents such as traffic violations or disorderly disputes between husbands and wives seemed to create a more serious situation than existed prior to the police attempt to control the situation. A family dispute might have been merely noisy prior to the entrance of a police officer. After his entrance, personal violence often became more likely to occur in all possible combinations and permutations of assaulter and assaultee. In this type of situation police often found it difficult to be an impartial and disinterested third party. Patrolmen were often assaulted by a wife armed with a frying pan when they used "necessary force in restraining" a husband who, moments before, had been loudly denouncing his wife and publicly calling into question her species membership. [5, p. 169]

The skills needed in support areas of intervention are professional skills. Police should have a sophisticated and educated conception of human needs and function in order to perform support activities. At the present time dependence on "common sense" rather than training for handling of human problems persists among police trainers in American police academies:

Since the tasks of developing and maintaining these [interpersonal] skills is an extremely difficult one, many academy personnel involved in the selection and training of recruits tended to treat the matter as one of having common sense or not having it. They assumed that common sense is something that you have or you do not. That is, an ability that cannot be developed or taught.[5,p.220]

The reliance on skills that "cannot be developed or taught" in performance of support activities by the police is not in consonance with the experience of mental health professionals, such as Bard, who have helped train police in performance of support service activities.[1,p.78]

Experiences in training police for support activities have pointed to the benefits of such training as well as the need for it. The Task Force report was explicit in its suggestions along these lines:

The quality of police service will not significantly improve until higher educational requirements are established for its personnel. . . . The complexity of the police task is as great as that of any other profession. The performance of this task requires more than physical prowess and common sense.[8,p.126]

The successes in such training indicate the value it has. Bard, in his report on the development of the Family Crisis Intervention Unit in the Twenty-fourth Precinct of the New York City Police Department had the following to say about the value of training:

It is our impression that increased professional responsibility increased job satisfaction. Mastery of technical skills and the challenge of decision making responsibility are conducive to high morale in all occupations. . . . It is our impression also that policemen themselves feel more secure and less defensive generally when they have professional skills equal to the increasing complexities of their role.[1,p.78]

There are indications of a need for training and also benefit in terms of police self-concept in more and better training for support roles of the police.

There is also benefit for the improvement of service delivery in the development of a policeman professionally trained to perform support functions:

By increasing the sensitivity and professional perceptiveness of policemen, an unusually early warning mechanism of identifying psychological and social pathology is made available to the community. . . . [The trained policeman] became a resource for a range of human problems. Their trained ability to discriminate among the problems and their knowledge of the options open to them permitted the officers to move in helpful directions and yet remain faithful to their basic peace-keeping mission.[1,p.79]

Many American police forces are not particularly enthusiastic about college-educated police, even those with incentives for police to get college educations. The police officers themselves are often increasingly enthusiastic about going to college while on the force. In Baltimore the community college schedules a number of classes, particularly those in the social sciences and humanities, so that people on "swing shifts" can keep up with the course work. Swing shift is what many police and fire personnel work, sometimes day shift, sometimes evenings and sometimes nights. Two sections of a course will be taught early and late by the same instructor and with the same syllabus. Students in the course can attend either session, depending on the shift that they are working that week. The courses are very popular, and a large percentage of the students in these sections are police. In 1978 Philadelphia had 8000 police officers. Of this some 500 had bachelor's degrees and about 2500 had attended some college. A 1974 study showed that nationwide about 46% of police officers had at least 1 year of college. The rate of increase in this percentage over the preceding years indicated that by the mid-1980s about 75% of police officers in the United States will have attained that educational level.[9] Police surveyed suggested that they felt the additional education also helps police prepare for other careers.

A police training guide suggests that policemen should try to assist the citizen who is engulfed by forces beyond his control to deal with them constructively.[2,p.80] This all suggests that one element of police represented by the LEAA and their advisors are leading in the direction of increasing the training of policemen in both quantity and quality so as to better equip them to relate to and understand people as well as to deal with an increasingly complex and changing society.

It should be emphasized that increasing educational levels and training requirements will not necessarily do the job. The Ford Foundation report suggests that there must be an increasing sophistication in the use of education for police. Hit-or-miss education will not do the job. The suggestion is that police receive university level education in the social sciences in general educational institutions and that police education focus on the integration of that material and its application to police work.[7]

One thing is clear. Police can work much more effectively when they are adequately educated and trained for this complex and important work.

In addition to proposals to add to police training there have been proposals for reorganizing the service delivery system and integrating police into it. The proposal was made in 1967 by the President's Commission on Law Enforcement and the Administration of Justice—Task Force on the Police. In the proposal there is discussion of reorganizing the human service delivery system to be a more completely integrated and responsive system in which the police play a major role. In the original concept the police were to be part of the intake screening unit of a general service system. However, there are a number of roles that police might conceivably play within such a system. The concept is to develop community service centers providing multiple services in local areas and feeding into a more comprehensive system. As part of the intake screening unit, police would refer persons to the unit with adequate information and "individual decision would then be made on what should be done in each case—whether the persons should be processed through court, treated at a hospital or mental health clinic, or given social counseling and help in finding a job or in going back to school."[8,p.163] Further, the proposal sees the police station as an integral part of a community service center:

Precinct stations might well be a part of community service centers. Meeting halls and athletic facilities could be opened to the public; other services, such as employment assistance or family counseling, could be in adjoining offices.[8,p.163]

This proposal is something to look to in plans for the future development of a less fragmented public support system than that which exists in the United States now.

A comparison of police work in the five countries studied might give support to such a scheme. We see that police are involved in a much smaller range of service activities in those countries with well-developed service systems (i.e., Britain, the Netherlands, and Israel). Though they still do get involved with people in need, this is a much smaller part of their task than that of police in the urban areas of the United States, as exemplified by Baltimore. This might indicate that the very heavy police involvement in such service activities in the United States is indeed a reflection of the inadequacy of the total service delivery system and the difficulty many people have in reaching it for help.

An alternative approach is taken in the Soviet Union. Many support activities are delegated to nonpolice agencies, in theory. Health, physical, and mental services are available at all times through health agencies. In all areas of the country there are three emergency phone numbers: 01 to 03. These bring the fire department, police department, physical health ambulance, or mental health ambulance to emergencies.[6] A response to the difficulties found in the human service delivery system might well be to divest the police of their responsibilities in these areas and develop a universal and equally accessible generalized alternative gateway to the human service delivery system. It is possible that it might be most reasonable for society to allocate its resources in this manner, particularly in light of the many questions within police systems and outside them as to whether the provision of support services is what the police should be doing. An additional question is whether the police are capable of handling the situations with which they are called on to deal in the most helpful and appropriate manner. Thus an alternative is the reorganization of the human service delivery system to handle most of the support activities police have been handling and leaving police forces primarily with law enforcement activities to perform. This would be dependent, naturally, on a rationalization of the service delivery system and simplification of access to it, far from guaranteed in the United States.

When one compares the problems of police in the United States and those in the other four countries examined, there is one striking observation. The police in the United States are plagued with many very difficult functional problems, while this is not true of police in the other countries. In the main the problems seem to stem from the way local autonomy has developed in policing in the United States and the coincidental multiplicity of agencies with policing powers and responsibilities. In none of the other countries are policing powers and responsibilities so dispersed, fragmental, duplicative, unstandardized, and disorganized. In none of these countries is it conceivable to have the kinds of police scandals that at times rock various American forces. This is primarily due to the checks that exist on local police through "supervision" by higher levels of government and mandates that more centralized governments have given local authorities for policing. It is, of course, probably unrealistic to expect the commitment to local autonomy to be weakened in the foreseeable future in the United States. However, a similar commitment has been successfully transmuted in the United Kingdom.

In the United Kingdom there was a similar development of locally autonomous police forces throughout the country. The philosophy of the new police, however, and the changes in society toward a more standardized approach to dealing with social issues led to the amalgamation of local forces and the final emergence of autonomous but regulated county forces. There is a similar pattern in the Netherlands. The growth of municipal police and even local direction of national police units was tempered by the guidance and support of the national government. This has ensured a minimum standard for all forces and a universality of police coverage and function that seems to be beneficial. It has not done away with a flexibility to respond to local needs and differences. Thus the police in Gloucestershire and Cheshire differ in many ways, as do the police of Groningen and Nijmegen. Nor has it done away with local autonomy. An example in the United States is the unified police system of Baltimore County, Maryland. The above examples have married local autonomy and general governmental guidance so that some of the bizarre variations in police forces within the country and the intendent strains on police work would be minimized.

The main fear, of course, is that of a "police state." However, local autonomy has not in any way inhibited the growth of police powers on higher levels of government. A police state could as easily develop from federal and state policing organizations as from more centralized and equally trained and supported local police organizations. It would also remove them from the political system more effectively and render them less subject to local conditions leading to corruption. County police forces are to all intents and purposes independent in the United Kingdom, and municipal forces are equally independent in the Netherlands. However, there is a great accountability to higher authorities and a sharing of information and other resources that at present is unlikely in the United States. The situation in both the United Kingdom and the Netherlands also does away with the multitude of policing agencies and levels found in the United States. These are certainly viable alternatives in equally democratic countries that could be examined for possible application with the United States.

This is particularly relevant in an age when most other instruments of government have made some attempt to adjust to the conditions of life in a modern, mobile society. Boundaries of towns and cities are irrelevant for most functions of life in the modern United States. It makes no sense for them to be the governing force in police organization. At the same time, local autonomy is not in essence threatened by rationalization of police organization into more standardized and reasonable units.

SUMMARY

Implications for further developments of police forces and the total supportive system in the societies examined deal mainly with the role that police should have in the support system of a society with the problems of local autonomy in the United States. It is suggested that police forces presently are a natural and integral, though often unacknowledged, element of the society support system as well as that of social control. They provide support service for many kinds of problems and are available at any time without a fee. They fill the gaps in service left by the other agencies of society. The extent to which they deal with a wide range of activities may reflect the inability of other institutions within the society to fulfill social needs. The responses to requests for service are provided relatively quickly, at the source of the problem and without need for prior diagnosis. At the same time police in the United States and elsewhere are generally not trained sufficiently to provide these services to their or the public's satisfaction. The problem is most acute in many forces in the United States. There are a number of ways to resolve the problems that therefore arise.

The choices for a future police role in support services are several in theory. Police forces can either continue to play a role in support activities, socially integrative activities, or attempt to abandon this responsibility. In essence there are three alternatives. One alternative is that police forces be more completely integrated into a reorganized service delivery system. A partial example is the relationship between police and social service agencies in Britain. A second alternative is that the human service delivery system remain the way it is in the various countries, whether with the police continuing to operate as they presently are or with more comprehensive training to better equip them to handle the support activities they already perform. A third alternative is replacing the police in the support system with alternative generalized service agencies. Training for police needs to reflect the increasingly complex role of police whether there is greater integration into the service system or not.

Implications for the United States specifically are that the current system of organization has led to many severe problems for both police and society. These problems are related to the complete local autonomy of generalized police forces and the multiplicity of policing agencies on all levels of government. Completely autonomous local police agencies lead to incomplete coverage, wide diversity in quality, standards, training, fragmentation, disorganization, duplication of effort and expenditures, and possibilities of corruption. It has led American police to feel alienated and frustrated and for citizens to feel similarly about police. Similar problems are not found in the more standardized and simpler though locally autonomous police systems of Britain and the Netherlands. Local autonomy can be compatible with accountability to higher authorities and amalgamation of forces as found in these two countries. It is suggested that rationalization of police systems into more standardized units with higher governmental influence might help solve some of the major problems of police work in the United States.

REFERENCES

1. Bard, M.: Training police as specialists in family crisis intervention, United States Department of Justice, Washington, D.C., 1970, U.S. Government Printing Office.
2. Berkley, G. E.: The democratic policeman, Boston, 1969, Beacon Press.
3. Canadian police argue, *Macleans*, October 1970, p. 1.
4. Fleming, T.: The policeman's lot, American Heritage **21**(2):4, 1970.
5. McNamara, J. H.: Uncertainties in police work. In Bordua, D. J., editor: The police: six sociological studies, New York, 1967, John Wiley & Sons, Inc.
6. Number of police have no effect on crimes, *New York Times*, February 24, 1975, p. E-5.
7. Policy of encouraging policemen to attend college challenged, *New York Times*, November 28, 1978, p. A-20.
8. President's Commission on Law Enforcement and the Administration of Justice, Task Force on the police: Task force report: the police, Washington, D.C., 1967, U.S. Government Printing Office.
9. In pursuit of degrees, not just criminals, *Philadelphia Inquirer*, September 25, 1978, p. 1-A.
10. Saunders, C. B., Jr.: Upgrading the American police, Washington, D.C., 1970, The Brookings Institute.
11. Shane, P. G.: The social functions of a civil agency, unpublished thesis, Baltimore, 1975, The Johns Hopkins University.
12. Wallach, I.: The police function in a Negro community, vol. 2, McLean, Va., 1970, Research Analysis Corp.
13. Westley, W. A.: Violence and the police: a sociological study of law, custom, and morality, Cambridge, Mass., 1970, MIT Press.
14. Whittemore, L. H.: COP!, New York, 1969, Fawcett World Library.
15. Whittington, H. G.: The police: ally or enemy of the comprehensive mental health center?, Mental Health **55**(1):55, 1971.
16. World Health Organization: Programme development in the mental health field, WHO Tech. Rep. Ser. 223, 1961.

Appendixes

Appendix A

Rural Indian police station, Punjab

Station: Nakodar (serves rural area)
Area: 12 × 15 miles
Villages: 133
Population: 400,000 to 500,000
Personnel: 12 constables, general duty; 3 clerks; 1 constable liaison with court; 3 detectives; 1 station head officer; 2 assistant subinspectors
Distribution of work: investigation, detection, prevention, prosecution of crimes
Duty: 24 hours, 7 days
Daily Diary: running account of work of station, kept by clerk (munshee) 24 hours per day.
At least every hour an entry is made, even if "Nothing to report."
Phone Calls—change of guard.

EXAMPLE OF DAILY DIARY
Sunday, November 7, 1971

8:00 AM	Daily Diary for day started.
	Building has been cleaned.
	Evidence and station in order.
	List of cognizable cases under investigation.
8:30	Departure of assistant Subinspector and three constables armed with rifles and 50-50 cartridges for patrol duty.
8:35	Departure of officer and assistant subinspector for patrol duty in Miranput.
9:00	Change of sentry.
10:00	No complaint.
10:30	Trunk call message to controller in Jullundur.
11:30	No complaint.
NOON	Change of sentry,
12:15 PM	Report by individual that he was physically abused, but no fractures with blunt weapon. Noncognizable. Assigned to assistant subinspector.
1:00	Return of patrol from Miranpur.
2:00	New constable and detectives reported for duty on transfer from other station with particulars on constable.
2:30	Departure of station head officer in connection with investigation of case FIR #400/71 under particular section.
3:00	Change of sentry.
4:00	Nothing to report.
4:15	Head constable arrived to get arms. Left on patrol of town.
5:00	Return of 8:30 AM patrol. Names of villages patrolled. Checked licenses (for arms) in general. Left two constables in area to check on bad characters, habitual offenders.

5:30	Dusk patrol left.
5:35	Home guard left on patrol.
5:40	Phone message to control.
5:45	Home guard members report.
6 PM	Report of who is present on patrol, etc.
6:15	Return of 2:30 PM patrol. Details of compromise made in noncognizable offense.
6:20	Departure of assistant subinspector for Amritsar for testifying in court in a case under cognizable offense (attempt at murder).
6:25	Departure of station head officer for dusk patrol.
6:45	Report of head constable on recovery of illicit alcoholic beverages and request to enter case in FIR.
7:45	No report.
8:45	No report.
9:00	Change of sentry.
9:45	Clerk to sleep. Left Daily Dairy with assistant. Station head officer returned after patrol. Took unconscious drunk to hospital.
9:55	Arrival of head constable (see 6:45 PM).
10:00	Arrival of assistant subinspector in (see 5:30 PM). Preventive patrol; no incidents.
10:15	Head constable (see 4:15 PM) returned. No incidents.
10:30	Call control in Jullundur.
Midnight	Change of sentry.
2:00 AM	No report.
3:00	Change of sentry.
5:00	No report.
5:30	Call to control.
6:00	Change of sentry.
6:30	Constable sent to serve summons for cognizable offense.
7:00	Roll call: who present, on patrol.
7:30	Call to deputy superintendent of police for discussion of cognizable case.
8:00	Close of Daily Diary.
	Account of money on hand.

Patrol diary: Jerusalem, November 24, 1971

Time	Incident	Action taken
6 0700	Army draft card found by patrolman	Lost-and-found department
7 0709	Suspected thief apprehended at youth hostel by regional patrolman	Suspect handed to investigation branch
8 0715	Damage caused on Cordova Road, Gigat Shaul (notified by citizen)	Criminal investigation file opened by sergeant major
9 0730	Road blocked at 5, R St. (notified by citizen)	Car left before police arrived
10 0739	Suspect (stolen) motor car found	Transferred by unit to car pound
11 0745	Fire at residence	False alarm
12 0820	Internee at mental institution escaped	Found by patrol and returned to hospital
13 0850	Trees being uprooted in K district (citizen complaint)	Investigated by patrolman and found legitimate; case closed
15 0850	Traffic accident, no injuries	Drivers exchanged information; no file opened
16 0939	Parking on pavement in residential area	No cars found on investigation
17 0935	Assault and battery at residence (notified by citizen)	No complainant or attacker found
18 0940	Public disturbance and damage caused in TV building	Investigation file opened by sergeant major
19 0940	Traffic accident, damage only (TA/DO)	TA file opened by patrolman
20 0955	Public disturbance in B St.	Disturbee removed from premises and warned not to repeat, case closed (R & W)
21 0955	Alarm at bank in residential area	Technical fault
22 1000	TA/DO	Reported to complaint officer (CO)
23 1000	Motor scooter suspected of being stolen	Transferred to pound
24 1002	Street dispute in business area	Officer mediated and effected compromise
25 1005	Business dispute	Officer mediated and effected compromise
26 1012	Complaint person bothering another in market	Investigation file opened at complainant's insistance
27 1040	Damage in residential area	Complainant cancelled complaint when patrolman came
28 1115	Traffic accident, injury	Referred to traffic department
29 1115	Disturbance at community center	Investigation file opened (trespassing)
30 1120	Disturbance in private home	Complaint withdrawn by phone

31	1122	Quarrel between neighbors in residential area	Suggested civil action
32	1127	Suspicious death at hospital	Transferred to investigation department
33	1145	Lost child	Held at police station until reclaimed
34	1145	TA/DO	Traffic file opened
35	1203	Assault and battery in residentail area	Compromise reached
36	1210	Disturbance at national health clinic	Disturbed R & W
37	1235	Disturbance at business area	Disturbed R & W
38	1250	Police assist, dispute in business area	Compromise reached
39	1310	Neighbor dispute in residential area	Both sides warned to keep peace
40	1325	Assault and battery at ritual bath; incident result of contempt of court (disobeyed court order)	Transferred to investigation department
41	1355	Stolen motor scooter found	Transferred to pound
42	1410	Lost child	Held at station until reclaimed
43	1410	TA/DO	Complainant withdrew complaint

Police log: Haifa, Israel, November 24, 1971

Time		Incident	Action taken
17	0715	Execution of message (wireless), residential area	Carried out
18	0715	Burglary, residential	Criminal Investigation Division
19	0730	Damage to property (shop)	Complaints office
20	0740	Threat, residential	Settled
21	0810	Conflict, business area	Complaints office
22	0830	Burglary, residential area	Criminal Investigation Division
23	0845	Conflict, residential area	Help refused
CO	0845	Conflict (came to station), residential	Dealt with by complaints officer
24	0900	Suspicious persons at school	Nothing suspicious found
25	0905	Breach of peace, garage	Settled
26	1015	Insult, business area	Settled
27	1015	Police assistance requested	Given
28	1035	Execution of message (wireless)	Carried out
29	1120	Threat, residential suburb	Settled
30	1150	Execution of message (wireless)	Carried out
31	1200	Breach of peace	Settled
CO	1200	Assault	Dealt with by complaints officer (CO)
32	1205	Found wallet	Lost-and-Found Department
33	1210	Execution of message (wireless)	Carried out
34	1210	Police assistance	Settled
35	1215	Breach of peace, port area	Settled
CO	1215	Disorderly behavior	Complaints officer
36	1250	Search for addresses	Passed to officer
37	1300	Execution of written message	Carried out
38	1305	Transfer of detainee from port to complaints officer	Carried out
39	1310	Conflict, residential	Settled
40	1310	Suspicion of stolen scooter	Not stolen
41	1410	Traffic accident, injury	Traffic section
42	1310	Willful damage to property	Dealt with by complaints officer

Bibliography

Abrecht, M. E.: The making of a woman cop, New York, 1976, William Morrow & Co., Inc.

Abu-Lughod, J. L.: Testing the theory of social area analysis: the ecology of Cairo, Egypt, in Am. Sociolog. Rev. 34:198, 1969.

Aiken, M., and Alford, R.: Community structure and innovation: the case of urban renewal, Am. Sociolog. Rev. 35:650, 1970.

Anderson, D.: Public institutions: their war against the development of black youth, Am. J. Orthopsychiatry 41(1)65, 1971.

Arm, W.: The policemen: an inside look at his role in a modern society, New York, 1969, E. P. Dutton & Co., Inc.

Articles on disturbances and murder in Borough Park, *New York Times*, December 2-6, 1978, p. 1.

Balch, R.: The police personality: fact or fiction? J. Criminal Law, Crimonol. Pol. Sci. 63:1, 1972.

Baltimore Sun, January 16, 1973, p. A20.

Banton, M.: The policeman in the community, New York, 1961, Basic Books, Inc., Publishers.

Bard, M.: Training police as specialists in family crisis intervention, United States Department of Justice, Washington, D.C., 1970, U.S. Government Printing Office.

Bayley, D. H.: Forces of order: police behavior in Japan and the United States, Berkeley, Calif., 1978, University of California Press.

Bayley, D. H.: The police and political development in Europe, unpublished draft, Denver, 1970, University of Denver.

Bayley, D. H.: The police and political development in India, Princeton, N.J., 1969, Princeton University Press.

Berkley, G. E.: The democratic policeman, Boston, 1969, Beacon Press.

Billingsley, A.: Family functioning in the low income black community, Social Casework December 1969, p. 563.

Billingsley, R.: Black families and white social science. In Ladner, J., editor: The death of white sociology, New York, 1968, Vintage Books, Random House, Inc.

Billingsley, A.: Black families in white America. Englewood Cliffs, N.J., 1968, Prentice-Hall, Inc.

Bittner, E.: The functions of the police in modern society, Washington, D.C., 1970, National Institute of Mental Health, U.S. Government Printing Office.

Black, A.: The people and the police, New York, 1968, McGraw-Hill Book Co.

Boorstin, D. J.: The Americans: the colonial experience, New York, 1958, Vintage Books, Random House, Inc.

Bordua, D. J., editor: The police: six sociological essays, New York, 1967, John Wiley & Sons, Inc.

Buoma, D.: Kids and cops, Grand Rapids, Mich., 1969, Wm. B. Eerdmans Publishing Co.

Calhoun, J. B.: Plight of the Ik and Kaiadilb, Smithsonian 3:8, November 1972.

Canadian police argue, Macleans, October 1970, p. 1. Catching runaways before the street gets them, *New York Times*, April 13, 1978, p. B1.

Cavan, R. S.: Juvenile delinquency: development, treatment and control, ed. 2, New York, 1968, J. B. Lippincott Co.

Cheshire Police Authority: The Cheshire constabulary, Wilmslow, England, 1970, Cheshire County Council.

Church Assembly Board for Social Responsibility: Police: a social study, Oxford, England, 1967, Church Army Press.

Clark, J. P.: Isolation of the police. In Quinney, R., editor: Crime and justice in society, Boston, 1969, Little, Brown & Co.

Coleman, J. S.: Resources for social change, New York, 1971, Interscience, John Wiley & Sons, Inc.

Commissie ter Bestudering van het Politievraagstuk: Report (verslag) presented by joint request of the Ministries of Justice and Interior, October 1, 1948, The Hague, 1948, Staatsdrukkerij & Uitgeverijbedrijf.

Cop on the beat: a dying breed? *Philadelphia Inquirer*, December 17, 1978, p. 1H.

Critchely, T. A.: A history of police in England and Wales: 900-1966, London, 1967, Constable & Co., Ltd.

Cumming, E., Cumming, I., and Edell, L.: Policeman as philosopher, guide and friend. In Quinney, R., editor: The social reality of crime, Boston, 1970, Little, Brown & Co.

Duff, D. V.: Bailing with a teaspoon, London, 1953, John Long Ltd.

Durkheim, E.: Suicide, Glencoe, Ill., 1951, The Free Press.

Durkheim, E.: The division of labor in society, Glencoe, Ill., 1947, The Free Press.

Elkins, A. M., and Papanek, G. O.: Consultation with the police: an example of community psychiatry practice, Am. J. Psychiatry 123:531-535, 1966.

Elson, A., and Elson, M.: Educating teachers and children in law: an approach to reduced alienation in lower city schools, Am. J. Orthopsychiatry 40(5):870, 1970.

Faris, R. E. L., and Dunham, H. W.: Mental disorders in urban areas, Chicago, 1939, University of Chicago Press.

Fijnaut, C.: The rebuilding of the Dutch police, Neth. J. Criminol. 18(3):119-130, 18(5):320-324, 1976.

Fleming, T.: The policeman's lot, American Heritage 21(2):4, 1970.

Gloucestershire Constabulary: Chief Constable's report on the police establishment with criminal and other statistics for the year ended 31 December 1978, County Police Headquarters, Cheltenham, England, February 1979.

Gloucestershire Constabulary: Child abuse, Gloucester, England, 1977, Gloucestershire Constabulary, Juvenile Liaison Department, Northern Division.

Granovetter, M. S.: Alienation reconsidered: the strength of weak ties, Unpublished draft, Cambridge, Mass., 1969, Harvard University, Department of Social Relations.

Hearing on police to reopen, *Philadelphia Inquirer*, December 18, 1978, p. 1C.

Hewitt, W. H.: British police administration, Springfield, Ill., 1965, Charles C Thomas, Publisher.

Hill, R. B.: The strength of black families, New York, 1972, Emerson Hall Publishers, Inc.

The homicide files, *Philadelphia Inquirer*, April 24-27, 1978.

Hovav, M., and Amir, M.: Israel police: history and analysis, Police Studies 2(2):5-31, 1979.

Israel Police: Annual report 1970, Jerusalem, 1971, Israel Police Publications Section.

Israel Police: Annual report 1969, Jerusalem, 1970, Israel Police Publications Section.

Johnston, J., and Harris, M.: What does a policeman do? New York, 1959, Dodd, Mead & Co.

Kahn, A.: Planning community services for children in trouble, New York, 1963, Columbia University Press.

Katzenbach, N. de B.: The challenge of crime in a free society, New York, 1968, Avon Books.

Kingdom of the Netherlands, Ministry of Foreign Affairs: Police, civil defense, fire services: 5, The Hague, 1973-1974, Netherlands Government Printing Office.

Klein, H.: The police: damned if they do—damned if they don't, New York, 1968, Crown Publishers, Inc.

Knebel, F.: Police in crisis, Look Magazine, February 3, 1968.

Kosa, J., Antonovsky, A., and Zola, I. K.: Poverty and Health, Cambridge, Mass., 1969, Harvard University Press.

Leighton, A.: The character of danger, New York, 1963, Basic Books, Inc.

Leighton, A., et al.: My name is legion, New York, 1959, Basic Books, Inc.

Lieberman, R.: Police as a community mental health resource, Comm. Mental Health J. 5: 111-120, 1969.

Linton, R.: Culture and mental disorders, Springfield, Ill., 1959, Charles C Thomas Publisher.

Lipsett, P., and Steinbrunner, M.: An experiment in police-community relations: a small group approach, Comm. Mental Health J. 5(2): 172, 1969.

Lower Eastside Neighbors Association (LENA): Study of utilization of social services, unpublished study, 1956.

Martin, J. P., and Wilson, G.: The police: a study in manpower, London, 1969, William Heinemann, Ltd.

McNamara, J. H.: Uncertainties in police work: the relevance of police recruits' backgrounds and training. In Bordua, D. J., editor: The police: six sociological essays, New York, 1967, John Wiley & Sons, Inc.

Melville, W. L.: History of the police in England, London, 1901, Patterson Smith.

Mental health training program prompts police, Today's Health 48:84, 1970.

Merton, R. K.: Social theory and social structure,

1958 enlarged edition, New York, 1968, The Free Press.

Metropolitan Police Office, Great Britain: Reports of the Commissioner of Police of the Metropolis, 1958-62, London, 1958-1962, Her Majesty's Stationery Office.

More policemen in Borough Park—temporarily, *New York Times*, December 6, 1978, pp. 1, B3.

Move shootout articles, *Philadelphia Inquirer*, August 1978.

Municipality of Jerusalem: The City of Jerusalem: some statistics and comparisons, Jerusalem, 1971, Israel Communications.

National Institute of Mental Health: First United States Mental Health Mission to the Soviet Union, Washington, D.C., 1965, U.S. Government Printing Office.

Newark police officers appeal to fear, *New York Times*, November 22, 1978, p. A1.

Newman, L., and Steinberg, L.: Consultation with the police on human relations training, Am. J. Psychiatry, **126:**1421, April 1970.

New Orleans police strike ends, *New York Times*, March 5, 1979, p. 1.

Niederhoffer, A.: Behind the shield: the police in urban society, New York, 1967, Doubleday & Co., Inc.

Number of police have no effects on crime, *New York Times*, February 24, 1974, p. E5.

Nyrop, R. F., editor: Israel: a country study, ed. 2, Washington, D.C., 1979, U.S. Government Printing Office.

Patterson cops tied to arson, slumlord racket, *New York Post*, March 7, 1979, p. 18.

Perrick, F.: The post war foundations of the municipal police in the Netherlands, Chapter 5, 1976.

Plan to reorganize U.S. law enforcement is studied, *New York Times*, May 24, 1978, p. A20.

Police strike broken, *Philadelphia Inquirer*, March 5, 1979, p. 1.

Policy of encouraging policemen to attend college challenged, *New York Times*, November 28, 1978, p. A20.

Port Authority of New York and New Jersey Police Department: Third and final interim report—1977: youth assistance project, Division of Criminal Justice Services (DCJS), Grant #G-98393.

President's Commission on Law Enforcement and the Administration of Justice, Task Force on the Police: Task force report: the police, Washington, D.C., 1967, U.S. Government Printing Office.

President's Commission on Law Enforcement and the Administration of Justice: The challenge of crime in a free society, Washington, D.C., February 1967, U.S. Government Printing Office.

A public hearing on police "crisis," *Philadelphia Inquirer*, December 12, 1978, p. 1.

In pursuit of degrees, not just criminals, *Philadelphia Inquirer*, September 25, 1978, p. 1A.

Relations between police and public, training materials, Police Training College, Police Training College, Northern Zone: Phillaur, Punjab, India, 1967.

Quinney, R., editor: The social reality of crime, Boston, 1970, Little, Brown & Co.

Reiss, A. J., Jr., and Bordua, D. J.: Environment and organization: a perspective on the police. In Bordua, D. J., editor: The police: six sociological essays, New York, 1969, John Wiley & Sons, Inc.

Reith, C.: A new study of police history, London, 1956, Oliver & Boyd.

Reorganization of Miami police, *New York Times*, April 11, 1971, p. 24.

Rubinstein, J.: City police, New York, 1973, Farrar, Straus & Giroux, Inc.

Sager, C. J., Brayboy, T., and Waxenberg, B.: Black ghetto families in therapy, New York, 1970, Grove Press, Inc.

Saunders, C. B., Jr.: Upgrading the American police, Washington, D.C., 1970, The Brookings Institute.

Shane, P. G.: The social functions of a civil agency: a study of police forces in England, India, Israel and the United States, unpublished thesis, Baltimore, 1975, The Johns Hopkins University.

Shils, E.: The theory of mass society, Diogenes, **39:**45-53, Fall 1962.

Sikes, M., and Cleveland, S.: Human relations training for police and community, Am. Psychol. **23:**766, 1968.

Silver, A.: The demand for order in civil society. In Bordua, D. J., editor: The police: six sociological essays, New York, 1967, John Wiley & Sons, Inc.

Skolnick, J. H.: Justice without trial: law enforcement in democratic society, New York, 1967, John Wiley & Sons, Inc.

Smith, B.: Police systems in the United States: second revised edition, New York, 1960, Harper & Row, Publishers.

Solomon's judgment: now women can seek any job, *Philadelphia Inquirer*, January 10, 1980, p. 1.

Steward-Brown, R.: The serjeants of the police in medieval England and Wales, Manchester, England, 1963, Manchester University Press.

Study: law enforcement in chaos, *Philadelphia Inquirer,* January 7, 1979, p. 7C.

Study on police: some things just never change, *New York Times,* February 24, 1974, p. E5.

Talbott, J., and Talbott, S.: Training police in community relations and urban problems, Am. J. Psychiatry 127(7):894, January 1971.

They don't rely on just nightsticks anymore, *Philadelphia Inquirer,* December 17, 1978, p. 20A.

Van Der Burg, F. H.: Preventive justice and local police, dissertation, University of Utrecht, March 22, 1961.

Van Reenen, P., personal correspondence, April 12, 1979.

Van Reenen, P.: Overheidsgeweld, Alphen aan den Rijn, Netherlands, 1979, Samson Uitgeverij.

Wallach, I.: The police function in a Negro community, vol. 2, McLean, Va., 1970, Research Analysis Corp.

Webster, J. A.: Police task and time study, J. Criminal Law, Criminol. Pol. Sci. 61(1):94-100, 1970.

Werthman, C., and Piliavan, I.: Gang members and the police. In Bordua, D. J., editor: the police: six sociological essays, New York, 1967, John Wiley & Sons, Inc.

Westley, W. A.: Violence and the police: a sociological study of law, custom and morality, Cambridge, Mass., 1970, MIT Press.

Whittemore, L. H.: Cop!, New York, 1969, Fawcett World Library.

Whittington, H. G.: The police: ally or enemy of the comprehensive mental health center?, Mental Health 55(1):55, 1971.

World Health Organization: Programme development in the mental health field, WHO Tech. Rep. Ser. 223, 1961.

Index

A

American Civil War, 153
Anglo-Saxon policing system, 10
Antiviolence, development of, 13
Ashkenazim, 101

B

Balfour declaration, 103
Baltimore
  ethnic character of, 172-173
  police in, socioecological analysis of, 172-173; *see also* United States, police in
  police distribution in, 172
  police work in, 152-153
Bentham, Jeremy, 13
Bonaparte, Napoleon, in Netherlands, 123
Bow Street Runners, 9
Britain; *see also* England
  changing role of police in, 27-28
  development of police force in, 10-17
  government of, 56
  history of, 56
  history of modern police in, 61-62
  Indian revolt against, 3
  police force in
    data categories of, 63, 65
    development of, 56-76
    operation of, 63-65
    organization of, 62-63
  police function in, 35
  police work in, 3
    administrative aspects of, 71
    distribution of, 59
    incidence of, per 1000 population per month, 60
    law enforcement and, 69, 70, 71-72
    problems of, 74-75
    rural-urban breakdown of, 67-68
    sample monthly breakdown, 66
    support activities and, 69, 70, 71-72
    urban vs. rural, 73
  policewomen in, 64-65
  religion in, 58

British Police Order of 1925, 106
Buddhism, 77

C

Calhoun, Patrick, 13
Celtic policing system, 10
Central Intelligence Agency (CIA), 157
Chadwick, Edwin, 13
Cheshire, study of police work in, 58; *see also* Britain, police force in; Britain, police work in
Church of England, 58
Civil War, American, 153
Civilian review boards, development of, 36
Coast Guard, United States, 157
Collective responsibility
  Anglo-Saxon policing system and, 10
  Norman policing system and, 10
Common Market of Western Europe, 121
Consensual crime, 4
Constable, parish, 11
Crime
  consensual, 4
  types of, 164
  victimless, 4
  violent, 164

D

Dacoitism in India, 3
Democratic Party National Convention, 29
Drug Enforcement Agency (DEA), 157
Dueling, outlawing of, 13

E

East India Company, policing powers of, 84
England; *see also* Britain
  medieval, law enforcement in, 10-11
  police history in, 9-17

F

Family crisis intervention, 198
Federal Bureau of Investigation, 35, 157
Frankpledge system, 10

215